BLAMELESS

BY

SAM SITLER

BLAMELESS

BY

SAM SITLER

This book is dedicated in the memory of Charles James Kirk.

May we all be bold and speak truth, no matter the cost.

Prologue

Crenshaw-on-Ribble started life as an island just outside of the Ribble Estuary in South Lancashire between Blackpool and Preston. Before Roman times, the island was uninhabited, avoided by the native Britons as the dwelling place of dark spirits. The Romans, undaunted by the inferior gods of the conquered natives, settled there anyway, founding the Port of Ensenadum, a vital checkpoint on the northwestern coast of Brittania for people and goods coming in, as well as the perfect protected launching point for expeditions and conquests into Caledonia and Hibernia. The port was known for dangerous shallows southeast of the island, claiming many a ship in those days.

When the Romans left the island, the village and its port fell into ruins. There was no more need to defend the area or launch raids. Sometime between the evacuation of Roman rule and the arrival of the Angles and Saxons, the shallows between the south of the island and mainland surfaced, connecting Ensenadum to the west coast of Northumbria.

Now a peninsula, a new village was erected in the late Ninth Century upon the ruins of the old Roman settlement. Its founder, Æthelstan Crowswood, found that the shallows that had become land had displaced much of the water on the northeast side, deepening what would become a new harbor. Æthelstan became a great landowner with the riches from his harbor, charging seafarers and fishermen to dock at the safe haven. By 1025, Æthelstan Crowswood was one of Cnut's wealthiest thegns. In his honor, the King of the North Sea Empire officially named the settlement Crawshaw, after its founder and benefactor.

Though Crawshaw was a prosperous harbor, it could never really expand beyond the bounds of the peninsula, nor could it rival bigger ports like Liverpool or Bristol with their large open river mouths. Additionally, there was only one road in and one road out. The isthmus that had surfaced in the early medieval ages was narrow, and the ground was soft; and any other land along the coastline was marshy tidal estuary. As a result, Crawshaw remained a just village.

After the Norman Conquest, it was found that there was a competing Crawshaw in the region, that being Crawshawbooth on the eastern side of the county in the Pennines. It was then decided that the tiny coastal village would be named Crawshaw on Ribble to differentiate it. As the English language evolved, so did the name until it arrived at its present name of Crenshaw-on-Ribble in the late Sixteenth Century.

With the Industrial Revolution came more attempts to turn Crenshaw-on-Ribble into a harbor that could at least compete with places like Barrow or Scarborough, but any attempt to dredge the harbor was met with lost equipment and more shifting sand. An iron bridge was erected in the 1850s in a bid to bring a railroad into the village to serve the fishing industry, but that sunk down and eventually collapsed into the harbor within a year.

During the Second World War, Crenshaw saw action as a beach-mounted gun fired upon a U-boat that had surfaced. It is unknown whether or not the shot connected, but the inhabitants never saw another U-boat ever again.

After the war, many of the old medieval roads were torn up and paved over. This caused quite a stir when the main road coming into town was widened and many of the ancient buildings were torn down to make room for it. Angered at the destruction of their home without even being consulted, the villagers banded together and physically blocked the construction equipment from proceeding with their work. To that end, the main road in is a modern two-lane highway only about halfway across the south of the peninsula (actually built over the old paved bridge), where it reverts back to its original form, albeit paved over with asphalt in lieu of cobblestones. Additionally, the new main road extends across the isthmus, nearly taking up the whole landmass. To accomplish this, road crews drilled down deep into the bedrock to build a solid foundation. Then, a type of ground-level bridge was built to keep up with the ever-moving sandbar.

After the decolonization of the British Empire, Crenshaw-on-Ribble found itself growing upwards. Several more centuries-old buildings were condemned and demolished to make way for immigrants from India, Pakistan, and Nigeria. The quaint little Northern fishing village was becoming urbanized.

The new arrivals brought a sort of human capital to the small village, and the townies accepted them as their own. This first wave of arrivals integrated and became full-fledged Englishmen, save for their complexion and the spices in their food. To them, Crenshaw-on-Ribble was their village, and it had always been their village. They were English, and they had never been anything but English. It was "God save the Queen" from here on out.

This happy arrangement lasted all of three or four years when another wave came. Crenshaw-on-Ribble had little vacancies, and they spilled out onto the street. The once-clean village became littered with humanity and garbage. The old folk – native and immigrant alike – were appalled by the lack of respect these young-ins possessed.

It soon became an unspoken rule that if you were a female, especially a young, pretty female, you stayed inside after dark. 'Twasn't polite to talk about such things. That didn't mean anybody didn't try. Lord knows a few went to the police, but they went ignored. Crenshaw-on-Ribble was a welcoming community to all races, creeds, nationalities, and sexual orientations, and it was only proper to welcome all races, creeds, nationalities, and sexual orientations.

For forty years, Crenshaw-on-Ribble continued on as if nothing was happening. Elephant in the room? What elephant? The air's just gotten a bit denser in the middle. Hmm, I wonder why I can't see t' telly from me sofa. Oi, you ain't hatemongerin' about them poor migrants, now.

Part 1
Love and Hate

I t was a bitterly cold morning in the harbor. *A thick layer of fog had settled over the water, obscuring the sight of anyone brave enough to venture out. Old Man Hutchins was in the doghouse again – something about his drinking problem, or so he thought. He didn't have a drinking problem; they had a problem with him drinking, but the old lady always thought he'd knocked back a few too many up at Fat Terry's. He could take care of himself. He was not drunk. He was perfectly sober. He even told her as much.*

"I'm soberly perfect, stupid bint," he slurred as she slammed the door on his back. "Keep me from me own house. I can take it. It's my house. You'll be sorry. You'll see."

Whatever she would see, nobody knew.

Reggie Hutchins owned a small fishing boat he'd docked in the harbor. It wasn't much, but it was the perfect place to hang after a night of drowning his liver if his wife didn't want him at home. He could sit on deck for hours with just a pole and a bottle of beer, or two, or three, and ruminate — if his brain allowed him to ruminate. If he got tired or woke up from the common unplanned nap, he could head below deck to a small cabin and sleep off the booze.

Reggie managed to climb aboard this morning without falling in — a true miracle these days. He slurred out a sea shanty as he started the motor. The little boat puttered as the old man piloted it out of the marina, miraculously missing another fishing vessel by inches. Now in the open water of the harbor, he cut the throttle and ambled to the deck.

Perhaps Sybil would let him back home if he brought dinner with him. Smoked fish always sounded good, and he could hang with even the best of anglers, even if he was three sheets to the wind. Luckily for him, he always kept a pole and some bait inside the boat, just in case he got the itch to use the boat for its intended purpose while he was out and forgot his good equipment at home.

Within twenty minutes, he stumbled back out on the deck and took a seat. He cast his hook into the harbor and settled in with a bottle of Chang's. Nothing out there but the squawk of a few seagulls obscured by the fog. It was another five minutes, and there was no movement from the line. That wouldn't do. Old Man Hutchins drew the line back in. After a few attempts at casting his line, one that nearly impaled his right cheek, he successfully launched the hook and line back into the harbor.

A miracle! Immediately, the line went taut. Even through his drunken haze, Old Man Hutchins could see it. He started to reel in his prize. Bugger was heavy, that was for sure. Had to be a marlin. Did they even live all the way up here? He'd hooked one in Baja years ago, but never here. It had to be at least a hundred pounds. Hopefully it wasn't a sea turtle. No, they were never here either. Would be a shame though, cute little buggers they are. Sea lion? No, not nearly heavy enough.

It was strange though. The fish wasn't putting up a fight. Oh well, it was his lucky day, so what did it matter? In short order, the fish banged up against the hull. It was time to lift it up out of its home and into his.

Hutchins began reeling his catch up the side of the boat. His heartrate increased as he'd finally see the trophy he had won. Sure was a hefty bugger, no matter what it was. Maybe he'd have it mounted at Fat Terry's after he gutted it. Had to be a marlin. It would feed him and Sybil for weeks, and he'd be able to tell his drinking mates at the pub that that was his catch.

6

Old Man Hutchins let out a scream of terror as he finally came face to face with what he'd caught.

Chapter 1
Back to the Grind

Verity Baker felt around the counter for her hair tie. It was one of those kinds of days – the kind where you've spent so much time on everything else that there's no time left for a flourish on the finishing touch. Verity knew she'd left a hair tie on here last night, and the cat was in no wise allowed in the bathroom. She looked high and low. No sign of the stupid band of elastic in any of the cabinets either.

Verity rushed out of her room, the caramel hair falling unkempt all around her face. There had to be a hair tie around here somewhere. As she stumbled into her sitting room, she noticed the little girl sitting on the edge of the sofa.

"Hallie, what're you still doing here?" she scolded.

8

"Hi, mum," the eight-year-old, Verity's exact miniature, addressed her. "I, uh, missed the bus."

Verity breathed a silent f-bomb under her breath. She didn't have time for this.

"Bloody Nora, Hallie!" she exclaimed out loud. "I'm already late! Where's my hair tie?"

It was then she saw the little band of elastic holding Hallie's hair back. For some reason, she was now even more agitated.

"Are you serious right now, Hallie? Where's yours? That was my last one!"

"Oliver took it," Hallie explained.

"How many times have I told you to make sure the bloody cat stays off of your vanity?" Verity scolded. "Come on, we're late. I'll just have to figure something else out."

Verity took Hallie by the wrist and led her out to the car. She had gotten so uptight in the last several months, but who could blame her? It's not like Elliott was ever reliable or responsible. The idiot barely took care of Hallie as it was, but at least he got her to school on time. He could at least do that one single job. This wasn't how it was supposed to be. Elliott was to be the bread winner while she enjoyed making a home for him and Hallie. At least, that's what she wanted, but that world had been dead for nearly fifty years, only remaining on life support through cheesy daytime television reruns and banned novels. But now where was Elliott? How do you not have to work and still leave that life?

"Look, Mummy, I'm sorry I took your hair tie," Hallie apologized once the car had reached highway speeds.

"Hallie, you don't have to apologize," said Verity. "I know it was an accident. I'm just a little bit stressed, and you need to be more careful."

"Because of your job?"

"Well, it's been over a month since I've been there. You'll see one day. You leave work for a couple days, and you dread going back. The first day or two is always the hardest."

"It's like coming back after Christmas holiday!" Hallie exclaimed, as if she had solved the problem of the world's greatest math equation.

"Exactly like that," Verity replied.

Verity stopped in a no parking zone in front of the school and whisked Hallie inside.

"Be good. Don't do anything I wouldn't do," she said as she pecked the girl on the forehead.

"Like what?" Hallie asked, confused.

"You know the rules," said Verity as she ran out.

Verity rushed back out to her car. The three minutes inside were enough for a parking enforcer to leave a ticket on her windshield.

"Bloody Nora," she growled though gritted teeth.

If there was a diagnosis to be made, then what Verity was experiencing was an onset of a terrible case of the Mondays all on a Friday. Verity took a look at the ticket. That's another £50 down the drain. She crumpled the note up and tossed it into the passenger seat. Then it began to rain. It was a Friday that screamed "Monday".

Verity checked her watch. She was supposed to be at the station fifteen minutes ago. To top things off, it was still a half hour to Preston. People always drove slow on the A roads as well. If she could reach under the pedals and charge up enough velocity, she would kick herself in the shins for not having moved closer since Elliott left. Then again, she would have had plenty of time if both she and Hallie were ready. Then again, if people would actually drive instead of doing whatever must be so much more important at the point, whether it be looking at their phones or screwing with the radio, she'd make it to Preston in no time.

Verity's Vauxhall Astra flew into the parking lot of the Lancashire Constabulary doing Mach Mohammed, sparks flying from the undercarriage as it bottomed out on the small rise from road surface to car park. Forty-five minutes late, just as she had estimated. As Verity climbed out of the little car, the wind blew her loose hair all over her face. The fibers of hair stung her eyes like little needles, and she found various hairs in her mouth as she tried to brush it all away. Holding her locks in one hand, she slammed the door, only to notice the tail her cardigan, which had been picked up by the heavy winds, hadn't left the car with her. She heard a gut-wrenching rip as the door kept the tail in place. Forget it, she'd just leave the cardigan there for later. She slipped out of the cardigan, slivering as the cold rain started peppering her.

"Oi, Verity!" a familiar voice called.

"Hey, Josh," she replied to the cheery beat cop, trying to ignore him so she could actually get in and work.

"Good to see you back," Josh continued.

"Charmed, I'm sure," Verity replied dryly.

"Is everything alright?" Josh asked.

"Now, why the devil would you go and ask a question like that?" Verity finally snapped. "Look at me! I'm a mess! My hair's all tangled because my kid couldn't keep her stupid cat off the table. I got a bleedin' parking ticket for leaving my car running in a no-parking zone for three minutes! And now I'm forty-five minutes late because people on the A roads don't understand that the roads are for driving, not texting and mucking about! And now, my favorite cardigan that I picked out last night specifically for my first day back at work is not only stuck in the door of my car, but probably damaged beyond repair because of this stupid wind. Is everything alright? No! Now, please, Josh, I know you're being kind, but I need to get into work."

"I'm so sorry, Verity, I didn't know."

"And how could you?" Verity sighed. "I'm sorry, it's not your fault. Thanks for caring, Josh."

"Anytime. Hey, if Elliott ever shows up around here, I'll break his legs for you," Josh joked. "Just keep it quiet. I need this job."

"You're a true hero, Josh. Just be sure to find a way to do it slowly."

As Verity approached the main building, she noticed something different. She knew everybody's cars. That's how she could tell who was at work and keep tabs on things. There were some people she wanted to avoid; others, she knew it would be a great day if they were in for work. It was the usual assortment of Vauxhall Astras, Ford Focuses, and Škoda Fabias, but among them was a brand-new Mustang Dark Horse. It was gray, as was most cars these days. She looked it up and down. Steering wheel was on the right, so it was bought here in England, but she didn't recognize the muscle car that stood out like a sore thumb among all of the European compacts and super minis.

"Oi, Josh, any idea who's that is?"

"No idea, Verity, but whoever it is had enough saved up to drop seventy-five grand on it."

"No way they're making payments on our salary, right?" Verity added. "Know anyone here with a taste for American muscle?"

"Not a clue," Josh replied, "but I'll get right on that investigation. Let me guess, it's a new guy."

"I guess I might find out when I go inside," said Verity.

"You do that," Josh chuckled.

"Oh, and Josh."

"Yeah, mate?"

"Thanks for being friendly and taking that beating from me. If you can handle that kind of abuse from me, then Louisa is the luckiest girl alive."

"I'll tell her you said that."

Verity suddenly remembered that she was late, and she rushed through the doors. Her speed in finding her desk created a wake, sending any loose papers flying into the walkway. Oh well, that mess would have to be cleaned up later. She sat down at her desk and powered her computer on as quickly as possible.

"Not a good look on your first day back from leave," came a voice from behind her.

Verity turned around to see her chief supervisor, Detective Investigator Brandon Whiteaker. Not entirely by choice, the man projected authority. When he served in the Royal Navy twenty-five years ago, he was a heavyweight boxing champion. Now at the Lancashire Constabulary, he towered over everyone.

"Fifty minutes past start time," he continued. "I ought to reprimand you for it."

"I'm so sorry, Whit, I just…"

"But, you know, it's your first day back, and you haven't exactly had it easy the last couple of months, so I think we could let this slide for today."

"I don't know what to say."

"Honestly, if I were you, I'd shut up and get to work as if you'd arrived at eight."

"Thanks, Whit."

"Oh, and by the way, I have an assignment for you, so meet me in my office in ten minutes," he told her. "Perhaps, you should visit the loo. You look a mess."

Verity blushed at the comment on her appearance. That was why she either wore her hair in a bun or put a hair tie in it. She excused herself and disappeared into the bathroom.

She had a good look at herself. Something had changed in the last month. Was it stress? Even with working as a police detective, seeing the things they see, she'd always looked young. It wasn't uncommon for some guy to hit on her, only for Elliott to appear out of nowhere and set him in his place. That's it. It was Elliott. Even for all of his foibles, he made her feel loved. But apparently, that was all a ruse. That spark, that love of life was gone. In its place, a palpable sadness. Elliott never truly loved her, that was true. Being some man's unwitting beard for so many years turned out to be a devastating blow, no matter how much time to recover they gave her.

Verity finished by tying her hair in a messy bun. It looked unprofessional, like she was about to spend the day cleaning house, not investigating crime, but not as bad as walking around with a bird's nest on top of your head.

As Verity walked into Whit's office, she noticed someone had beaten her to it. All she saw at first was the back of his head – a thick crop of black hair and a pair of shoulders covered with a blue turtleneck.

"Ah, Verity, meet your new partner," said Whit.

The new guy stood up, and she was able to take him in. He was dark with brown eyes to match his darkness. He had a combination of English and Hispanic features, and he only stood about four inches over her. He held out his hand to greet her.

"Denny Lawton," he greeted her in an American accent. "Pleased to meet you. Whit says you're one of his best."

"Uh, Verity Baker," she returned the greeting. "So, Whit what did you want to see me about?"

"Well, first, you two have a seat," Whit instructed.

Verity sat down in her seat uneasily, Denny waiting for her to take her seat. This new guy seemed strangely old fashioned. She wondered if he thought she didn't even belong here, like she should be at home, raising fifty kids and keeping house all while wearing a sundress. Nobody ever stood when women entered the room anymore, or even stayed standing until a woman was seated.

"Now, your supervisor, Martin, has decided to retire," Whit began. "DC Baker, I'm sorry we didn't save you any cake from the retirement party. That being said, the higher powers have not decided on a replacement, even though they've had several months of knowledge of DS Oatman's retirement. That being said, you'll report directly to me until they decide they want to start cutting checks for someone to fill that position."

Whit turned on the television behind his desk. It was the BBC. Apparently, it was a local report. The headline said it all: "BODY OF ANNIE LOVE FOUND IN CRENSHAW HARBOUR". There was footage of a small fishing vessel approaching the marina, surrounded by a couple speed boats from His Majesty's Coastguard.

"First day, and I get something like this?" said Denny.

"Yeah, we already have CSU over there, but she definitely wasn't killed there. They're already saying she's been dead for a couple days, meaning she was probably killed out in the sea. Old Man Hutchins fished her out earlier this morning. Apparently, Sybil kicked him out, and he went to drown his sorrows in a bottle of Chang's and some peace and quiet."

"So, you're wanting us to figure out what happened before she washed up in the harbor?" asked Verity.

"That about sums it up," said Whit. "And by the way, they didn't show this on the telly, thank God, but the left side of her face had been completely blown away. She didn't drown, if that's any consolation."

"I don't think it's any less horrific," Denny added, "but at least she didn't suffer."

"That's what we hope," Whit replied.

"Shotgun?" Denny asked.

"That's what they're thinking," Whit answered.

"So, this Annie Love," Denny began, "sorry, I'm new here, but she's..."

"Daughter of Ian Love," Verity answered for Whit, "the man challenging our current MP, Michael Lorde, for his seat in the House of Commons. So, this is high profile."

"Thank you Verity, that's right, "said Whit. "Anyway, you two had better get down there," Whit continued. "Oh, and you'd better not dilly dally. From what I understand, people like to take their time on the A road."

"I'll keep that in mind," Verity replied sarcastically as she stood up.

"Hold up," Denny said as he stood up behind Verity, "was her family notified?"

"They haven't even had a chance to identify the body yet," Whit replied. "They're in the process of getting her safely to land so the coroner can get a good look."

"Crap, I hate the press," Denny muttered.

He threw on a blazer and ran off after Verity. The woman was obviously in a mood to get out of here as quickly as possible and to avoid anyone and everyone while doing so.

"Hey, wait up," he called.

Verity grabbed a tumbler from her desk and filled it with water. Denny caught up to her.

"You ready?" he asked.

"First off, stop being so friendly," she scolded him. "Second, today's not the day to be so gung-ho or whatever. Just relax and leave inconspicuously."

"Well, excuse me, princess," Denny mocked her.

"Denny, I'm really not in the mood, and you're already making this partnership a living hell; so, could you please just act normal or something?"

"You want out of here?" Denny pressed. "Then let's go. It's too stuffy in here for my taste anyway."

Denny reached down and grabbed a backpack. He took a look back at Verity and cracked a smile. She rolled her eyes at the cheesiness.

"Shall we go?" he asked.

Verity rolled her eyes again and followed Denny out.

"First things first," Denny began, "we're partners. That means no matter what, I will always have your back. Second, I don't do the whole pussyfooting around. I call it as I see it. Black man kills a white kid, it's just as evil as a white man killing a black kid. You read me? Hey, where you going?"

Verity had wandered off to the line of official Škoda Scala police cars. It was normal routine: going out on assignment, you took an official vehicle. Apparently, this was foreign to Denny.

"I'm going to get us a car," Verity replied.

"Whit said he wanted us to get there fast," said Denny. "You think that's possible in some Eurotrash like that?"

"Oh, and what did the all-knowing magical Yank have in mind?"

Denny said nothing. He just held up a key fob with a silver running horse on it and pressed the unlock button. The horn on the gray Mustang parked out front chirped, and the parking lights came on.

"You know we're not really supposed to use our own vehicles on official police business, right?" Verity recited.

"Meh, better to ask forgiveness than permission," said Denny as he opened the passenger door for Verity.

"You're impossible," Verity muttered.

"Yeah, exactly what my mom used to say."

Chapter 2
Love and Death

Denny had hidden a Kojak light in his backpack. If the roaring V8 wouldn't wake people up, the flashing red bubblegum machine and the siren would. At any rate, they would make Crenshaw-on-Ribble within fifteen minutes if Denny could actually open up the throttle.

"Would be very nice if these people would wake the heck up!" he shouted to the wind.

"Welcome to Lancashire," Verity said dryly.

"Get off your phone!" Denny shouted to no one in particular.

Even with the clear sign of emergency services behind them, people did very little to clear the way. It was as if people were just there to be there, no particular place to go. Denny scowled at each and every motorist as he passed them, as if it were a personal affront to him that they would have the temerity to block him from official police business.

"Oh well, I've seen worse," Denny resigned. "Get on I-5 in Portland, and people will literally stop for no reason. Like, people will stop just to let someone merge onto the freeway. Trying to get over the Marquam Bridge is like a gamble with your life. It's like they've found something interesting to look at that no one else can see. Wanna go from Beaverton to Troutdale? Too bad, we're not letting you over."

"You know, something tells me they'd move if we were actually in an official police vehicle," Verity rebutted. "You know, I don't associate a loud sports car with a blinking red light on top with moving because the police are coming. Just a thought."

"Lesson learned," replied Denny. "I still much more prefer this, if you don't mind. So much more comfortable than those Scalas they have you driving."

"Yes, I'm sure a car designed for commuting has a much rougher ride than a sports car," Verity drawled on sarcastically.

"Still better and faster," Denny ignored the comment.

"Do you even know where you're going?" asked Verity.

"I'd hope so," Denny replied. "I live in Crenshaw."

"You don't say. How long? I've never seen you around."

"Well, I've only been here a week or so," Denny explained. "I've spent the last few days getting to know the lay of the land if I wasn't unpacking."

"Makes sense," replied Verity. "It's my first day back after a month."

"What a coincidence! It's my first day on the job here."

"Where were you before?"

"Did Whit not tell you?"

"I was in the office literally ten minutes when I got called into Whit's office, so no."

"Officer exchange," Denny proudly explained as he turned off onto the isthmus causeway. "They sent some poor fool from here to fill in for me at the Portland Police Bureau. He's probably getting pummeled by some soy boy Fa thug right now."

"Fa?"

18

"I refuse to call those fascists anti-fascist," said Denny. "Anyway, Portland's a city at war, so investigating a girl with half her face blown off is a nice change of pace, don't you think?"

"Great, well I hope you get used to working without a gun," Verity chuckled.

"I almost feel naked without it," Denny replied, "but I can manage."

"Turn right here, or you'll have to fight through the narrower streets," Verity instructed, pointing at a turn-off to the harbor.

"Right-o."

"So, why Crenshaw? I mean, you've no roots here, so why somewhere an half an hour from work?"

"It reminds me of home," Denny replied. "I grew up on the Oregon Coast in Astoria. I like watching the sunset over the ocean."

"So, it's worth the long commute?"

"Very much."

"Still, if you're only here on exchange, I just find it odd to not find a place closer to Preston."

"Well, I guess I want to live it up. Don't have any other responsibilities besides work and bills. I bought a house here, and I'll have equity should I return to the States. Anyway, I need something to do during my free time."

"Okay, you win," said Verity. "Oh, turn here."

"So, this is the harbor?" said Denny.

"This would be our tiny harbor," Verity confirmed.

"Reminds me of Depoe Bay," Denny commented.

"If you don't mind, let me take the lead," Verity instructed.

"Why's that?" asked Denny.

"Because, at the end of the day, I'm still a local," Verity explained.

"Have it your way, Princess," Denny replied in sarcasm.

"And stop calling me that," Verity scolded.

"Right, right, Queen Verity of the Seven Precincts of Crenshaw and Its Assorted Ghettos."

"Bloody Nora, it's like living with a twelve-year-old," Verity muttered under her breath. "Anyway, I know, or knew, this Annie Love."

"You do now?"

19

"Annabelle Love, daughter of Ian and Harriet Love, remember? The man running for MP? She was the sweetest thing," Verity explained. "Top student in her school, most likely to succeed. We were all sure she'd be Miss England one day. Everybody in the area loved her. Why, she had boys chasing here around all day."

"Any reason she'd go missing like that?"

"With her character, no, but she did have a little sister, Agatha, who's her polar opposite."

"Do you suspect foul play?"

"I sure hope not."

The marina was filled to the gills with police boats and police vehicles. There were enough blue lights to convince someone not in the know that there was some kind of rave going down at the harbor. Not only did the two detectives have that to contend with, but just about every news agency in the UK was there. The Kojak light did very little to clear the way. Denny revved the big V8, waking a few people from the *Guardian* out of their stupor. Slowly but surely, a path cleared for the muscle car. Denny made it through the gauntlet and pulled up short of the police tape and killed the motor.

Neither Denny nor Verity shared a word as they simultaneously exited the car and approached the crime scene. Together, they flashed their badges, and a uniformed officer lifted the tape. They were just in time. Annie Love's corpse was being covered up on a stretcher that was, in turn, being prepared to be loaded into a meat wagon. Verity flashed her badge at the medic. No words were needed as the medic got the message. He lifted the sheet covering Annie's face.

True to Whit's word, the poor girl was missing the left half of her face; in its place, a void that took up a quarter of the circumference of her head with what remained of her brain beyond that. Hanks of her blonde hair were plastered here and there, some over her right eye and some in the hole that was once the left half of her face. Her right jaw hung stupidly as the force of whatever damaged her face also broke the bone on that side. She must have been conscious when whatever took her life killed her, because the expression that was left frozen on the right half of her face was one of pure terror. Verity turned around to compose herself before taking it all in head on.

"She's been dead for three days at least," the medic said. "Some poor geezer found her bloated body floating in the marina next to his boat."

"Old Man Hutchins, Whit told us," said Denny.

"Yeah, that's right," the medic replied.

"Got a cause of death?" asked Verity.

"Well, absent an autopsy, I'd say it were a shotgun wound," the medic continued, "but we won't know until we get her in for autopsy. For all we know, she could've fallen into the water and been hit by a boat propeller. Either way, it's safe to say that losing a good portion of her head did her in."

"So, we're hoping this was just an accident with a boat, right?" asked Denny.

"How do you mean?" the medic answered with a question.

"I mean, as tragic as this is, I feel like a murder would be worse for everyone around," Denny explained, "If this was a murder, that means that this could go deep."

"How so?" Verity joined in the interrogation.

"Think about it," Denny continued, "why would anyone want to kill this girl?"

"Are you saying you don't want to investigate?" asked Verity.

"Not at all," Denny defended himself. "I'm ninety percent sure this was a murder. I just want to start asking questions."

"Has the family been notified?" Verity asked the medic.

"At the same time as the rest of the country," the medic replied. "Bloody cameras got through the lines before we ever did. Old bloke who found her talked to them first. He knew it were Annie."

"Thanks, no thanks, am I right?" Denny commented.

"And how did they identify her?" Verity asked. "I mean, how did the media themselves know it was Annie?"

"Well, that's the fun part," the medic explained. "Our friend recognized her from all them missing persons posters and told the BBC who she was. We don't actually have a positive I.D. That only makes this whole thing even more of a living hell, I'm sure you'd imagine. This whole thing is already a big mess, and we're not even an hour into it."

21

As if Denny and Verity summoned them, Annie's parents arrived. Distraught would be putting it lightly. They rushed past security and past crime scene investigators.

"Our baby!" the Mrs. Love cried. "Where's our baby!"

"Cover her up!" Verity whispered to the medic.

"Harriet! Slow down!" Mister Love yelled to his wife.

"Please, please, no!" Harriet Love cried, oblivious to her husband's pleas. "She can't be dead. My baby can't be dead!"

"Whatever you do," Verity whispered to the medic, "do not, I repeat, do not show them the left half. If they must see, only uncover the right half. They don't need to be seeing her like that."

The medic nodded in agreement.

"Please, not me wee bairn!" Harriet cried, digging into a more ancient part of her soul. "Not Annie! Not my perfect little Annie!"

Harriet, a diminutive woman who was much stronger than she appeared, shoved Denny aside.

"Please, ma'am!" Denny cried, turning to hold her back. "You don't want to."

"Harriet, listen t' officer," Mister Love said apologetically, grabbing at her hand to restrain her.

Verity nodded at the medic who then pulled the right half of the sheet from Annie's face.

A wordless, soundless cry emitted from Harriet Love's mouth. Her lower jaw trembled as she grappled with the horrible truth. Forget the emergency personnel blocking her, she loosed herself from Mr. Love's grip and barged past Denny and Verity. She leapt onto the corpse of her favorite daughter, emitting an awful shriek of pain and agony. Everything hurt, mentally, physically, and spiritually. The force of her impact pulled the rest of blanket from what was left of Annie's face. The agony of loss was replaced with horror as the grotesque extent of her daughter's end met her face to face. At this point, Harriet Love's cries could no longer be described as human, the very features of her face twisted beyond any recognition. A sickly howl of fear and sorrow escaped the woman's mouth as she leaned next to the gurney, her legs turning to jelly.

"Cover her up! Cover her up!" Ian Love shouted.

The medic obeyed the victim's father. Harriet Love collapsed to the ground, convulsing in sobs and howls. Mister Love picked his wife up off the ground, burrowing her into his chest.

"I'm so sorry, Mister Love," Verity apologized.

Ian Love looked Verity directly in the eye. Verity, for her part, felt as if the man was beaming a laser directly into her soul.

"Detective…" he began, searching for her name.

"Baker," Verity replied.

"Detective Baker," Ian Love continued, "please, however possible, find whoever did this."

"Whoever it was, we'll find him and make sure he pays for this," Denny said in an official, yet reassuring tone.

Verity never turned her head. Instead, she just moved her eyes toward Denny, shooting a glance at him. Denny seemed not to notice, which only intensified her cold blue gaze.

"Mister Love," Verity turned to the old man, "we will do whatever we can. You have our word."

"That's all I want," said Ian Love as he turned away and walked his wife back to the street level.

"If that's everything," Verity turned back to the medic, "I guess we'd better get going. We'll be by the morgue once they figure out what actually happened."

Without a word, Verity turned around and headed back up the dock to the street level. Denny hesitated a second and then followed. Verity beat Denny to the car and yanked on the door handle, nearly dislocating her arm.

"Unlock it, please," she spat at Denny.

Denny obeyed her and unlocked the car as he approached. Verity ripped the door open and climbed into the car. Denny followed suit. He started the motor but hesitated to put the car into gear. He could feel the palpable tension in the air. He could hear the blood pumping through his temples, his mouth drying out as if he had swallowed a whole bag of cotton balls. After a moment of silence, Verity spoke.

"What the devil is wrong with you?" she growled.

"What do you mean?"

"I told you to let me take the lead."

"Which I did."

"And then you butted into the conversation as if you know everything that's going on. News flash: you don't!"

"Am I part of this investigation or not?"

"And then you promise the victim's parents that we'll find whoever did this."

"Are we not supposed to do that."

"You don't understand, Lawton. We don't even know if she was murdered. Second, we can't make any promises other than we'll do our best. Now we have a distraught family counting on us to find and arrest somebody, anybody."

"You saw the look on her face. Something terrible happened, and it was by someone else's hand. There's no way she got caught up in a boat propeller or whatever B.S. they want to spin so that this isn't a murder, and you know it. Anyway, where I come from, we don't screw around. We solve cases."

"Well, we're not where you're from, are we?"

"You know, maybe we should see if they can't find us different partners if you're going to be like this. I can't work like this. We can go back to Preston and see if Whit won't reassign us somewhere else, right?"

"If I'm going to be like this? We've not been together for an hour, and you're begging for another partner?"

"If I can't do my job, why would I want you as a partner?"

"If you would just be patient, you can do your job. This isn't some cop show where we find the murderer in an hour. You're not in Hollywood anymore."

Denny started to snicker.

"What?" Verity's anger turned to confusion. "What's so funny?"

"Hollywood?" Denny chuckled. "Girl, Hollywood's about a thousand miles from where I live."

"Is that what this is all about?"

"Verity, I apologize. Next time, I'll keep my mouth shut and let you take the lead with the locals. Just please go home and study a map for a little bit."

"You're incorrigible!" Verity scolded.

"Well, I've called worse," Denny laughed. "Where to next, Princess?"

24

"To the gallows where I'll have you beheaded if you keep that up, ye vile peasant" Verity finally got in on the joke. "Let's get going. There's a pub on the north side of the village. I have a friend who may know a few things."

Chapter 3
A Basket of Deplorables

It took nearly a half hour to clear out of the marina. If people weren't hyperfocused on the apparent murder, they were more than enamored with the rare muscle car plying through the crowds. Denny revved the motor a few times to get some people's attention, the loud roar waking them up. People immediately fled from the beast unseen, as if they thought some kaiju had risen from the harbor and was about to devour them. Finally free of the mob, Denny still kept it slow as he traveled over the ancient cobblestone streets of medieval Crenshaw.

"Just who is this guy at the pub you want to see?" Denny asked.

"An old friend," Verity replied. "Knows a bit about the underworld."

"So, an informant?" Denny confirmed.

"In so many words," Verity said. "It's not so much that he's a criminal. He just has a bunch of criminals that frequent his pub."

"Can we trust him?"

"He's never steered me wrong before."

"There's a first time for everything," said Denny. "Suppose something big happened here, and he wants to cover his skin."

"You really need to relax, new guy. You promised to let me take the lead. I know these people a lot better than you. Please don't embarrass me."

"See, I'm afraid we're going to get into some *Star Wars* cantina situation here," Denny chuckled.

"That's why you need to let me take the lead," Verity continued. "They hear that accent, and they'll never take you seriously again."

"Like you?"

"Make a left here. No, not like me. I think you take this thing seriously, perhaps a bit too seriously."

"How so?"

"Because you are pulling out all the stops today. Great, you're asking questions. You look like a cop, walk like a cop," she sniffed the air in the car, "maybe you smell like a cop, but I can't get past this new car scent. You're trying too hard. These are my people, and they only trust me because I grew up with them and built a relationship with them. You wouldn't expect me to come to Seattle, or Vancouver…"

"Portland," Denny interrupted.

"Portland," Verity corrected herself. "You wouldn't expect me to come to Portland and start talking to every criminal lowlife in town as if we were best mates for twenty years."

"Who am I? Lurch? Just the silent muscle behind you?"

"If you could for now, please. It's right up here."

Denny pulled in behind a Chevette, a piece of garbage that he was surprised even still existed. The pub looked like just the place some lowlife scum would hang out. Far from the quaint establishments that pass for English and Irish pubs on the Oregon Coast, Fat Terry's looked ancient, as if it had been there since before the Norman invasion. Denny could have sworn the crumbling tile roof was somehow a new addition, like there had just recently been a thatched roof.

Inside, it was dark, lit mainly by oil lamps and a few dying incandescent bulbs. Denny expected to find some rough and tumble customers wearing bowler hats and sporting walrus moustaches and mutton chops. The patronage was nothing less than Denny expected, sans the bowler hats and mutton chops. Deep down inside, his chivalrous instincts kicked in, his eyes narrowing on anyone who might look at Verity the wrong way, ready to square off with a quick throat punch or a roundhouse kick. This was no cute holiday spot, rather a place for the lowly of Crenshaw-on-Ribble to gather after a day of doing whatever the lowly of Crenshaw-on-Ribble do.

The bartender (whom Denny surmised must be Fat Terry himself) looked all the part of what Denny pictured a bartender at this establishment looked like. Hunched over and bulky, he didn't seem to have a smooth bit on him – more like lumps of flesh and whatever else – lacking in symmetry. Even his eyes were mismatched, one squinty while the other stared directly into your soul. Denny question whether or not he was looking at a human, and not one of Tolkien's creations. Heck, he was probably the one responsible for taking the Hobbits to Isengard himself.

"Ey up!" the bartender cried. "Look 'oo's come 'round 'ere now. Why, it's Veri'y Troof and 'er new pet."

"Cut the crap, Terry," Verity spat back at him. "We're here strictly on business."

Terry turned his glance to Denny, who at this point was doing an exceptional job at keeping a poker face.

"What 'bout you, boy?" he growled at Denny. "You 'avin' a bi' o' fun wiv' 'er?"

Denny broke his glance away from the empty air and stared directly into Terry's good eye.

"What?" Denny asked, but he masked it to sound like "Wot?"

"I said, 'you 'avin' a bi' o' fun wif' this lass?"

"Right, I heard you," Denny began just slightly under his breath, using some generic British accent mask to his heritage, "but last I checked, the lady was talking to you."

Verity grabbed Denny's lower left arm and gave it a great squeeze. Denny, for his part, was confused. He was never all that great on the non-verbal communication, as many of the women in his life could attest. He couldn't tell if Verity wanted him to shut up or if she was concerned for her safety and wanted his protection. He decided he could work with both.

"Listen 'ere, you bein' new and all, let me tell you 'ow it all works. Now, I'm talkin' to ye, and you answer me questions, yeah."

Terry stepped out from behind the bar. For looking like Quasimodo, he moved rather well.

"Now, 'ere in me pub," Terry continued, "we don't take kindly to interlopers. And you, my friend, are new 'round 'ere."

"Look, Terry," Verity pleaded, "we just want to ask a couple questions."

"Shut your mouth, cow," Terry growled at Verity.

"Come on, Terry, just two pints," Verity nearly whined. "We'll even pay double for both. Just let us ask a couple questions."

"Sit down then," said Terry. "Just know I don't like 'im. 'E's all... I can't place it."

Terry turned around and set about grabbing two beer mugs.

"Thanks for having my back, but I got this," Verity whispered to Denny.

Terry returned with two mugs of beer and slammed them down onto the bar. Denny grimaced at the sight of the alcohol.

"What's wrong, boy?" Terry laughed. "Ain't never 'ad real beer before? 'Ere, I'll take this back and run to t' loo if you want that American rubbish. Or be'er yet, I'll bring ye out a cuppa apple juice. Pu' i' all in a sippy cup if ye like."

"How'd you know he was American?" asked Verity.

"Look at him." Terry chuckled. "Look at 'ow 'e carries 'imself. Walks 'round like 'e owns t' 'ole place, lah."

"Does he now? He looks like a scared child to me," Verity chuckled.

It was then Denny knew Verity had planned this all along. If she could control him, what else could she do? Either way, Denny felt smaller than a flea. It was as if he were just the child accompanying mommy to some meeting where he had to sit and be quiet.

"Oh, come off it, Verity," Terry chuckled. "Don't be too harsh on the boy. Look at him."

"Denny, it's okay," Verity chuckled. "You can talk to him. He's a friend."

"Friend's a very loose term," Terry said, "mainly because of all these knuckleheads we got 'round 'ere."

"Very reassuring," Denny mumbled.

"Anyway, Ver, what was it you needed?"

"Agatha Love," Verity answered. "Know where she is?"

"Aggie Love?" Terry scratched his rough chin. "You know, I ain't seen 'er 'round lately. Well, as you know, I would never allow a child in me establishment."

"Cut the crap, Terry, you and I both know you have minors coming in all the time."

"Allegedly," Terry defended himself. "Anyway, I think you and I both know where she been, 'oo she been 'angin' out with, lah. And you and I bofe know I can't exactly say where she is, even though we all know, wivout certain repercussions."

"Look, can you just give us a straight answer?" Denny finally snapped.

"Dennis! Not now!" Verity snapped back. "Let me handle it."

"Oi, you'd be'er listen to t' lady," Terry chuckled. "She may look small, but she is fierce. She'll 'ave your 'ead were you not watchin'."

"I'm sorry about Denny," said Verity. "He's a bit eager. It's his first day and all."

"Hey, I'm a merciful guy. It's these other cretin's you'd better be watchin', lah."

Denny turned around and scanned the pub. Sure, he looked suspicious. He came in with all that swagger, and then when some brew was set in front of him, he refused to touch it. Denny felt his gorge rise as he looked down into the ale. He picked up the mug and put it to his lips. Whatever was in there was warm and bitter. Whatever Fat Terry had planned for it couldn't be any worse than what was already in here. He took a sip of the beer. He felt his tongue wrench as the beverage passed through his mouth. He slammed the mug down again.

"Maybe we'll just stick wiv a Coke or sommat next time you come in, amigo," Terry chuckled as he took the mug away. "You're not strong enough for this Bri'ish Brew."

30

Verity hid her face from Denny, but he could tell all he needed to know through the trembling. She was laughing at him – making a mockery of him. This whole enterprise had become a disaster.

"Verity, do we have what we need?" asked Denny.

"As far as we can get," she replied, barely able to answer through her uncontrollable giggling.

"Well, I'm glad we got to chat," Denny said to Terry, "but me and my partner have a murder to solve, and a chat to have before we continue solving that murder. Thank you very much for all you've done."

"Come back any time, me boy," Terry laughed. "We'll make sure you get sommat you can drink."

Denny tore out of the pub. He was furious. It was almost as if some code of honor had been broken. He marched straight to his Mustang and climbed in. Verity had barely shut the door to the pub when he started the engine. For fear of being left behind, she ripped the passenger door open and jumped in. Instead of taking off, Denny just sat there with the engine idling, the purr of the big V8 almost soothing to him. He was quiet. Verity couldn't tell if he was blushing or not, but he didn't need to; he wore his true feeling on his face like a mask. He sat there, staring into space.

"When I say I have your back," he finally broke the silence, "it's because I expect my partner to be there for me. I don't expect my back to be stabbed."

"Come on, Denny, it's not like I left you alone."

"Verity, you humiliated me in front of those people."

"Oh, so you're mad about your fragile male ego?"

"No, it's not like that!" Denny snapped. "If things went bad in there, I was ready to put my life on the line for you. The way Terry talked to you, the looks he gave you; I was ready to jump that bar and beat the living crap out of him if he tried anything. I don't know how you view things, but I don't take this kind of crap as a joke. So, when it's all a ruse to haze me in front of the whole village, it's a bit unnerving and makes me not want to act like a gentleman towards you. Oh, and that's another thing."

31

Verity turned her head and rolled her eyes, preparing for a lecture from Denny as if she were his sixteen-year-old daughter preparing to meet some boy he didn't like for a date.

"I don't care if you're a slut on the street or the bloody queen of England," Denny continued, "you are a lady, and I will always respect you as such."

"Oh, like you just did back there," Verity said, pointing to her door, which she herself had to open, as if she hadn't been opening doors herself her entire life.

"Don't push it," he said. "I get it. I messed up back at the marina. I opened my big mouth. But why is it that when I keep my mouth shut and respect you that you turn around and do something like that? This isn't about some fragile male ego. This is about me being able to trust you and have my back. I need to know I can trust you, Princess."

"I'm sorry you feel that way," Verity sighed in resignation. "It won't happen again."

"Verity, everybody in my life up to this point has betrayed me. I don't know you all that well, but you seem a good person. Please don't add yourself to that list."

Verity put her right hand on Denny's left. He felt a surge of blood pass through his heart. No, this was Verity's way of comforting him, nothing more, nothing less.

"I believe we have an understanding," Verity said.

"Thank you."

"And I will say, you handled yourself marvelously in there."

"Did I? Because I feel like I was a deer in headlights the whole time. You actually trust those wombats?"

"Just Terry, to a degree."

Suddenly, Verity's phone rang.

"Yes," she answered. "Oh," her expression changed to a grimace. "Thank you, we'll head there now."

"So, anyway, what did he mean by you know exactly where Agatha is?"

"I can't confirm nor deny where she is, Denny. However, I think we need to make a run by the Love residence. They're done with the investigation at the morgue."

"What's the news?"

"We're investigating a murder," Verity answered. "They found buckshot in Annie Love's brain. That was no boat propeller."

"Well, you're the local who knows everybody," said Denny, his chipper mood returning. "Point the way, Princess."

"You know, I might get used to you calling me that, Peasant."

Chapter 4
House of Love

Ian and Harriet Love had done well for themselves. Their house was a sprawling two-story right on the western edge of the peninsula with a stunning view of the Irish Sea visible through a floor-to-ceiling picture window at the back of the foyer. In the pull-around driveway, all manner of luxury vehicles were parked – Rolls Royces, Bentleys, Land Rovers, Benzes, and a few exotics Denny couldn't quite place. There were palm trees lining the drive, tall palms at least twenty feet tall. Denny was surprised by the occasional pint-sized irrigated palm he'd see in someone's front yard back home or the occasional trip to In-N-Out, but he had no idea they could even grow them this far north, or even this tall for that matter. That was all he could see when he first pulled in. Despite the $90,000 muscle car he drove, this place made him feel ghetto. Beyond the front drive, the mansion was made of red brick. It loomed three stories over them, dominating at least nine thousand square feet on the ground floor of the two-acre tract of land.

"Keep my mouth shut?" he asked Verity as they pulled into the drive.

"Just don't make any more promises we're not sure we can deliver on," replied Verity.

"Forgive me if I hyperfocus on all this," Denny chuckled as he coasted the Mustang in neutral before bringing it to a stop next to a classic Mercedes Gullwing. "I might be too awestruck to say anything."

"It may be best if you talk to Mister Love," Verity explained, "you know, man to man. You seem his type."

"His type?"

"I just think you'd connect with him."

"Over the cars?"

"Isn't that what you guys like to talk about?"

"Look, Princess, I've been a cop for over ten years," Denny almost snapped. "I know how to interview witnesses."

"Just don't make any promises."

"Yes, Mom."

Verity rolled her eyes at Denny's insolence. The jury was still out on whether or not she could work with him.

Denny led the way to the front door. It was a ten-foot-tall slab of mahogany construction, adorned with a golden knocker. Naturally, there was a doorbell button placed off to the side. Denny hit the button. The chimes sounded like Big Ben at noon.

A old hunched-over butler answered the door. Dressed in all black, save for his button-up dress shirt, he wore a carnation on his lapel. Denny and Verity flashed their Lancashire Constabulary badges. The old man got the message.

"Right this way," he said as he turned to lead the pair inside.

"Hello, *Downton Abbey*," Denny whispered to Verity.

The whole family was gathered in the great room, as well as some of the house staff. Harriet Love took front and center, dressed in black mourning clothes, the kind you only see in those Victorian dramas on

35

the BBC and PBS, Ian Love standing over her, puffing on an old pipe and massaging her back to comfort the weeping woman.

"Did you expect anything less?" Verity whispered back.

Harriet Love looked up from her weeping at the two detectives. A maid handed her a tumbler of water, the plastic vessel detracting from the antique setting. Clearly, she had dehydrated herself from crying all morning.

"Hello," Denny said awkwardly, "DC Lawton and Baker, Lancashire Constabulary. We were wondering if we could ask some questions of Mister and Missus Love."

"Have you found the man who did this?" asked Harriet through deep gulps of air, trying to compose herself.

"That's what we want to talk about," Verity stepped in. "We're hoping we could talk to you two alone."

Harriet looked up at Ian. He nodded in approval at her. Perhaps Denny's big mouth had served some purpose. They seemed to trust the two detectives.

"If I could speak to Missus Love, sir," Verity continued. "Just a few questions."

"Harriet?" Ian Love addressed his wife.

"I'm fine," she reassured him.

"With you, DC Lawton?" Ian Love asked, pointing to himself.

"Yes, sir," Denny replied.

Verity rolled her eyes. He was so American. Nobody was called "sir" unless they were nobility, not even a rich commoner like Ian Love.

Denny followed Mister Love through the corridors of the house. It looked straightforward on the outside, but in reality, the house was a maze. Denny wondered if he'd ever find his way back to the great room by himself. He figured he had better get to asking questions sooner rather than later.

"So, you and Harriet?" Denny began. "How long have you been together?"

"Thirty years," Ian Love replied. "Thirty mostly-good years."

"Through better or worse," Denny added.

"I'm afraid this is the 'worse' part we talked about in those vows, Detective."

"You seem to be holding together rather well," Denny commented as the turned yet another corner.

"I have to, Detective Lawton," Ian continued. "My Harriet, she's always had somewhat of a weak constitution. I'm afraid this may have pushed her over the edge."

"And that's all just for her?" Denny asked.

"To be honest," Ian answered, "a bit of it's for the cameras. See, I'm running for Parliament, and I can't look weak."

"Politics, then?"

"Like I said, a small bit of it. I'll be honest, I had the picture-perfect family – beautiful wife, beautiful, perfect daughter."

Ian led Denny through a door and flipped on a light. The bright LEDs revealed a massive car collection. The gathering on the drive was just the tip of the iceberg. Denny kept his composure from the obvious distraction and continued asking questions.

"Your happy place?" he asked.

"You could say that," Ian replied. "It's my hobby. I'll go to Pebble Beach on occasion, maybe Mecum or Barret-Jackson. See that Cobra over there?" He pointed to a Shelby Daytona. "Know how much I paid for that?"

"I could only imagine," Denny replied.

"£3 million. It's an original too, no replicas here. You into cars too? I see you're driving one of them new Mustangs."

"As much as I can," Denny said. "I've always been too busy for a hobby. I drove a 2015 Tacoma back home. Police work kind of keeps you busy, not to mention family and church."

"Oh. Your family here?"

"It's a long story," Denny replied. "They're back home in Oregon. I'm here on an exchange program."

"I see. Anyway, you have any questions for me?"

"Yes, I might cut to the chase, seeing you're the one being interviewed here."

"Whatever it takes to resolve this quickly. I feel if Harriet at least had some closure, she'd be okay. Annie was her favorite, you know."

"That's just it," said Denny. "You say Annie was her favorite, but you have another, right?"

"Yes, her younger sister, Aggie. She's, how do we put this, a special case."

"How so?"

"Well, you know, you can raise two children in the exact same environment, give them equal amounts of love and attention, nurture them all the same, and they still turn out different. I only say Annie was the favorite because she acted like it. Well, that and she was our first after thirteen years of trying. Never got into any trouble. Prize student, helped out the community, never had to be asked to do what she was supposed to do. She even had boys kicking down the door wanting to take her out. Like I said, made us the picture-perfect family. Aggie, on the other hand."

"Complete opposite?"

"Polar opposites," Ian continued. "God knows I love the poor girl, but something's told her she had to be different. Terrible student, useless around the house, useless to the community for that matter. I found a crack pipe in her room a couple months ago. People she's chosen to be around are terrible too."

"Have you seen her around lately?"

"Not for a week or so. Now, before you go getting any ideas, no, we didn't kick her out or disown her. Agatha's like a cat. She comes and goes as she pleases, but let me tell you, I've wanted to kick her out from time to time. We make sure there's no drugs in this house, I tell you."

"Well, we're not here sniffing out any drugs," said Denny. "Don't worry about that. I'm trying to find your daughter's killer."

"Well, know if you find drugs, we want nothing to do with them. I can't stand the stuff."

"So, do you have any idea where Aggy is?"

"I hate it," was all Ian said.

"You hate what?"

"All this," Ian continued. "You know, she weren't all that bad. She was a sweet girl up until she realized she were a woman and knew exactly what a woman could do. She started slipping four years ago, but she didn't take the dive until about three years ago when she started running around that Hassan character."

"Hassan?"

"Yes, Hassan Abdul," Ian replied. "He's one of the migrants – Afghan boy, I think. Could be Pakistani or Indian. Who knows? Sometimes they all just blend together and intermingle to become one. Hangs around some abandoned warehouses near the docks."

"What's he to Aggy?"

"She'd like to think he's her boyfriend."

"And how old is this Hassan Abdul?"

"Twenty-three, I believe."

"And you're okay with what amounts to statutory rape?"

"Not at all, but like I said, Aggy's like a housecat. She comes and goes as she pleases. Even if I said anything, I don't think she'd listen. Also, I think you're forgetting age of consent here is sixteen."

"Sorry, had a little lapse there. I come from a state where it's still eighteen. I still think it's sick."

"Not a problem," Ian replied. "I don't like it either. Were it up to me, age of consent would be forty, and that's after the father's dead and out of the picture. Look, what's worse: me letting her go and hang out with some guy who may be too old for her or locking here away in this house like a prison?"

"Do you really want my honest assessment, Mister Love? Because you won't like it. I worked vice for ten of my eleven years with the Portland Police Bureau. I've watched this scenario play out more often that I'd like."

"What are you implying, Detective?"

"This Hassan Abdul is a pimp."

Ian Love recoiled in disgust.

"My Aggie may be a little wayward," Ian said defiantly, "but she's no prostitute."

"I didn't say it with any certainty," Denny defended himself, "but I am speaking from experience. It doesn't have to be that way. Let me talk to Aggie. She may know some things."

"What would she know?"

"Well, did Annie and Aggie ever hang out?"

"Hardly," Ian scoffed. "Like I said, those two were night and day. Annie tried to be the perfect older sister and steer Aggie toward the straight and narrow, but I think she just gave up at some point. No, Annie would've never hung out with Aggie."

39

"So, do you have any idea what Annie was doing the day she went missing?"

"Look, I've already told the detectives the first time when she went missing three days ago."

"Yeah, and this is only my first day on the job, Mister Love, so just humor me for a few minutes more. Remember, I barely know anything about this place, or anyone for that matter."

"She was here writing a college entrance paper for Cambridge, if you must know."

"Legit. Did she go anywhere, talk to anyone?"

"I don't know," Ian Love said defiantly.

"What about her phone? Did you check her phone?"

"Bloody Nora, Detective! She took the bloody thing with her, and it's probably now at the bottom of the bloody Irish Sea! You're interrogating me as if I had something to do with this."

"Mister Love, I want to find out what happened to Annie. I have to ask hard questions if we want to get to the truth. Do you understand? We have no reason to suspect you'd do anything. I just need to know so I can bring justice and closure to you."

"She was murdered and then dumped out at sea. It's that simple. No, I don't know who would do this. Everybody loved her. I know it's cliché, but that's the truth. My little Annie."

Ian Love lost his composure and burst into tears.

"My little baby Annie!" he sobbed. "Why? Why did it have to be you? My perfect little angel?"

Denny caught the man as he collapsed in sorrow, and every ounce of that stoic and stiff British upper lip vanished. Ian Love shuddered as he continued his lament. This must have been the point where the truth had finally hit him. His little girl was never coming home. All the work and love he had put into her, along with Harriet, over the past seventeen years was gone. It was clear that any suspicions on Ian and Harriet Love's part were completely unfounded. A guilty man would never break down like this. Hollywood can never portray accurately the agonizing sounds Ian Love was making. The emotional pain was tantamount to physical pain, as if he were being torn limb from limb and disemboweled, all while alive and conscious.

"Mister Love, I can't make any guarantees," Denny pleaded, "but I will stop at nothing to find the monster who did this."

"Anything you need, Detective Lawton, you can have," Ian Love trembled as he tried to compose himself.

"I just need to make sure you don't know where Aggie is. Just need to double check and cover all my bases, if you catch my drift. I honestly think she can help us here."

"I don't know," said Mister Love as he stood up to lead Denny out of the garage and back down the hallway, "but whatever you do, bring her home. She's still our baby. Help us heal our family."

"I'll try."

Ian Love dried his tears and led Denny back to the great room. Harriet's tears had dried as well, and she was sharing tea with all of the women, Verity and the maids included. At least the mood had lightened somewhat. Hopefully, this was Verity's doing. Hopefully, she had tabs on Agatha's whereabouts.

"DC Baker, you ready?" asked Denny.

"I'm sorry, Missus Love, I must excuse myself," she told Harriet politely.

"Oh, thank you, Detectives," she addressed both Denny and Verity. "Please stop by for tea anytime."

"We'd love to," replied Verity as she rejoined Denny.

"Thank you, Detectives," Ian called as the two detectives turned to leave. "And remember, don't make yourselves strangers. If we find anything out, you'll be the first people we call."

And with that, Denny and Verity left the house and headed back to the Mustang. He remembered to open the passenger door for Verity this time before climbing in on his side. Denny waited a few seconds to start the motor.

"So, how did it go for you?" he asked Verity.

"Splendid," Verity replied. "We had tea, talked about Annie. Mostly stuff I already knew."

"Anything about Aggie?"

"She knows nothing of her whereabouts, just that she comes and goes as she pleases. You?"

"Same, but I do have a name – someone she may be with."

"Who's that?"

"Hassan Abdul."

Verity's expression turned sour at this news.

"What's wrong?" asked Denny.

"Hassan's an interesting character."

"I say we go and check him out," said Denny.

"Hey, I'm a bit hungry. I didn't have time for breakfast, and it's getting late. Want some chips?"

"What aren't you telling me, Princess?"

"I'll tell you over lunch," Verity answered.

Denny looked at his watch and sighed in resignation.

"Over lunch then," he said. "Point the way."

Chapter 5
Fish and Chips and Vinegar

I love fish and chips, don't you?" Verity said as she dabbed her lips with a napkin. "Especially here. You know, this is the best place to get them in all of Lancashire. Seriously, Denny, nothing compares to the fish and chips they have here in Crenshaw."

Denny almost completely ignored Verity's words. She was hiding something. He knew it. For her to go from 0 to 100 with almost the snap of a finger, opening up about something that had no bearing on any of the day's previous events, it didn't add up unless she was redirecting. Either that, or she believed in completely severing break time from work. That could be possible. Even working deep in the slime of humanity, it's not every day a detective sees the corpse of a girl with half her face blown off or the unspeakable anguish of two parents who lost their pride and joy in such a cruel way.

"I know," Denny replied, "you've told me a million times since we've been here."

"And yet, you've barely touched yours," she scolded.

"I go to Mo's whenever I'm back home," Denny argued as he took a bite of the fried fish. "I can get deep-fried cod and French fries anywhere in Astoria."

"But this is the real deal," Verity shot back. "Authentic English fish and chips."

"Yeah, and if I go a couple hours south to Newport, I can get authentic Irish bangers and mash at Nye Beach. Princess, this is great and all, but my mind's on work."

"Not while you're on break, it isn't," Verity reminded him. "Now, enjoy your lunch. It's my money."

"Oh, no, it isn't. I don't let a woman pay my bills, work partner or not."

"So mysterious," Verity chuckled. "Anyway, it's already been a long morning, and I've been working with a stranger. So, who is Detective Dennis Lawton?"

"Who is Hassan Abdul?"

"Now, wait a minute. We'll get to that soon enough. We're on break. Relax."

"What are you hiding, Princess?"

"He's nobody."

"Verity, I can see it in your eyes. You're hiding something."

"Look, he's just a local, one of the migrants. He's nobody important."

"Then why not just look into him? Why are you avoiding the subject? What, is he your lover or something?"

"No!" Verity almost shouted before shifting her eyes around as if she were scanning the area. "Look, you're new here. It's a lot for you to get all tangled up in. And you're a really nice guy and all…"

"Stop stalling, Baker," Denny interrupted. "Who is Hassan Abdul?"

"Denny, we don't talk about Hassan. As far as we know, it's a dead-end case."

44

"Bullcrap!" Denny shouted, slamming his fist on the table. He tried to sink back into his chair as people stared at him. "Why is this such a big secret?" he whispered.

Verity leaned in. She looked Denny dead in the eyes.

"Hassan Abdul is an Afghan migrant. He runs one of the local gangs," Verity whispered. "He keeps somewhat of a harem. Well, I guess you could call it a harem. He likes local girls, English, Scottish, Indian, maybe a few whites from the Continent. Okay, he's indiscriminate, as long as they're young and fresh."

"So, why don't we check into him?" Denny asked. "We could have this solved in a day. Why are you stalling this?"

"You don't get it, do you? How do I put this? Hassan Abdul is part of what we would call a 'protected class'. As far as we know, he is an upstanding citizen, a part of the beautiful tapestry that makes up the citizenry of Crenshaw-on-Ribble."

Even Verity couldn't hide the unspoken disdain and sarcasm that most everybody showed to unscrupulous migrants in the area.

"Same crap I've heard before," Denny shot back.

"Then you know why we don't talk about him."

"I know the why. I just think it's all a load of bullcrap."

"Go after him. You won't get anywhere."

"Why's that?"

"Because nobody will help you."

"Nobody?"

"Like I said, Denny, nobody talks about Hassan Abdul."

"You'll back me up."

"What makes you think that?"

"Because you're my partner, and I'd rush into a burning building for you."

"Sweet, but no."

"So, what? This is just a dead end now? What do we tell the Loves? 'Sorry, your daughter died by a shotgun magically going off in her face'. Or how about this? 'We're so sorry, but your daughter's killer had a high melanin count, so he was too stupid to understand the gravity of the situation'. Does that sound reasonable to you?"

"You make it sound as if Hassan Abdul's already guilty," Verity argued.

45

"You defend him like he's got nothing to hide, Princess, as if what we already know about him isn't reason enough to maybe suspect that there's a connection. So, what? Maybe he's innocent. I'm not wanting to approach this as if he's guilty. I want to know where Agatha Love is. We're not arresting him for statutory. She's what? Sixteen? Well, if they are sleeping, which I can tell by the context of everything going on here, then so what. If he knows where Agatha Love is, that's all I want. We find Agatha, we're closer to finding Annie's killer."

"And what if he did kill Annie Love?" asked Verity. "No, what if he's just an accessory?"

"Then we cross that bridge when we come to it. Look, I know they're rich, and Ian Love is running for Parliament, and the whole county is probably suffering from 'rich white girl syndrome', but the Loves are good people. You saw how Harriet Love was. If anything, they deserve to know."

"Why are you being so bold about this?"

"Because I worked in vice for ten years," Denny answered. "I'm good at this. I know a trail when I smell it, and something just does not seem right with this Abdul situation."

"So, you come to my country and try to play the white knight?"

"Who's saying I'm playing the white knight?"

"Your first day on the job, and you're going after a local like some sort of bloodhound."

"Because people deserve closure. Do you know how many families I've seen torn apart by drugs, alcohol, gambling, and every other vice out there?"

Verity stared Denny down, understanding the rhetorical.

"I can't count how many. Girls out there on the street, barely old enough to need tampons; yet, there they are on the corner. You try to stop it, try to get them to go home; but you can't save them all. One day, you see that poor girl dead in the gutter, or washed up near Vanport or Sauvie Island. That never leaves you – that once-living, breathing girl who had her whole life ahead of her, this person you actually knew and had full-on conversations with, who had intelligence, who could think, reason, and speak, who had a family – a mom, a dad, maybe some brothers and sisters, all gone and thrown into the river like a bag full of dirty diapers and crap. That girl should've been just

46

hanging out with friends, getting into pre-teen shenanigans. Instead, she's sold herself for practically nothing."

"So, you're on a crusade?" Verity asked timidly.

"I guess you could say I'm on a mission from God. At least, that's what I tell myself. You know, I was a deacon back in Oregon. Yeah, a church deacon at a Baptist church in Lake Oswego. Know how often I found myself at odds with my calling? Too many times to count. I'm not sure if you know your Bible, but one of the qualifications of an elder is to be blameless. Now, we weren't pastors, but they held us to the same high standard as church leadership. That being said, I found it hard to be blameless being in that muck. I just had to leave it to the hope that people knew what I was about. There was an understanding that I was above board, but let's be real, you see the pastor parked in front of the liquor store, and you think the worst, even if he was actually going into the Safeway next door and there was no parking."

"I'm sorry, I don't understand," Verity replied.

"This world sucks, and this is some nasty business."

"And you're wanting to save Aggie Love," Verity concluded.

"Those poor people have already lost one daughter," Denny continued. "Why should they suffer the loss of another?"

"Because she's the black sheep of the family," Verity answered. "You don't know Aggie Love. She's the exact opposite of her sister."

"People can change."

"Not when they're that far gone."

"I've seen worse. I've returned teenaged hookers to their parents, and they've gone back to school and graduated with honors. It can be done."

"I promise you're wasting your time."

"How so?"

"Do you really know what kind of person Aggie Love is?"

"No, Princess, enlighten me."

Verity took a deep breath. For the life of her, she could not figure out why this newcomer was pursuing this one insignificant human so doggedly.

"Agatha Amelia Love, born 3 September, 2009," Verity began as if she were a text-to-speech program from the police files. "Born to Harriet Veronica Love (née Nielson) and Ian Peter Love of Crenshaw-on-Ribble, Lancashire, England, United Kingdom. Younger sister of the late Annabelle Violet Love of Crenshaw-on-Ribble. First entered into system 14 February, 2021 for petty theft. Arrested 25 April, 2022 for possession of illegal cannabis. Since then, arrests too many to list in this one sitting. Now, do you understand why we don't care about Aggie Love? She's a lost cause."

"Saul of Tarsus," Denny began. "Born to a Jewish Family in Tarsus, a major city in Asia Minor, of the Tribe of Benjamin, a Pharisee of Pharisees, killed countless Christians before, himself, converting to Christianity and then helping spread the new movement to Europe."

"Did you seriously just use a Bible character to prove your point?" Verity asked incredulously.

"And that's just in the Bible," Denny continued. "Wait until I tell you about the coked-up walker that visited my church once and became a Sunday school teacher. Threw away the coca and heroin and turned to Jesus. Now, she's happily married with three beautiful kids. Verity, nobody's a lost cause. Everybody has value. Everyone's worth saving."

"You know," Verity began, "you're starting to grow on me, and I don't know if I should hate it or embrace it."

"So, you'll take me to Hassan Abdul?" asked Denny.

"If you tell me who you actually are."

"Okay, should I just tell you my police file? I'm Dennis Carl Lawton, born September 30, 1992 in Astoria, Oregon to Brian and Marisol Lawton. I have eleven years with the Portland Police Bureau, ten years with vice, and now I've been transferred overseas to the Lancashire Constabulary on an officer exchange program. Father of three, recently divorced…"

"Divorced?" Verity interrupted.

"Yeah, really put a damper on the whole deacon thing too. She took the kids, the house, both the cars, even the dog. Left me the stocks and bonds though. We were smart and invested in crypto when nobody cared about it. I cashed out when I moved here, bought a nice little cottage by the sea and that Stang. All clean, no alimony, just a child support check every month."

"I get it," Verity replied. "I'm recently divorced too. My husband decided he needed to find his real self and split for Brighton. His new boyfriend was even more important than our daughter."

"I would give anything to see my kids again," said Denny. "My wife was eight months along when she ended the marriage. I have a kid that I've never even met."

"And you've never tried to see them?"

"My ex has full custody. Not just that, but she has a restraining order against me."

"Why would she do that?"

"Because someone convinced her that I was a terrible person because I worked vice. Apparently, I'm a dirty, rotten sinner because I spend my days around harlots and boozers. Wasn't a problem for ten years, and now all of a sudden, it is. And you know the worst part about it, Princess? It was my best friend that convinced her I was so bad, and then the jack wagon turned around and married her."

"So, you've come here to get away from it all?"

"In a way, yes. I kind of wanted a change of scenery."

"So, you volunteered first thing?"

"I guess you could say that. I didn't run."

"I never said you did."

"I know how it looks. My life back home sucks, and I move halfway around the world. I just needed a new start."

"Well, you've certainly made an impression."

"So, what about you, since we're wasting our breaktime?" Denny shot back.

"Well, I've been in Crenshaw all my life. I was married for nine years until, as I've told you, my husband left me and my eight-year-old daughter. I've been with the LC for six years."

"Okay, so now that we know each other a little better," Denny started as he dropped some cash on the table and glanced toward his Mustang, "can we go?"

"You're really dead set on finding Aggie Love, aren't you?"

"For all we know, Aggie could've been away with someone else when Annie disappeared. I just want to know. I just want the Loves to have answers."

"You know," Verity added, "I have a feeling you're going to find more than you want to know, and it's not going to end well for anybody."

"Well, the truth will inevitably come out, so why wait?" said Denny as he stood up.

"If they start asking questions, Denny, I had nothing to do with this."

"Be a bystander," said Denny. "That way, if things go south, you have plausible deniability."

"You're really guilt tripping me, aren't you?" Verity shot back as she followed Denny to the car.

"If that's what you want to call it," Denny chuckled.

"That's not fair," Verity laughed.

"See, now you get it. Hey, I told you what I was about the moment we met. I don't mess around. I'm a cop. It's my job to make sure evildoers are brought to justice, and there's an evildoer here in Crenshaw."

"And you want to find him?"

"That's the idea, Princess."

Chapter 6
Hassan Abdul

For such a small space, the peninsula of Crenshaw-on-Ribble held a diverse landscape. In the northern and eastern portions, there was a traditional English seaside town, untouched by the Industrial Age, save for some paved road and electric lighting. On the west side, there were luxury homes overlooking the Irish Sea. On the south side, it was all brutalist post-war grunge. Apartments, warehouses, and a wide highway marked the destruction of historic Crenshaw.

Hassan Abdul was a resident of these parts. At least, he lived somewhere in the area. He never gave any definite address; there was nothing in the registry. However, everyone knew where he and his gang hung out.

The whole place reminded Denny of the Pearl District – grungy warehouses with a veneer of hipster trendiness slapped on the outside. In front of the warehouses were gathered men that slightly resembled him, if only in complexion. They were gathered around a fleet of Bentleys, at least one from each current model they produced, sometimes three or four – all in different colors.

"Guy must like his Bentleys," Denny commented.

"He's been said to have a penchant for finer things," Verity replied. "This is just his main hangout. It's rumored he has an actual mansion somewhere on the mainland."

The Afghans gathered outside glared at the stranger. Denny instinctively felt for his weapon, only to feel momentary shock at the reminder that he couldn't carry one here. Nothing new – he had had loads of situations in vice where he had to go in unarmed. At that point, his only weapons were his brain and possibly his knuckles. If things went south, there was always the likelihood that one of the thugs was illegally packing, and he could surprise them and disarm them. He had had that training before.

"You sure you want to see Hassan?" Verity whispered.

"Now more than ever," Denny replied as he reached for his badge.

Two burly men with brown faces obscured by thick black beards blocked the main doors of the warehouse. Denny flashed his badge.

"I'm here to see Hassan Abdul," he announced confidently.

The two muscle men stared him down, their brown hooded eyes gleaming with fire.

"He's not in trouble," Verity added. "We just think he may know the whereabouts of a person of interest."

The two guards turned to each other and started conversing through whispers in a foreign language that sounded to Denny like gibberish with some coughing and hacking thrown into the mix.

"Put your arms out," one of the guards instructed.

Denny and Verity obeyed the command as the two guards started to frisk them. One of them drew Denny's visible ire as he paused around Verity's breasts. Of course, he would. Any other day, that piece of trash wouldn't be recognizable as a human after Denny got done with him. If Denny had his way, that fool would be singing soprano in the choir eternal if he put his hands on a woman like that.

52

"They're clean," the other guard said.

"Don't do anything you'll regret," Denny's guard instructed the two cops.

The doors opened, leading to a dark hallway.

"You know he did that just so he could touch you, right?" Denny whispered.

"Comes with the territory," Verity replied.

"Doesn't have to," said Denny.

"You wanted to see Hassan Abdul. You're going to see Hassan Abdul."

"You didn't have to follow me if you knew he was going to touch you like that."

"What happened to 'I have your back if you have mine'?"

"Had I known they were going to have a little extra fun with you," Denny argued back, "I would've told you to stay in the car."

"Doesn't work like that, Lawton."

"He better not meet me in a dark alley then," Denny hissed. "I've spent enough time with thugs like these to know how to make a fool disappear."

Hassan Abdul possessed none of the visual qualities of a leader. Short and stalky, he looked like a little demon spawn, like a little gremlin that would jump onto your back at lightning speed and not let go. He was dressed in a Manchester United sweatshirt, blue jeans, and a black Carhartt beanie, definitely not the type of person that looked like he enjoyed the finer things. He appeared more like a soccer hooligan who'd just returned from an afternoon match. He did, though, keep a keffiyeh wrapped around his shoulders; that was the only thing that told Denny that maybe this guy wasn't a local.

For Denny, though, it was the eyes. It was definitely the eyes – two white orbs with big brown irises and dark beady pupils. They were the eyes of a demon. That was it. That was what seemed so threatening about this guy when it came to his person. If it came to a fight, Denny was sure he could take him.

Abdul was seated on an old-yet-plush couch in the middle of a large empty room of the warehouse, as if he were a king in court. The fine furniture felt as out of place of this industrial hellhole as did the Bentleys – the king of a third-world industrial hellhole. Hassan Abdul

53

had his arm wrapped around the back of a young coffee-colored woman – obviously a pick from his alleged harem. With a snap of his fingers, she left him to give him privacy while he embraced his new visitors.

"Ah, welcome, my friends," he said in a warm, yet somehow threatening tone. He had a high-pitched, yet mellifluous voice that was an odd mixture of his native Afghan accent and some of the local dialect.

Even more threatening was a third muscle man to Hassan's right – obviously his main body guard. The man was even bigger than the two guards outside. His long black beard extended full down to his diaphragm. Instead of the grungy hood clothes Abdul wore, the guard was dressed to the nines – a navy-blue Hickey Freeman suit with a matching tie and Johnston & Murphy Oxfords. Breaking from his western business attire, he wore a small Taqiyah. He was packing heat, no doubt. That jacket could easily conceal a handgun holstered in a pair of suspenders. That would make sense. Hassan Abdul wouldn't need to worry about the need to carry or being caught illegally carrying if "Bluto" had his back.

"Detective Constable Dennis Lawton," Denny held out his badge. "This is my partner, DC Verity Baker."

"How's it going, Verity?" Hassan addressed Verity.

"Not too bad, Hassan," Verity replied. "Just showing this Yank around the village, getting him acquainted with all you lot."

"Right, I forgot everyone knows everyone here," Denny chuckled.

"Well, it comes with the territory," Hassan replied.

"Where have I heard that before?" Denny talked through the side of his mouth to Verity.

"So, what brings you to my humble abode?" Hassan asked, spreading his arms to gesture to the empty warehouse as if it were a palace.

"We came to ask a couple questions," Denny replied. "Nothing bad or incriminating."

"Oh?" Hassan replied as he theatrically recoiled.

"We just wanted to see if you may have an idea of where Agatha Love is."

"What makes you think I would know?" asked Hassan.

"We've been told she hangs out here," said Denny. "A couple of people say they've seen her with you."

"Hey, Habib," Hassan gestured to his body guard, "you know who this Infidel's talking about?"

"It is quite possible," Habib replied with a knowing grin.

"Look, we think she may be in danger," Denny pleaded. "You heard about her sister, right?"

"Oh yeah, poor Annie," Hassan nodded. "Yeah, I seen it on the telly. Poor girl. Real shame too. Ah, yes, yes, I know who you're talking about now. Aggie Love – sweet girl she is. Knows how to have a good time."

"We have a feeling that given what Agatha's been involved in, there may be a connection to Annie's murder."

"And you think you one my boys down there is to blame."

"Oh, no, not at all," Denny recoiled. "No, we don't have any suspects at the moment."

"Good, because let me tell you something, Detective Lawton. Aggie Love hangs out with anyone and everyone who'll give her a good time. Okay? She craves attention. You had better get that through your skull before you go accusing any of my boys. She don't hang out with just us, you know. You might wanna check out some of the blokes out in Banks."

"Do you or do you not know where she is?" asked Denny. "That's all I want to know."

"I've no clue, and if I did, you'd be the first to know."

Denny made direct eye contact with Hassan. He couldn't figure out the reason if this guy had nothing to do with it that he seemed disingenuous. He had to be playing with his mind. Something was off here. Sure, it was obvious that things here weren't strictly legal; everyone knew that. There just seemed to be more to the story.

"Mister Abdul," Denny continued, "just how do you make your money?"

"What do you say back in America? 'I plead the Fifth'?"

"Well, the 'Fifth' doesn't exactly apply out here. I was just interested in how a man who lives in a place like this has such a fine taste in British machinery."

"My Bentleys?"

"Yeah, I was just wondering how you came by them. You just seem to have quite the affinity for fine British craftsmanship."

"Honestly, if that's what you want to know," Hassan shot back. "You can run the registration. It's all legal, bought and paid for."

Denny took another good look in Hassan's eyes. That part was true. There was nothing left here.

"Well, Verity," said Denny, "I think that's all the help Mister Abdul can give us today. Thank you for your time, sir."

Hassan extended his right hand, and Denny shook it. Even this seemed disingenuous. It was as if Hassan were trying to convince Denny he was truly on his side. That wasn't happening today. He had shaken hands with guys like this enough times to know when the handshake was meaningful.

"Detective, if there is any way I can help you, let me know, and I will gladly provide any information I may have."

Denny thanked Hassan and followed Verity out. The muscle men were still there. These idiots were so easy to read. They were thirsty – thirsty for the attractive brunette he accompanied that wasn't available to either of them. He could see it behind their dead eyes. They had already undressed her in their minds, had their way with her, and discarded her for their next hunk of human meat. Denny instinctually took Verity's hand as if to protect her as he led her to the Mustang.

"Denny! What're you doing?" she demanded.

"Just get in the car," he instructed.

Safely inside the fortress of the car, Denny let out a long breath.

"Now, can you please explain to me what the devil's gotten into you?" Verity asked.

"He's lying," said Denny.

"Is he now?" Verity rolled her eyes.

"You couldn't tell?"

"Search the system," Verity argued. "We have nothing on him. Those cars will come back clean."

"That's the problem," Denny shot back. "Why don't we? You know, why don't we search the system for further things? Are the cars registered here as fleet vehicles? Why is there no actual home address? Where does he sleep at night? Clearly, there's something going on in there that he doesn't want us to know about."

"And we can't do nothing about it without proof."

Denny sighed as he fired up the engine. The bangers were staring him down again. They wanted him gone. He agreed with that assessment and put the car in first.

"So," Verity began, "what did you pick up, Supercop?"

"You know how you can just tell someone's lying by looking in their eyes?"

"We all know that," Verity rolled her eyes.

"Yeah, the eyes are the window to the soul. He knows something. I've seen that look in every pimp I had to bust."

"Look," Verity continued, "I know it all looks bad. He's definitely not ethical, but he keeps it all legal. The girls, he may have a 'harem'," she air quoted, "but he isn't a polygamist on paper, and none of them are underage that we know of. He doesn't have any thefts on his record."

"Who owns the warehouse?" Denny asked.

"He does," Verity replied. "Old run-down warehouses sold for dirt cheap. Check the records. He paid £10,000 for it in 2015. I bet you're going to ask how he makes his money, since he didn't seem to keen to answer you in that regard. He owns a couple chip shops in the area – even has a couple carts in Blackpool. He's clean, Denny. He just lives differently than we'd expect."

"Do you know how many people I've arrested that were 'clean', Verity? Do you know how many politicians, pastors, and parents I've gone after who didn't have any record until I caught them meeting up with children? I'm not looking for something on him, but I feel like I'm going to stumble on it."

"You've really come here to tear this community apart, haven't you?"

Denny couldn't tell if Verity was being serious. He held his tongue for a second before letting out a big sigh.

"I just showed up here and was assigned a case. If I wanted to tear this community apart, whoever killed Annie Love already beat me to it."

By now, it was getting late. It was Friday, and it was time to go home. Verity chuckled at the irony.

"What's so funny?" Denny asked.

"It's my Monday and my Friday," she replied. "One day back on the job, and I already get a day off."

"Same here, I guess," said Denny. "What do you guys do around here on the weekend?"

"I take care of my daughter," Verity answered. "She needs all the attention she can get."

"Uh-huh," Denny acknowledged as he guided the Mustang into his parking spot.

"And what are you planning on tomorrow?" Verity asked, trying to guide the conversation away from the gang leader.

"More unpacking, getting settled in," Denny replied as he killed the motor.

"Sounds like you'll have loads of fun," Verity chuckled.

"So, uh, same time Monday?" Denny asked.

"It's a date," said Verity as they left the car and walked into the office.

"I'll write up the report," said Denny as he sat at his desk.

"Oh, you'd do that for me?" Verity gushed in jest.

"I'm a fast typist," Denny bragged.

"Good, because I need to make sure my daughter actually made it home today. She missed the bus this morning."

"Have a great weekend," Denny bade her. "I'll let you know if I find anything out."

Verity turned to leave. This place was getting to her, and she had only spent not even twenty minutes here this morning. She was about to head out the door, but she felt the wind change. At least, that's what it felt like. She was so close to being out of here. Someone was walking up behind her.

"Oi, Baker, please see me in my office," came the voice from behind her.

Chapter 7

The Real Dennis Lawton

Whit's office seemed cold. Who was Verity kidding? It always seemed cold. Can't have such a dark business feel so warm, you know. DI Whiteaker always kept his decorations sparse – a commendation from the Royal Navy, a part of golden gloves hanging from a thumb tack in the wall, and a picture of he and his family that he always had facing him. The office was plain. Apart from his decoration, it was dark wood paneling and a very plain desk with a computer monitor on top. It was clean. Detective Inspector Brandon Whiteaker was here to work, and that was all.

"So, how'd it go, Baker?" he asked Verity as he sat back in his office chair.

"Where do I start?" Verity sighed as she rolled her eyes.

"Train wreck, was he?" Whit chuckled.

"You knew you were pairing me with a boy scout, didn't you?"

"Well, they told me he was their best," said Whit.

"He's a bleedin' bloodhound!" Verity exclaimed.

"Bleedin' bloodhound," Whit chuckled.

"He's literally tearing the whole village apart!"

"You want this case shut, don't you?"

"But he's running his mouth…"

"He's an American," Whit interrupted. "It's what they do."

"And he's so sure of himself," Verity continued, "bulldozing through everything like he owns the place. He told the Loves that he'd find Annie's killer before we even knew she was murdered."

"A slip-up," Whit commented. "He's a little off his game, I see."

"Then he goes on this whole witch-hunt," Verity said. "Pressed me to take him and see Hassan Abdul."

"Isn't he that Pakistani?"

"Afghan," Verity corrected.

"Yes, Afghan," White repeated.

"Yes, he's a migrant."

"What did he want with a migrant?"

"Our investigation led that way. See, we were trying to determine the whereabouts of Agatha Love."

"Think she's connected to the murder?"

"We thought she could be in a round-about way. Fat Terry and Ian Love both told us she hangs out around Hassan Abdul."

"And your new partner thought they might be connected," Whit concluded.

"He said he didn't think Hassan had anything to do with it."

"And you think different?"

"Denny changed his mind. Says he can tell Hassan is lying or, at least, he knows more than he's letting on. Nobody knows where Agatha Love is, but Denny is convinced Hassan actually does and is just covering for something nefarious."

Whit sat back in his chair, clearly troubled by this.

"This isn't good."

"I told him to leave well-enough alone," Verity explained, "but he was so gung-ho about catching a killer."

'Did you two dig up any more leads?"

"Hassan was our last stop."

Whit let out a four-letter expletive.

"Verity, whatever you do, please make sure he leaves Hassan Abdul alone."

"Whit, I know we generally avoid him, but is there any other good reason he'll take other than that's just what we do?"

"Do you want the official reason or the true reason?"

"Whit, you've always shot straight with me."

"He's brown. That's it. The reason we don't investigate him, even though we know he's up to something, is because he's brown. Do you know what happens when a white cop cuffs a brown criminal?"

"Social media?" Verity replied.

"Social media," Whit confirmed. "People get ahold of it, edit it to fit their narrative, and create a story. So, while we have one piece of scum off the street, hundreds of thousands more come out of the woodwork to take his place. Happens every time. A criminal dies, looks sympathetic, and the people riot."

"So, what if he did have something to do with Annie's murder?" asked Verity. "It's not like she was a common whore. She was a top student, popular girl. She comes from a family with some money."

"You don't think I know that? I've had reporters all day asking me about the case. Of course, the care we've put into it has come up several times based on who the victim is. Look at this." Whit held up a pack of cigarettes. "I've been trying to quit. Three packs already I've smoked today."

"So, you're saying we need to find another suspect."

"Do you have any suspects?"

"Not officially. I think Denny was dead set that Hassan Abdul was a suspect. We're trying to locate Agatha Love. I think she's the link in this case."

"What makes you think that?"

"Think about it, Whit. She's out doing whatever. She was the one we all thought would end up a corpse floating in the harbor."

"So, if you find Aggie Love, you'll be closer to finding who killed Annie Love."

"That's what we're thinking."

"If we don't hear anything about her over the next few days or so, go out to the mainland," Whit instructed. "I hear she likes to travel to Banks and get into trouble there."

Verity stared at Whit blankly. It was as if he'd had the answers all day.

"Did you…"

"You could've called me," Whit chuckled.

"I'm sorry," Verity apologized. "It's Denny. He's just so fast."

"Is he now?"

"It's like following a toddler around. You know how that is? It's like one thing to the next with no break. Didn't even want to sit and enjoy his lunch break."

"Sounds like he wants to find his man."

"Not to mention, he doesn't follow protocol."

"How so?"

"We were speeding around in that big boy toy of his – that Mustang – all day like this was the bloomin' Indianapolis 500."

"Sounds serious," Whit commented, obviously bored with Verity's rant.

"Aren't you even the least bit concerned?" asked Verity.

"Why should I be?" asked Whit. "I trust him."

"Why do you trust him? He's barely been here a day."

"Because his police chief back in Oregon assured me that he was the best."

"Then why send their best man to some forgotten backwater in bloody Lancashire? I mean, if they were going to exchange their best man, why not something more prestigious like Manchester, the Metro, or even Scotland Yard?"

Whit looked out the window. Denny was walking to his car, his backpack thrown over his shoulder. The American climbed into the Mustang and backed out. The squealing tires and roaring V8 echoed as he peeled off toward home.

"Can I tell you something in the strictest of confidence?" Whit asked.

"What's the secret Whit?"

"So, the reason he's here isn't because he wanted some change of scenery or the fact that he's a great cop. Granted, I think we made out like bandits with him. He's great at his job."

"Stop stalling, Whit."

Whit took a deep breath. He knew this was going to hurt, emotionally and physically if Verity had her way.

"Verity, Dennis Lawton is under investigation."

"Investigation? For what?"

"I need you to relax."

He could tell she had tensed up. What he was about to tell her would send her through the roof if she was high-strung.

"DC Lawton was accused of raping a prostitute."

"And you paired me with him?" Verity started to raise her voice in anger. "You put me in a car with a suspected rapist? What about my safety, Whit?"

"Verity, sit down."

"The heck I'm sitting down! You're unbelievable!"

"As is the accusation."

"How so?" asked Verity as she took her seat.

"He didn't do it."

"How can you be so sure?"

"Because his chief swore to me that he didn't."

"Oh, so now we're just going on promises? What did you do? Scout's honor? Is that what we're basing workplace safety on now?"

"Verity, the guy has a clean record."

"And so did many of the lowlifes he arrested back in Portland, as he attested. And as have many of the people I've taken in. A clean record means absolutely nothing."

"It's not in his character to do what they said he did. It's a prostitute's word against a trusted cop. Not only that, Dennis Lawton walked the talk. He was faithful to his wife. He was a deacon in his church. Never had a complaint, and he's been working vice for ten years. And just now, he gets accused of rape? Please. There is no way for a second that I'd believe that. It's shaky at best."

"Then why did they send him away?"

"Because the investigation went sour. The prostitute found some friends that wanted a piece of the action. The DA and mayor weren't friends of his either – something about the fact that he had no filter and hurt everybody's feelings. His wife found out. She dumped him on the spot."

"He told me she took everything he had except for his crypto."

"He lucked out there."

"I just can't believe you'd put me with him."

"Look, Verity, if you want to go solo or get a different partner, I totally understand. I put you in an awkward spot. I'm sorry."

"I just wish I'd been told all this. It's hard returning to work after an absence on a Friday."

"DC Baker, I promise you that you're working with the best when you have Dennis Lawton by your side. The books all prove it. Absent this small hiccup, you'll solve that murder."

"What if it comes to investigating Hassan Abdul?" asked Verity. "What if he actually does have something to do with this?"

"Let's cross that bridge when we come to it," Whit brushed her concern off.

"It's all a lot to take in," Verity concluded.

"Go home, Baker," Whit instructed. "It's only been a day, and you look like you haven't had a day off in a month. Which is funny, because I just got done paying you to stay home for a month. Go home, have a glass of wine. Enjoy the weekend."

"If you insist," Verity chuckled.

"Hey, good work, Baker," said Whit as he stood up and extended his hand. "Welcome back."

Verity shook Whit's hand and walked out. She sat down at her desk and fired up her computer. There was just one thing the wanted. She delved into the address book. There it was: 28 Ocean Breeze Lane, Crenshaw-on-Ribble. She would be making a visit in the morning.

As Verity walked out to her car, a chill set in. Josh was just returning from his beat. Still a happy soul, he was.

"Oi, Verity!" he called.

"Josh, how are you?"

"Honestly?"

"Yes, of course, honestly."

His face turned downcast.

"I had to arrest an old man today," he replied.

64

"What for?"

"Social media posts," Josh explained. "It was so innocuous too. He just posted a news article about a murder in New York."

"Okay? Nothing to do with anything here. What was so bad about what he posted?"

"Apparently, it was an Arab-on-white crime. He posted the story, and someone complained anonymously. Said it was distressin' to them or some rubbish like that."

"Oh, Josh, I'm so sorry."

"I hate being all business-like and all that. I hated putting the cuffs on him. It felt like his arms would break if I just touched them. I was just followin' orders, but I feel like that's what the Nazis would've said."

"Was it all that bad?"

"Verity, I feel like we're losing our purpose here. I became a cop to help people. Nowadays, I feel like all we do is arrest people for not paying their television license or for hurting the wrong people's feelings. I'm sick of it."

"Josh, I think we've all earned a good weekend. You get in there, do your paperwork, and go home. Louisa's probably worried sick about you."

"If you insist, Ver."

Verity finally reached her car. Rain was starting to patter down. This just wasn't right. An old man was arrested for something so petty. Here she was, working with a man who would say something ten times worse than whatever that old geezer had posted, and he'd say it loud and proud.

Verity took stock of the day. She couldn't decide whether it had been a success or a disaster. Sure, their investigation had gone far, but at what cost? Agatha Love was nowhere to be found, Denny (and by extension she) was on Hassan Abdul's bad side, and they were still far from determining Annie Love's killer.

"Oh, Denny," she sighed out loud as she thought about his stupidity. That was another thing. He came in here guns blazing like he was ready to take on the world. He truly seemed like he was all on the side of truth and justice. Now, she even questioned her safety with him. Could what Whit said be trusted? Was he capable of hurting a woman? Of course, he was. Almost all men are. The question wasn't whether or not he was capable, but whether or not he had the character to keep his hands off. Oh, she saw the way he glared at that guard when he took extra time frisking her; but she wasn't sure. Could that all be an act?

Verity's thoughts returned to the poor old man that Josh had had to arrest. That was over a stupid social media post. Denny was leading them into even more dangerous waters. She could tell he wanted to poke the bear further. If they arrest an old man for merely posting a news article from the *New York Post*, what would they do when a cop accuses a Muslim migrant of murder?

Part 2
Finding Myself

This time, it was for real. At least, it was the confirmation of what she had expected for a long time. It just didn't seem real now that it was all out in the open like this. The women's cosmetics, the phone calls, long nights away from home, the secrecy. She had spent the better part of nine years almost hoping it was another woman. She could work it out with him then. It could be excused within reason. She reasoned that she wasn't always her chipper self every day and that she wasn't always a peach to live with. But another man? Did she really know who he was at this point? Had she actually loved a closeted homosexual who played at her heart? She actually bore a child by him? Was it actually 'making love' at that point if he didn't actually love the woman he was making love with? Nine years of living a foul lie.

"Look, I really feel like I'm finding my true self," he excused himself, spinning by rote the line they all recite nowadays to avoid accountability.

"That's a lie, Elliott, and you know it!" she shouted at him. "You're lying to me, and you're lying to yourself."

"I've been lying to myself for years, Verity. I have to live my truth now. It's the only way I can actually be me."

"You made a promise to me. Shoot, you made a promise before man and God, if He even exists. Does that not mean anything?"

"It was all a mistake. I didn't know."

"Nine years, and you're just now figuring that out — that you didn't know what you were doing? What, did you just think getting married to a woman and having sex with her would make the gay magically go away? Is that it? After all we've done. Your own daughter? You had a baby with me, and now all of a sudden, you're gay? You're giving up all this for what?"

"To live my truth."

"Truth is here staring you right back in your stupid face. There is no way on God's green earth that this is true, none of it."

Elliott tossed his suitcase into the back of his Land Rover. This was really it. He was leaving. This just didn't seem fair.

"One of these days, you're going to come back from Brighton, or wherever you've run off to and try to start where you left off," Verity spat as she grabbed Elliott by the arm, "and you're going to find everyone's moved on. Then you'll see how sad of a man you really are. You'll find yourself alone and see that nobody loves you because you pushed away everything that was good and decent in your life. You believe this lie about yourself, and you've just decided to change. This isn't how it's supposed to work."

"I'm sorry, Verity, but this is me."

"I can't do this anymore," she cried, the tears finally starting to well up. "I can't put up with this fight. Nine freaking years, I tried fighting for you."

"Then don't," Elliott replied, completely indifferent to her suffering. "Live your life."

Elliott felt the sting on his cheek a few seconds before he registered what had happened. He turned to see Verity waving her hand in pain.

"Then go on, go and live your truth, whatever that means," Verity hissed. "I swear, you will never come back to this world when you've hit rock bottom. I swear it on my blood. You will never see your daughter again, you selfish puke.

"Good-bye, Verity," was all he had to say as he turned and climbed into his Land Rover.

Verity watched for what seemed like hours, if not days, as the Land Rover disappeared down the road. Here she was now, alone. Her daughter, fatherless. Her bed, empty. It was going to be a long year.

Chapter 8
That's Not Me

Verity double checked the evidence as she pulled up to the modest beachside bungalow. She had half expected a street-block-sized American flag waving from a 200-foot flagpole in the front yard, maybe a few "Trump-Vance 2024" yard signs for some odd reason. Instead, the Mustang parked in front of the house was all the evidence she needed. Heck, it was the only one in town.

"Stay in the car, yeah," Verity said as she turned around to talk to Hallie. "I'll be just a few moments."

"But do I have to?" Hallie groaned.

"Just a few minutes," Verity matched her energy. "I need to talk to someone from work."

"But it's a Saturday," Hallie complained. "You don't work on a Saturday."

"Just a few minutes, then we'll go to the seaside."

Before Hallie could say another word, Verity had closed the door and walked up the stone path to the front of the house. For oceanfront property, this was probably the cheapest house on the peninsula — clean but very modest. The door was solid oak. That was for sure. It didn't resonate when she knocked on it. Moreover, she wrung her hand from the pain of punching solid wood with it.

Verity was greeted with a totally different Denny Lawton. It was 9 in the morning, and he was wearing a Trailblazers t-shirt and matching shorts. His hair looked like a big black bird's nest. He'd left his five o'clock shadow unshaven this morning. She decided she liked that look. Who was she kidding? This guy was a potential danger for her, and she just caught herself mooning over him.

"Come to pick me up for work?" Denny chuckled.

"No, I came to talk to you," was Verity's curt reply, trying to get her attraction for his tough guy stubble out of her mind.

"Good, because last I checked, it was Saturday."

"I won't be long," Verity continued.

"Good, because I'm cooking breakfast," Denny said. "Why don't you come in?"

"I'm really in a hurry."

"I insist."

"Denny, I'm really in a hurry."

"Hey, you showed up at my door on our day off. I at least gotta share some breakfast."

"Denny," Verity groaned.

"Five minutes, that's all," Denny pleaded.

Verity looked back to her car. Hallie was engrossed with something on her phone. What hurt would five minutes do?

"Alright," she conceded, and she entered the house, leaving the door open.

Denny was back in his kitchen. Verity hadn't noticed before, but he was covered in some white powder. Cocaine? No, it couldn't be. That short suspicion was disproven when she saw a bowl of that

71

powder mixed with some water and black pepper. It was flour and baking powder.

"Sorry you caught me at a bad time," Denny said. "I made a late-night ASDA run. Breakfast is almost ready."

"What is it?" Verity asked as she sat down at the bar.

"Biscuits and gravy – my grandma's recipe," Denny answered. "I've got some ground sausage on the stove. Hopefully it should all be ready in a couple minutes."

"Did you do it?" Verity asked, completely ignoring Denny's offer.

"What? Did I do what?" he asked as he continued to stir the bowl of gravy. "Make this breakfast all by myself?"

"Did you rape her?"

"Rape who? Verity, I've only been here for, like, a week and a half."

"I talked to Whit."

"I didn't do it," Denny said, as if he all of a sudden caught what Verity was putting across to him, as if she'd been accusing him all day long.

"That's it? You didn't do it? That's all you're going to say? Not didn't do what? Not who I think you raped?"

Denny stopped stirring and slammed the bowl down onto the counter. He took a deep breath. He paused for a while, as if for dramatic effect.

"Mummy?" a voice echoed through the house, causing both Denny and Verity to jump.

"Bloody Nora, Hallie! I told you to wait in the car," Verity scolded her daughter.

"I'm sorry, I got bored," Hallie excused herself.

"With Amazon?"

"I've finished all the episodes of *Blue Peter* you downloaded," Hallie explained.

"'Hallie' is it?" Denny asked. "Hey, I've got a TV in the living room with BBC iPlayer on it. There's plenty of *Blue Peter* for you to watch while me and your mom have a chat. Remote's on the couch."

Without a word, Hallie made a b-line for the living room. Denny and Verity stood in silence until the sounds from the children's program could drown out their conversation.

"What do you mean you didn't do it?" asked Verity. "How am I supposed to feel safe when my partner is an accused rapist."

"'Accused' is the key word," Denny shot back.

"'Accused' is enough to make me glance over my shoulder every time I'm with you," Verity argued.

"Did anything I said or did yesterday give you any reason to doubt that I am who I say I am?" Denny asked.

Verity took a deep breath, running through the events the day prior. True, he had behaved like the perfect gentleman; and she could see the fire of anger in his eyes when Hassan's guard manhandled her. Was it anger because a lady was being violated, or was it jealousy that he couldn't get his hands on her? No, that was definitely a man who would defend her. And that was another thing. What was that all about him promising to have her back? Would a rapist do that? From the nine or ten hours she had spent with him the previous day, which wasn't much to go on, he couldn't be. Verity sighed.

"You were nothing but a gentleman to me yesterday," Verity replied. "Who are you?"

"I told you," Denny began as he poured the gravy mixture into a pan along with the ground sausage and set it on simmer, "I'm Detective Constable Dennis Lawton. You know who I am. Coffee? It's black."

"Yes, please. But the actual you," Verity pressed him, tears almost coming to her eyes. "I want to know exactly why you are here. Why you? How does Portland's best vice cop get accused of rape so that he's exchanged for our worst?"

"You really wanna know?"

"Yes."

"Here," said Denny as he split two biscuits and poured the gravy over them, "it's a long story. I hope you're hungry."

She was an informant – a hooker, twenty-five years old. You know, we all had them – informants, that is. Anyway, I'd worked with her for a couple years, had a good rapport. See, I try to get as many of them off the streets before it's too late. You know, they just seem to get younger and younger.

Now, I knew who her pimp was. Off the record, everybody knew who he was. She was just small potatoes compared to him. I knew once I got to him, actually proved it all in broad daylight and arrested him, I'd lose an informant; but, you know, at that point, it wouldn't matter. I wanted him – Aloysius Cephas McFarland was his name. Went by "Sticky". I'm sure you know that "Aloysius" isn't exactly a gangster's name, and "Cephas" sounds like some old grandpa. Goes to prove that no matter how good your mama's intentions are in giving you such a high name, you can still become lower dirt.

So, this girl, Michaela Roberts, she's my informant. She'd been on the streets for almost as long as I'd been a cop. By the time I'd gotten to her, she was twenty-one and in way too deep. You'd think she was twenty years older than she was because the drugs sucked all of the life out of her. I hated seeing her like that, you know. So much potential.

"Church Man!" she'd always say in this raspy, lispy voice when she saw me. She was missing about half of her teeth. The half of the remaining teeth were either brown or black with decay.

Yeah, she knew she could never turn a trick with me. I hate to brag, but she envied my wife and said so many times. Was I attracted to her? Heck no! See, I'm of the opinion that the face is the first physical feature that should draw a man to a woman; and I'm not so sorry to say that it didn't suit me. You know, sunken eyes and no teeth just don't hit it for me for some weird reason. I don't know.

On some level, I think she knew she was stuck because she was so willing to help me get other girls out of it. She knew who was dealing, who was putting themselves out, and who was pimping. She knew she was owned, so helping me was her way of rebelling against the man. We put some low-level guys out of business – sent many girls home, but none of these guys ever snitched on Sticky.

So, here we were. It was a Sunday after church. Talia, my wife, she'd been feeling the pregnancy all day and wanted a rest. She was eight months along and just wanted this baby out of her. Her back was killing her, and she'd been on her feet all day helping in Sunday school and junior church. I was on my own for lunch that day, which was fine. My two already-born kids were more than happy with a delivery pizza. I sat them down in front of the TV to watch some *VeggieTales* while I made the order.

74

Now, I generally like to keep my work and homelife separate, for obvious reasons. You know, I can't have my three-year-old listening to some story about how some kid who saw no way out blew his brains out with a sawed-off shotgun. You know, there's just something about blood and gore that doesn't beat the wholesomeness of *Bear and the Big Blue House*.

I was putting in the order for the pizza and breadsticks when my work phone buzzed in my pocket. I always kept both phones with me, because even when I'm off-duty, I'm on-call. I ignored it and continued with the order. These kinds of calls can usually wait, even if it's a big deal. After a couple seconds, the buzzing stopped. I was about to put in my debit card info when it buzzed again. I ignored it. My kids are important, and I just had a feeling it was something that would distract me in a major way. I didn't need that right now. Boy, was my prediction right.

The buzzing stopped again. I hit "Place Order" and set my phone down. I pulled out my work phone and received a start when the stupid thing started buzzing again. I looked at the readout. It was Michaela.

"*PLZ HELP!!!*" was all it said.

"*WHERE R U?*" I typed back.

"*HOTEL STUMPTOWN*" she texted back.

Hotel Stumptown, that was in the Pearl District – the part of the Pearl District that hadn't been revived yet. Graffiti, homeless camps, tweakers getting all up in your face. This was bad. What could she want? It was all empty run-down warehouses, kind of like Hassan's place.

"*What's wrong?*" I messaged.

I went and grabbed my keys. Informants didn't just text me out of the blue if there wasn't something terribly wrong, especially on a Sunday. Sure, they wanted to get something out of me, but that came at a price: information; and I was the one who solicited it, not the other way around.

BUZZ

I looked at my phone again.

"*HE KNOWS*"

This was bad. "He" could only be one him: her pimp, Sticky McFarland. He was a bad dude, alright. He was legendary for what he did to girls he didn't think were loyal. One of his prostitutes informing on him would earn the poor girl the worst unspeakable things. As bad as the things you've probably seen are, I'll spare you the gritty details. I'll just advise you to read Judges 19 in your own spare time.

"Babe, something came up at work," I said as I ran into the room to tell my wife.

"What is it?" Talia groggily asked.

"I can't talk about it," I replied.

Talia knew what I did for work. She knew I worked in that cesspool called vice, but I never went in depth on what actually went down. I guess that wasn't the wisest decision. I wanted to protect her, but I feel like if she knew at least a little bit of what I did, things wouldn't have gone as far south as they did.

"I'll be back in an hour," I told her. "Pizza should be here in about twenty-five minutes if you can just answer the door."

"I can do that," she croaked.

"You're the best," I said.

I leaned over and kissed her. She pulled me down for a better kiss. I miss that. There was something so reassuring in that kiss. It was like all of the trust she had in me was sealed inside that one kiss. I wanted to stay there like that all afternoon, were it not for the urgency of Michaela's text message. It was the last real satisfying kiss I'd ever have from her.

It was only about twenty minutes from my house in Milwaukie to the Pearl District. Traffic was light, and I beat the GPS. The warehouse was one of our normal rendezvous points. She kept a room up in one of the old offices. I entered through the back as usual. See, I was still dressed in my Sunday best. I looked even less like a vice cop in that get-up. I didn't have time to change due to the urgency of the message, and I stuck out like a sore thumb.

Michaela was in her office. When I got there, she appeared frantic, but something seemed off. It was like there was another presence there. Also, the frantic attitude, it all seemed so forced. But seriously, I could feel a third person there that I couldn't immediately see.

"Please, you have to help me!" the hooker cried as she grabbed me by the lapel and pulled me toward her.

I instinctively put my hands up in protest to push her off of me. This was highly unusual, not like her. Foul breath from her rotting teeth made me more eager to beat it. I was too late. I felt a hard size-13 foot on my butt, and Michaela and I were sent flailing into her desk. I saw a camera flash, and I knew. She had started to disrobe during her fall back, my hands up in defense still on her. I found myself on top of her, my lips centimeters from hers. I turned around. Sticky was right there with his phone. He got the photo, and he was recording the rest of the exchange on video. I could see the bright light of his phone camera.

"You lousy!" I yelled at him.

"Did you really think you'd bring me down?" he laughed. "You had to be smarter than that."

"Michaela! You didn't!"

"I'm sorry, Church Man," she apologized, "but I knew if you got to Sticky, I'd be out of a job."

I couldn't tell if she was serious or if Sticky had threatened her. Maybe both things were true at once. Either way, I was screwed.

"I think I have enough here," Sticky chuckled.

I lunged at him.

"Ah, ah, ah," he mocked. "Wouldn't want to add police brutality on your rap."

He gestured at Michaela that it was time to go. It was like he was calling his dog the way he did it.

"Ah, look Michaela!" he laughed as he looked at his phone. "Your picture already has over a hundred likes, not to mention what we'll get once I edit and post to my *Insta*."

I wanted to chase Sticky out of there. I wanted to smash his phone. That would've been a bad decision that would've just made the situation worse. Destroying evidence was out of the question. I'd just have to wait for the hammer to drop.

I drove straight home. Talia was up and making sure the dishes were clean from the kids' lunch. Man, she was amazing. I hugged her as hard as I could without hurting the baby. She had no idea what had happened, but she still tried to comfort me, whatever it was that was bothering me.

I could barely focus at church that evening. I could barely sleep. Even with Talia right there cuddling me, I felt like the biggest failure. I'd never hurt her. I'd never hurt anyone.

The hammer dropped as soon as I came in on Monday. The chief knew it was all bogus. He knows who I am. He knows my character. He knows the investigation. Sticky is a piece of garbage, but it's the social media that did it in for me. I was put on leave. I had to tell Talia. That was when she started to feel distant. I had to tell her why I was on leave.

See, I had a buddy from church named Rick Johnson. He was one of my closest friends. Talia and I would do stuff with him and his wife. He was diagnosed with leukemia a couple years ago. It got really hairy some days. We almost lost him a couple times, but his wife, Julia, was right there every minute until she wasn't. He was on the mend, and she was on her way to OHSU to pick him up one day when a Prius cut off a semi on the Marquam Bridge. The truck lost control and overturned directly on top of their Corolla. Rick was devastated, as you'd imagine. Julia was a special lady. She gave and gave and gave, and when she had nothing else to give, she dug around for more and gave that – just a real special lady. The doctors declared Rick in remission a week later, but it was so bittersweet.

Fast-forward a week after the whole debacle with Sticky goes down. I'm in the doghouse with PPB and my wife. She's there, at least she says she believes me, but she's wary. I don't blame her. I really don't. But here comes Rick. See, he always liked Talia. I think if Julia wasn't in his life, he'd have tried to woo Talia – that is if I weren't in Talia's life. Now, see, here's where it gets interesting. I think those meds messed with Rick's brain. Obviously, Talia wasn't really able to think straight through all the stress overloading her pregnancy brain. He convinced her that I wasn't who I said I was. He convinced her to divorce me. He was very persuasive, and Talia blindsided me with the divorce papers.

Multnomah County was cruel. They granted full custody of the kids to her as well as our house and cars. I got to keep our stocks and bonds, as I told you. Rick also convinced her to put a restraining order on me. I didn't even get to see my baby born, my little girl. I always wanted to be a girl dad. Thanks a lot, buddy.

Meanwhile, back at the ranch, the investigation was starting to get serious. The mayor and the DA don't like me very much, so they pushed a full investigation, and the chief chose me to come here to keep me away while they do their thing. And now I'm sitting here in this nice little house talking to you.

Verity sat there in shock. She had barely touched her biscuits. It almost seemed like a tall tale, but also in line with the man she'd spent the day with on Friday.

"Your own best friend?" she asked in shock.

"Hey, you're letting the biscuits get cold," Denny laughed. "Yes, Rick was my best friend. It's funny. All the people I'd expect to have my back, the second they heard I'd been accused abandoned me. The people I'd think would be most suspicious, the ones who'd love to bring me down, they believed me and fought for me."

"And your kids?" Verity asked between bites of her breakfast.

"I catch the livestream of the church services back home," Denny explained. "Occasionally, they do a Royal Riders performance. It's this Wednesday night kids' program our church runs. They do Bible stories and singing. Every month, they do a song or two in the main service. It's the only way I can get around the restraining order. Talia blocked me everywhere else."

"What about your parents? Are they still in your life?"

"Long story. They wanted me to come home after the divorce, but I don't particularly feel like going back to live in Astoria. I just feel like it'd be like admitting defeat. But also, I could kind of start to see them believing the stories about me too. See, I'm the middle child of three, the rebel. I was the son that didn't go to Bible college or become a pastor. My older brother, Mike, he's a pastor of a Spanish church in Tillamook, and my younger Brother, Alan, he's a church planter in Monmouth. But hey, I was still a deacon, if that counted."

"Do you think you'll be cleared?"

"I don't see why not," Denny replied confidently. "Look at Sticky's *Instagram*. It doesn't even look convincing. It looks like the social media of a guy who dominates women. But there is the fact that this opened the door for the DA to go after me. I wouldn't put it past him to dedicate every device he has in his arsenal to bring me down."

"I believe you, Denny. I just needed to know. I wanted to know I could trust you. I'll be honest. I put on the façade of a strong, independent woman, but even I know I can't fight off a man were he to actually try and hurt me."

"Princess, I would never lay hands on you," said Denny as he held up both hands. "The only action these hands will see is when I get the satisfaction of gut punching one of Hassan's goons for getting handsy with you."

"Thank you for that reassurance," Verity chuckled.

"Hey, has Hallie eaten?" Denny asked, changing the subject.

"No, we were going to stop at the shop and get some fruit and granola before we hit the seaside."

"Does she want to try biscuits and gravy instead?"

"I could ask."

"Please do," said Denny. "I wasn't expecting visitors, but I'm afraid I made a bit too much for me to enjoy this morning."

"Hallie, we're done talking. You can come in!" Verity shouted.

Hallie came rushing into the kitchen, obviously bored of the thousands of hour of television available to her. Denny slid a plate across the bar.

"Breakfast is served," he said proudly.

"What is it?" the little girl asked.

"Biscuits and gravy," Denny answered. "Don't knock it 'til you try it."

"So, is this what you do? Make American food in your free time?" Verity asked with skepticism.

"Well, not exactly. I'm not one to make things from scratch, but biscuits and gravy just seemed good today," Denny answered.

"It's not bad," said Hallie.

"I'll take that as a compliment. Here, try it with some eggs," Denny said as he shoveled a cup or so of scrambled eggs onto Hallie's plate. "Come back tomorrow night, and I'll make you some of the best street tacos you've ever eaten. I got some carne asada marinating right now."

"You're inviting us over?" asked Verity.

"Why not? I need to work on my hosting, and this place gets quiet with just me here."

Verity looked down at Hallie. The little girl's mind was made up. It seemed her mind was already off of the seaside adventure and on whatever lay in store at Denny's place. Unlimited television and good food – what was the holdup?

"Invitation accepted," Verity chuckled.

Chapter 9
Agatha Love

As quickly as the investigation had progressed on Friday, it seemed like it had all stalled as soon as Monday morning hit. Without Agatha Love, there were no real leads. Nobody knew where the girl had gone off to. Either that, or no one was willing to spill the beans as to where she'd gone off to. They had even checked a few of her known haunts on the mainland – a few friends she hung with, but nobody had seen hide or hair of their own Agatha Love.

It was like Denny and Verity were going in circles. They'd visit the marina, then they'd visit the Love residence, then they'd check up with Fat Terry (who had actually warmed up to Denny and started serving him a spicy ginger beer he'd found), then they'd finish up by getting humiliated at Hassan's, virtually repeating Friday's itinerary with a few variations here and there.

"How does someone so prolific vanish like a fart in the wind?" asked Denny one Thursday afternoon after another humiliation from Hassan's muscle men.

"I don't know," replied Verity, "but it makes me more suspicious every day, like maybe she did have something to do with Annie's death."

"I really hope not," said Denny as he started the car. "As much as I want this investigation done quick, fast, and in a hurry, I don't want the Loves to be hurt even more finding out their only other daughter is a murderer. My goal is to bring this family back together and repair broken bridges, not tear it apart and leave it in shambles."

Hassan's answer had been pretty much the same as it had been Friday and every other day. "No, dirty Yank, I haven't seen her. She's probably off with some tosser on the mainland."

"Did you ever consider going anywhere else on the mainland?" asked Verity. "Hassan mentioned someone in Banks, but we never heard of any of her friends there."

"Do you actually think we could find her there?"

"Well, Hassan mentioned she knew some guys out in Banks," Verity explained. "That's all I have on that lead."

"Well, at least we finally got something more specific out of those guys today," Denny added. "Wanna go and check it out?"

"It's worth a shot," said Verity. "I think I know who to talk to."

"One of your other pub buddies?"

"Shut up, you. It was one time, and Fat Terry's an old reliable informant."

"Whatever you say, Princess."

"Will you just get driving?" she giggled.

"Point the way, Your Majesty."

Traffic was light going over the causeway – first time it had been all week. People must not have much to do. Not fifteen minutes later, Denny and Verity found themselves in Banks, a village just off the A-road leading into Preston – the closest settlement to Crenshaw.

"Where do we start?" asked Denny.

"Try the local pub like I said," was Verity's response.

"Think I'll get the warm welcome I enjoyed at Terry's?"

"You'll never let me live that down, will you?" laughed Verity.

The first pub they came across was housed in an ancient building, much like Terry's. As they walked in, it seemed as if the party had stopped. The one thing Denny noticed was the amount of day drinkers here.

"Don't these people have jobs?" Denny whispered as they walked in, aware of the glares from the patrons.

"Not since the mills shut down and the immigrants came in," she whispered back.

If it were possible, the bartender here was uglier than Fat Terry. He eyed them suspiciously. Stood together, Terry and this guy would look like a comical pair. Terry was short and stout and looked like an unholy lovechild between a human and a walrus. This guy was tall and reedy, but still looked like Quasimodo had lent him his face.

"Two virgin Moscow mules," Denny ordered.

Now the bartender's glare was downright menacing, as if it were an affront to him order a soft drink in his establishment.

"Can't drink on the job," Verity told the bartender.

The bartender emitted an annoyed growl and turned around. He returned with two copper mugs of ginger beer and squeezed a couple fresh limes in them – a Moscow mule sans vodka.

"He doesn't seem like he wants to be bothered," Denny whispered to Verity.

"Oh, he's just sour because his wife left him," Verity explained out loud. "Told him she was leaving him because he looked like the White Orc, or was it Harvey Weinstein, eh, Jojo?"

"Bit of both, I'm afraid," Jojo, the bartender replied, picking up on Verity's humor.

"Are you going to drag me to every pub in Lancashire to intimidate me, Princess?" Denny chuckled.

"So, you never come 'round for pleasure, Ms. Baker, not since Elliott left," Jojo began, spitting a wad of phlegm at the mention of Verity's ex-husband. "So, what're you here for exactly?"

"Agatha Love," Verity replied. "Hassan said she runs with some blokes here in Banks."

"Right, I ain't seen her in a bit, not since… her poor sister," Jojo's countenance turned downcast. "What a pity."

"We think there may be a connection," Denny explained as he took a swig of his mule.

"Right, I see that," replied Jojo.

"When was the last time you saw her?" asked Denny.

"Let me think," Jojo reminisced. "I believe it were a week ago today."

"The day before Annie was found," Verity confirmed.

"Strike that!" Jojo exclaimed in a hushed voice. "Turn around."

Denny and Verity simultaneously turned in their chairs. Before them stood a teenaged girl, no older than sixteen. She looked tired, scared. She had bags under her eyes, and her shoulder-length blonde hair was every which way. She was dressed in an oversized Preston North End F.C. hoodie, itself moth-eaten and stained.

"Aggie!" Verity exclaimed just as hushed as Jojo.

Agatha blinked twice, then turned for the door. She barged her way out of the pub and onto the street. Denny wasted no time giving chase. He was less than two seconds behind, his Moscow mule left on the bar and his barstool rolling onto its side.

In a small village, there's very few places to hide. Agatha was so easy to spot. It was no contest. Denny, his sex being an automatic advantage, was stronger and faster than the petite teenager. That's not to say Agatha didn't have any speed. The girl could move when she was motivated, and she just happened to be motivated this day.

"Agatha Love, stop!" Denny shouted. "In the name of the Lancashire Constabulary!"

Agatha looked back. Denny was gaining on her. She found a burst of speed, like a street car taking a shot of nitrous.

"Aggie, we just need to ask some questions!" Denny yelled.

Agatha was so preoccupied with Denny that she took her focus off of where she was going. Her path was blocked, and she ran right into the arms of one DC Verity Baker.

"Let me go!" she shouted as she wriggled her arms, trying to connect her tiny fists with anything.

"Not until you answer our questions," said Verity.

"Nice thinking," Denny said as he caught up to the pair. "How'd you know where she was going?"

"Where else can you go here?" Verity chuckled.

Verity pulled the passenger seat forward and ushered Agatha into the back of the Mustang. She then took her spot as Denny started the car.

"Let's go for a drive," said Denny.

"You can't do this!" Agatha cried. "This is kidnapping!"

"Gosh, Princess, read her her rights," Denny groaned.

"You do not have to say anything," Verity began the Police Caution. "But it may harm your defense if you do not mention when questioned something which you later rely in court."

"I'm being arrested?" Agatha cried.

"Do you understand the rights, or not?" Denny asked.

"Yes, I know my rights, but why did you arrest me? I was just minding my own business. I did nothing wrong."

"Then you would mind answering a few questions," said Denny as he pulled away from the curb.

"I don't know anything," Agatha declared.

"Anything about what?" asked Verity.

"I, uh…"

"Come on, Aggie, we know who you run with. We also know your family misses you.," Denny said.

"Don't bring them into this," Agatha hissed. "Good riddance for them if I'm gone," she spat a wad of saliva onto the window.

"Hey! Don't spit in my car!" Denny snapped at her sharply.

"Agatha, they really miss you," said Verity. "You're all they have left."

"The wrong sister died," Agatha mumbled.

"Do you really think that?" Verity replied, only half shocked she would say that.

"Annie was always the goody two-shoes. Here I am doing what I want when I want. I'm already dropped out of school."

"You can go back and make something of yourself," Verity counseled.

"It's too late," said Agatha with a tear in her eye. "I'm not my sister and never will be."

86

"You do know why we want to question you?" Denny added.

"Is it about Annie?" Agatha questioned.

"Bingo," said Denny. "We've been looking all over for you for the last week. Nobody knows where you've been."

"I've been around," Agatha answered.

"When was the last time you saw your sister?" Denny pressed.

"I can't remember," was Agatha's obvious lie.

"Preston?" Denny asked Verity.

"Sounds good to me," Verity replied.

"A week ago," Agatha lied again.

"You can't be serious right now," Denny laughed before recomposing himself. "Aggie, your sister was a bloated corpse floating in the harbor a week ago. Try again."

"Come on, Aggie," Verity tried to encourage the girl, "we're not accusing you of any wrongdoing."

"Then why am I even here?"

"Just because you didn't kill her doesn't mean you don't know something," Verity explained.

"Look, we're not out to get you," said Denny. "We're the good guys."

"But what does this have to do with me?"

"Aggie, you're being obvious," said Verity.

"Is someone out to get you?" asked Denny. "Hassan? Habib? Someone else? Perhaps a spurned lover?"

"Nobody, I just don't remember when I saw her last."

"Kid," Denny continued, "you do realize this can make you a suspect. I'm throwing you a bone — a get-out-of-jail-free card. We're not accusing you of anything, but you're starting to act real suspicious if you ask me."

"Take me to my flat, and I'll tell you," Agatha demanded.

"So, we think we're in the position to start making demands?" asked Denny as he approached the intersection to the A-road and flipped the left turn signal on to head to Preston.

"Please, I'll tell you. Just take me to my flat."

"Denny, she did say 'please'," Verity tauntingly pleaded with him.

Denny flipped the turn signal to the right and headed out west back towards Crenshaw.

"You're in Crenshaw, right?" asked Denny.

"Yes," Agatha replied.

"Now, Aggie," Verity reapproached the subject, "when did you see Annie last?"

"I seen 'er last Monday," Agatha replied.

"What time?" asked Denny.

"I don't know," she said. "I think it were sometime in the evening, around eleven."

"So, the night before she disappeared?" asked Verity.

"Yeah, I was leaving the house," Agatha started to open up. "Daddy and I had been arguing."

Denny and Verity both made a mental note that besides their glaring differences, Agatha still referred to her father as "Daddy". At least they were sure "Daddy" was Ian Love. It may have been some other man, but they would both later conclude that she was definitely referring to her father with a term of endearment.

"What was the argument about?" asked Denny.

"They treat me like a child," Agatha complained. "I'm bloody sixteen years old. I'm my own woman, but they think I should be just like Annie. Just because we share a last name and the same DNA, I must obviously be the perfect little angel and get all the good grades and all the nice boys and be the queen of the bloody county."

"Well, I hate to break it to you," said Denny, "but you are a child."

"For your information again, I'm sixteen, and I'm legally emancipated."

"Doesn't seem your dad sees it that way," Denny argued.

"And that's the beauty of emancipation," Agatha said proudly. "I can come and go as I please, and it doesn't matter how he sees it.

The drive brought them through the warehouse district. Denny watched in the rearview mirror. He could see apprehension boil over in Agatha as they passed Hassan's joint. Another mental note.

My flat's just up the drive here," said Agatha as the warehouses turned into rundown flats.

"You really went from a seaside mansion to this?" asked Denny.

Agatha's flat was in the rundown apartments that had been slapped together in the 1980s to house the influx of immigrants. It reminded Denny of the Section 8 projects back home. Several pairs of eyes stared at the sleek muscle car trespassing on their domain. It seemed out of place as the only other cars here, owned by the few that could afford them, were old Vauxhalls and Minis.

"Who are you staying with?" asked Verity as Denny pulled the car to the curb. "We couldn't find a current address for you."

"Hassan pays for it," Agatha answered.

"That would explain why there's nothing in your name," said Denny. "Does Hassan do this for anyone else?"

"I'm not entirely sure. I do have a roommate, but she's Spanish, so she's just there. Can't understand a word she says. It's all so annoying."

"So, you're certain the last time you saw Annie alive was at eleven last Monday?" Verity pressed.

"Yes, that's when I seen her last," said Agatha. "Can I go now?"

Verity climbed out and pulled her seat forward.

"Listen, you're not in trouble," Verity reminded her. "We just want to find your sister's killer."

"I wish I could be more help," Agatha replied as she walked into the building.

Verity watched as the girl disappeared inside. Something was gnawing at her. She climbed back into the car, her heart heavy.

"What do you make of it?" she asked Denny.

"Honest truth? She's lying. At least, she's not telling the whole truth. She has a connection with Hassan. That makes me suspicious."

"What is it with you and Hassan?"

"Did you see her when we passed Hassan's place?"

"No."

"Her expression immediately changed. I could see it, especially in her eyes. She's scared of him, and yet he pays for her apartment. Verity, I worked vice for ten years. He's pimping her out."

"Come on, Denny! Hassan Abdul isn't pimping anybody out."

"You really wanna take that chance? You trust me, don't you? I don't have cause to make an arrest, but I'm even more suspicious. Either he's pimping her out or keeping her comfortable so she doesn't run from his harem."

"From his harem? Denny, do you really want to pursue this?"

"If it means finding Annie Love's killer, then yes."

"You're impossible!"

"I told you Hassan knew something. He said he didn't know where Annie was. Then it turns out he's footing the bill for her apartment. I'd say that's pretty freaking suspicious!"

"I'm not going down with you," Verity said bluntly.

"Who said we're going down?"

"Do you know what happens when you say the quiet part out loud here? You get silenced. You come over here with your American ways, guns blazing like a cowboy. Try it. Try and pin something on Hassan. Sure, you'll find the proof, but they'll make it disappear."

"Who's 'they'?"

"People bigger than us," said Verity. "The MP, Whit's bosses, I don't know, maybe the bloody king himself."

"That's cool," said Denny. "My job hasn't changed. I'm going to investigate Hassan."

"Why are you so obstinate?"

"Because I can't say I've done the investigation if I haven't done the investigation. It's a shame Hassan has to be part of it."

"They'll call you a racist. They'll drag your name through the mud and mine because of this."

"Well, let them. I'm brown. They can't touch me. My name's already been dragged through the mud back home."

"But me?"

"What happens if it turns out Hassan did, in fact, kill Annie Love?" asked Denny. "You haven't thought about that, have you? What if it was Habib or one of Hassan's other goons? Do we just ignore it because we don't want this multicultural project to look bad? Heck, it could've been some white bozo who decided to pull the trigger. Fact is, it doesn't matter what color you are, you are capable of evil. It's one of the blessings and curses that makes us all human; and to say one people group is incapable of doing some kind of evil, whether its murder or just everyday garden variety racism, is dehumanizing in its own messed-up way. Telling someone they are not free to think and be responsible for their actions is so degrading, because it basically tells those people that they're too stupid for common sense without allowing them the decency to be intelligent in the first place. That's why I don't care about how Hassan feels about this investigation or what people think about what we do with Hassan if he is guilty."

Verity looked Denny in the eyes. She could see the fire in them. He didn't care what happened to him. This was a man who had lost so much that he had nothing to lose. He had already shown he was willing to put himself in harm's way for her. What did she have to worry about?

"I'll file Hassan as a suspect," said Verity with a sigh.

"Let's go find that killer," said Denny as he put the car in gear, a big grin on his face.

Chapter 10
The Heck You Are

Denny sat at his desk as Verity typed up the report. He smiled at his partner as if he were the cat that ate the canary. Verity, for her part, made faces back at Denny, trying to figure out if this was all some joke. She still questioned why she was even going along with this.

"Why I let you talk me into this," she grumbled.

"Because you know if I typed it up, we'd all be in deep crap," Denny chuckled.

"Why's that?" Verity shot back.

"Because what I type won't be nice. You'll at least be able to twist it and use all of the fun little euphemisms I refuse to say."

"You know they're just going to crumple this up, toss it in the rubbish bin, and tell us to go find someone else, right? Like, you know they'll just say it's all rubbish."

"Call me naïve," Denny put in, "but isn't our job to bring criminals down?"

"Congratulations," Verity said dryly as she kept her eyes on the computer monitor, "you're a policeman. And yes, we are to bring criminals down; but you have to understand, we've opened our country to these people. They don't understand."

"This is starting to sound like all of these sweet little euphemisms I refuse to say. What don't they understand?" asked Denny, his temper starting to simmer.

"It's different in the Third World," Verity excused herself.

"That's a load of bull crap," Denny shot back, trying to keep the heat below 212°. "My abuelo came to the United States from Chihuahua with nothing but my abuela and the clothes on his back. He entered legally through El Paso and busted his butt to achieve the American Dream. He didn't know a lick of English when he came, but he learned it better than any American I know. Heck, listen to the old man talk, and you'd never know English was his second language. That's how good he learned it. And then when my mom and Tio Felipe were born, he was determined that they would be Americans. He made sure they knew English. He made sure they were Americans. He refused to teach them Spanish so that they would integrate into the culture fully. No Mexican flags were allowed at their house, but you'd be hard pressed to not find a big American flag flying on his front porch, especially on the Fourth of July. My abuelo was from the Third World, but he knew what was expected of him. I've already met plenty of people here that know what's expected of them. They're not here to conquer, but to take part in the culture."

"Look, I'm very proud of you 'abuelo' for assimilating," said Verity, almost discounting what Denny had just said, "but it's not always possible for everybody."

"Come on, Princess! It's just natural respect. Every culture has some form of hospitality. You're a guest, you respect your host. I'm a guest in this country, but you don't see me demanding we all start packing heat and using the Imperial System, now do you? You can't

93

tell me Hassan's goons feeling you up every time we go over there is just something to accept. Is that part of the cultural enrichment, Princess?"

"And you've been so respectful of our culture?" Verity shot back.

"You bet I have!"

"You've thrown yourself into this thing without even grasping our culture. You're so gung-ho of making sure Hassan is the one who did this without questioning whether or not it could've been someone else. Sure, you haven't made any demands of us, but don't come here saying you've totally respected us."

"For crap's sake, Princess!" Denny had had enough. "I'm doing my freaking job! I'm not going after Hassan just because he's a poor, innocent immigrant. I'm not going after him because he has more melanin in his skin that I do. I'm going after him because there's a pattern of behavior consistent with abuse – not just from him, but from his gang. I don't care what culture you're from. When you're here or anywhere in the West, you treat women with respect."

"So, you think Hassan pulled the trigger because he likes to have a little extra sex?"

"I don't have a motive yet," said Denny, "and that doesn't make any sense. It could be political. Ian Love's running for Parliament? It could totally be connected with that."

"How does that even connect?"

"I don't know for certain, but the fact that he's running on an anti-mass-immigration platform is a real good indicator that he's not a friend of Hassan Abdul."

"Why do you so want it to be him?"

"I don't want it to be anybody," Denny replied. "Shoot, if I had my druthers, Annie Love's death would've been a freak accident. Perhaps, she went out to the marina to hang out, fell in, drowned, and then was mutilated by a boat propeller. Unfortunately, reality dictates that she was murdered and dumped into the marina. And who knows? Maybe in the end, Hassan had nothing to do with it, but I have to look into it. The pattern and connection are there."

"So, what happens when we dig deeper, and we find Hassan innocent?"

"Then we move on," Denny replied. "Who knows? Maybe Hassan has nothing to do with it. Perhaps, it may have been one of his goons acting on his own. Either way, there's a connection. He's the gang leader."

"I still think it's career suicide," Verity shot back.

"Well, let's not forget I don't have much of a career left."

"And me? I very much do have a career here."

"Like I said earlier, I'll take responsibility."

"Your funeral."

"Nothing to lose. Anyway, remember what I told you our first day?"

"I don't know," Verity replied with the same lethargy, "you said so many stupid things your first day."

"Better to ask forgiveness than permission," Denny replied as he smiled thinly. "Don't you people believe in new guy privileges? I can say that since I'm a stupid brown immigrant that I didn't know better. I mean, that's how we're measuring the standard of right and wrong here, I presume. You know, connecting my intelligence level to my origin and darkness of my skin."

"Do you want to cause trouble 'round here?" Verity spat back.

"Princess, my morals are governed on what's right and wrong, not who's more oppressed. I don't believe that just because Hassan Abdul has more melanin than John Smith down the street that he should be automatically handed the privilege of being absolved of any and all wrongdoing. Now, you finish typing up the report as we agreed, and I will personally deliver it to Whit's desk in a gift basket with a couple Coronas and a bottle of Tapatio."

"You really want to get on everybody's bad side, don't you?"

"If that's what it takes to do the right thing. I'm not afraid of anyone, not even the king himself."

Denny never kept good on the promise of beer and hot sauce, but he did personally hand the typed-up report to Whit, who, as Verity had promised would happen, promptly crumpled it up and tossed it in the garbage bin the second he saw Hassan Abdul's name as a suspect.

"The heck you are!" he almost shouted.

"So, what happens if Hassan Abdul killed Annie Love?" Denny shot back, as if he'd readied his defense.

"Hassan Abdul is an upstanding member of this community, a pillar of society," Whit fought back.

"That's a load of bull crap, Whit, and you know it. An upstanding member of this community doesn't run a gang of thugs who like to manhandle women."

"What women? Who's doing that? I haven't seen it."

"I saw it with my own two eyes, Whit. You think I'm hallucinating? When they were 'searching' us," Denny put "searching" in air quotes, "his guards were all up in DC Baker's business. Come on, Whit, I worked vice for ten years. I've been on both sides of a pat-down. You and I both know you there's no reason to feel up a woman when you're doing one, unless you're actually feeling up a woman. Hassan Abdul is a piece of garbage, and he's a viable suspect in the murder of Annie Love."

By this time, a crowd had gathered outside of Whit's office as the conversation had turned into a passionate shouting match.

"Shut the door," Whit instructed as he closed the shades.

Denny did as Whit instructed. Whit took a seat back at his desk.

"Sit down," he instructed sharply. "DC Lawton, you are an amazing cop. Honestly, you're one of the best I've ever met. You've gotten more done in a week than a lot of my guys get done in a month. I took you on knowing what baggage you brought because I trusted your chief."

"Then you know why I suspect Hassan Abdul."

"I'm sure DC Baker tried to get you to drop it."

"All afternoon," said Denny. "Look, I'll tell you what I told her, I'm not into looking at the color of someone's skin to indicate guilt. I mean, look at me. If we governed strictly on what color your skin was and not on the content of your character, ICE would've thrown me in a van and sent me to Juarez. I don't care where Hassan Abdul's from. What I care about is who killed Annie Love and bringing that slobbering dog to justice."

Whit sat back in his desk chair and sighed, crossing his fingers and closing his eyes. Then, he leaned forward towards Denny.

"I've been waiting for the right man to say the quiet part out loud," said Whit with a satisfied groan.

"It shouldn't be quiet," said Denny. "I always thought it was common sense."

"Oh, it is common sense, don't get me wrong. Here's the bind. As much as I am in charge of this unit, I can only take that so far. Now, I could've easily filed away your report, but I'm not the ultimate power here in Lancashire."

"Politicians?" Denny filled in the imaginary blank.

"Politicians," Whit confirmed. "You see, people like Hassan Abdul do wonders for the local economy. When you're down at the House of Commons or up at your villa, you don't have to worry about what happens to society."

"Believe me, I know. I'm from a state where a tiny sliver of a county in the northwestern corner dictates what the rest of us does. It's like they don't realize there's actually more Oregon than Portland."

"There is absolutely no proof for what I'm about to tell you, so please keep this off the record until you have a solid case," Whit instructed.

"We don't make accusations until we know that we know that we know," Denny replied. "'Innocent until proven guilty'. Pretty sure that's enshrined in Common Law and the Constitution it's based off of."

"I am ninety percent sure Hassan Abdul is responsible for Annie Love's murder in some way, shape, or form and only eighty-nine percent sure he wasn't the one who pulled the trigger."

"What makes you say that, Boss?"

"She's not the first girl to go missing and turn up dead or not at all around here."

"What are you saying?"

"There's girls from the poor parts of the area," Whit continued. "They shack up with these guys, migrants, road men, and when these blokes are done with them, they're done with them."

"You don't think Annie Love shacked up with Hassan Abdul," Denny said with disgust.

"See, that's the part I don't get," said Whit. "Annie wasn't the type."

"Who is the type?"

97

"Agatha. DC Lawton, this has been going on for over forty years all over, not just in Crenshaw, but all around the county and even beyond in Yorkshire, Northumbria, and Cumbria. I just read a police report form Newcastle where a girl, her mother, and the baby of the man she was carrying on with were torched in a house fire set by the man she was carrying on with. Do you know what happens when people speak the truth about it?"

"Let me guess, it gets ignored?"

"Well, that's how it started."

"And how's it going? I mean, I think I have an inkling. I just want to see if what I saw in the news back home about that situation was true."

"You see these kids out here?" asked Whit as he directed Denny toward the window. He was pointing out the young uniformed officers heading back out on patrol. "These kids will do anything because it's what their orders were. I've held off, but it's getting harder and harder to resist these monsters at the top."

"So, let me get this straight," Denny cut in. "If I officially go after Hassan Abdul, that could essentially put me at risk of getting arrested?"

"They will crucify you."

"Who's they?"

"People with a lot more power and say-so than I have."

"I already told Verity I have nothing to lose, Whit. What do I have? I lost everything back home. I was expelled overseas to keep myself aloof from an investigation of a crime I didn't commit. The way I see it, I'm risking jail either here or there no matter what I do."

"And what about DC Baker?" asked Whit.

"What about her?"

"Do you mean to drag her down with you?"

"I'm figuring on some kind of plausible deniability."

"Then you had better give her a good alibi."

"I will."

"So, we're clear?"

"You mean, you're going to let me pursue this, no matter where it leads?"

"DC Lawton, you are exactly what this police force needs. That's another reason you came so highly recommended, besides the fact that the powers that be hate you over there. I know you'll do what's right, even if it leads to you arresting the bloody king, I trust you to take care of this and make sure the Love family receives the justice and closure they deserve."

"You're positive? This isn't some ruse to get me in trouble with the higher-ups, is it?"

"No, but I want this off the books until you've proven it. No reports, and I won't be able to protect you if you muck it all up."

"I won't screw it up."

"And don't drag Verity down with you."

"DC Baker?" asked Denny confused.

"Yes, DC Baker."

"You called her Verity."

Whit was taken aback by his lapse in professionalism. He searched his soul for an answer. It was unspoken – the concern he had for one of his brightest detectives. Denny could read it in his eyes.

"Just go get him," was all Whit had to say.

Chapter 11
Oh, Yes, We Are

Verity was pinching herself trying to imagine a world where Whit was still a sane, no-nonsense man. This was stupidity. Whit was always by-the-book – a people pleaser, in some ways. He was the last person who would ever break from convention and make the call. And yet, here they were, going to conduct an official investigation into one Hassan Abdul.

She looked over at Denny, who was beaming from ear to ear as he piloted his Mustang down the A-road. It seemed so off-putting. It was almost like he took some form of sick delight in being given unfettered access to Hassan Abdul. He'd said he wished Hassan was innocent. His face said otherwise.

"How're you going to play this?" she asked him.

"Same as always," Denny replied. "I'm just gonna straight up ask him what he knows about Annie and Aggie."

"You know he's going to give the same answer as always, right?"

"Initially," Denny said, still confident, "but I can push further. By the time I'm done with him, he'll know he's in trouble."

"Do you actually think he's going to play along?" Verity shot back.

"What do you mean?"

"'Oh, yes, Detective,'" she imitated Hassan poorly, with an Indian accent, "'I am putting a bullet in that poor girl's brain. I hate de white women infidels. Allahu Akbar.'"

"He's not going to confess," Denny chuckled, relieved that his dry humor was rubbing off on Verity, "but I will be lighting a fire under his butt. I want him to know he can't abuse women any longer and that his days are numbered."

"And you actually think he's going to make it easy on you?"

"I didn't say that, but if what I'm seeing is true, then I may put him on edge if he's never seen any accountability."

"I still say you're going to make more enemies than friends."

"I'm not here to make friends, Princess. You know that. I'm here to do a job and do it right."

"And you're okay with being public enemy number one if this goes south?"

"Won't be the first time."

"You're so impossible," Verity huffed as she sat back in her seat.

"Why are you so against this?" asked Denny. "Both you and Whit are pushing so hard against me doing my job, as if I still have something to lose. I already promised I'd leave you out of this, that I'd take the fall."

"He's dangerous," said Verity. "We don't talk about it, and I tried to be nice, but he's a dangerous man, Denny."

"Tell me something I don't know," Denny replied drolly. "Was it the body guards manhandling you? Or the other body guard holding me close to make me watch? Is it the big muscle-bound man-gorilla he keeps with him? Ooh, what about the clearly demonic look in his eyes? Princess, I've dealt with clowns like this before. I've dealt with politics like this before."

"Then you know what you're going into."

"Yeah, a situation where I can't defend myself or you because some dipstick thought it was a great idea to disarm the police."

Denny pulled up to the warehouse. It was such a familiar process to the two police that they didn't even question the situation. They walked up to the guards stationed out front, ready to submit theirselves to yet another humiliating search.

"DC Lawton and Baker," Denny said as he presented his badge to the guards. "We're here to speak to Mister Abdul."

"Mister Abdul ain't here," one of the guards sneered, a strange blend of British thug and Middle Eastern tinging his growl.

"Well, do you know where he is?" asked Verity.

The thugs ignored her.

"Hey, the lady asked you a question," Denny barked, his hatred and rage against these guys boiling to the surface. "Where is Hassan Abdul?"

Still no answer. It appeared their work was done.

"Tell me now, or I'll come back with a warrant. Do you really want to push me further?"

"Denny, let's just go," Verity prodded. "He'll be back."

"Screw you guys," Denny spat at them. "Waste of my time."

Denny opened the passenger door for Verity before climbing back into the driver's seat. He was angry, pure rage popping veins out on his forehead.

"Denny, what's wrong?" asked a concerned Verity, placing a comforting hand on his. "He's out. People go out. It happens. We'll come back, and talk to him then."

"It's more than that, Princess," Denny replied, his blood pressure steadying from Verity's touch. "Those are the kinds of people I hate. Did you see how they looked at you?"

"I know they didn't want to talk."

"They were just as disappointed they wouldn't have the chance to 'search' you," Denny explained. "I spent ten years taking clowns like this off of the street. And then, they sit there and waste my time. Official police business, and the second they know there's no benefit to them, they ignore us and waste our time."

"Well, it is their right," Verity pointed out.

Denny looked down and noticed consciously Verity's hand on his. He quickly withdrew it.

"I'm so sorry," Verity apologized. "I didn't mean anything by it."

"No, it's okay. It happens. Just takes me back a little, you know."

"Wanna talk about it?"

"Not on the clock," said Denny.

He started the car and pulled away from the curb.

"Where to next?" asked Verity, looking at her watch.

"Aggie's apartment," Denny replied.

"What're you going to find there?"

"I don't know exactly."

"Well, you do know it's getting late."

"What? Got a hot date?"

"I have a daughter, Lawton."

"I won't be long," said Denny. "I just want to talk to Aggie. I think she may be able to help us out here."

Denny still felt so out of place with his high-dollar muscle car parked among what looked like street legal go-karts, as much as he felt out of place among the higher-dollar exotics he found at the Love Mansion and Hassan's. The eyes were there too, eyes that said "You don't look like you belong here". Instinctively, Denny reached for his gun, only to remember he wasn't armed and hadn't been for several weeks. It must have been getting to him. The tenants all glared at him and Verity as they made their way to the main entrance. White folk were not an unusual sight here, rare, but not unusual. It was the car, the nice clothing that looked like it had just come off the shelf at Harrods, and the general sign of near-perfect hygiene. Denny had seen this before. They were hungry. This was what government efficiency had gotten them. He was rich by their standards. They were dirt poor. As much as he loved driving the Mustang and dressing smartly, he grew self-conscious. As well-off as he was, these were his people. These were the ones he spent time with day in and day out working vice – all at once a stranger and at home. He couldn't but help love them and only want to help them and give them his best.

Denny took Verity's hand, as if he thought he could protect her from a horde of zombies. As if she knew what he was on about, Verity gripped Denny's hand harder. He was not going to let anything happen to her. A cop and a lady all at once, she was.

The lobby of the apartment building was just as dingy. Like its exterior, it was no-frills and brutalist, slapped up in a hurry to house the incoming migrants. As soon as it was finished, the building was left alone to the sands of time, her owners putting in the bare minimum to keep it operational and to prevent the government from condemning it. The lights were barely on, and half of those that were on were flashing like a seizure-inducing strobe light, ready to give out at any second. It smelled like death, literally like rotting flesh, likely from a rat infestation that was stopped in its tracks, only to be left for bacteria and other smaller vermin to take care of the leftovers. If Hassan really wanted to provide for Agatha, he truly tried the bare minimum like the builders of this apartment complex.

"I wouldn't let my kids step foot in here," he whispered to Verity as they approached the receptionist.

"Me neither. I feel like just breathing will give me three or four different types of auto-immune diseases."

"Good afternoon, ma'am," said Denny as he presented his badge to an elderly Indian woman at the front desk.

The old crone looked the two detectives up and down suspiciously. Apparently, the police never came around here too often.

"DC Baker and Lawton," Verity put in.

"We're looking to speak to an Agatha Love," Denny continued, "if you could just tell us where her flat is."

"That is not information I can give without a warrant," the old lady replied.

"Look, she's not in trouble," said Denny. "We just have a few questions to ask her."

"Then kindly return with a warrant, and I will give you what you want."

"I'm not playing games here," said Denny as he turned away.

Denny scanned the lobby. There had to be a way to find Agatha. Sitting around would be a waste of valuable time already spent, and it wasn't like they could just waltz around a private building without a warrant knocking on every door until they got lucky.

"I'm very sorry about my partner," Verity apologized. "Typical American."

Denny, by this time, was across the lobby out of earshot. Even if he were in earshot of the slight against him, he wouldn't have heard it. Instead, he was tuned into the various conversations. So many different languages – Arabic, Pashto, Urdu, Hindi, not a lick of English. Then, something familiar perked his ears. Providence? No, but yes. Spanish, but a weird form of it that sounded like the speaker had a horrible lisp.

"Pardon me, ma'am," he called to the woman on the phone.

The young woman, a young brunette with olive skin and a turned-up nose, looked up, saw the smartly dressed man, pocketed her phone, and made a run for it.

"Stop!" Denny shouted as he gave chase. "Policia! Alto!"

The woman was deaf to his pleas as she tried for the elevator. Bloody thing was too slow for her as Denny closed in. She booked it for the stairwell. It was enough time for Denny to catch up to the woman and for Verity to catch up to Denny.

"Por favor! Por favor!" she pleaded, cowering against the stairwell door. "No habla Ingles. No sabo."

"Tsk-aah," was Denny's incredulous response.

The woman immediately shut up.

"Tu eres no bajo arresto," Denny told her in fluent Spanish. "¿Cuál es tu nombre?"

The woman stared blankly at Denny. Verity finally caught up to Denny. There was something about her calm, feminine demeanor compared to Denny's tough Meso-American scowl that seemed to calm the girl's fears.

"Isabella Mendes," the girl whispered nervously.

Verity stood behind Denny, trying to put on a motherly smile, as the American pulled out his phone and accessed the police database. He held up the phone and produced a picture of Agatha.

"Mira. ¿Conoces a Agatha Love?" he asked her.

Isabella stared at the phone for about ten seconds.

"Puede que en peligro," Denny continued.

"Es mi compañera de piso," Isabella replied. "Aquí."

The two detectives followed as the Spanish girl beckoned. She led them to a rundown elevator. There was no danger in her running, clearly. She'd already discovered she couldn't outrun Denny. She was quiet though, clearly intimidated by him.

The bell chimed as the lift arrived at its destination. This floor somehow seemed worse than the lobby. There was a smell. Was it death? Rotting food? Mold? Or was it all of the above? Another smell: cat urine. That could be a litany of things too. Isabella led the detectives into her flat. All this just to find Agatha sitting on the couch posing for selfies with a bottle of Crown Royal in her other hand.

"Hey, Aggie!" Verity tried to sound friendly.

"Bloody Nora, Issy!" Agatha shouted. "What are you two doing here?"

"We just want to ask you some questions, Aggie," Verity tried to reassure the girl. "Isabella was just being helpful."

Agatha huffed as she sagged back down into her broken-down sofa.

"Is that your Spanish flatmate you told us about?" Verity asked.

"That's Issy, and she's a bloody moron," Agatha replied angrily before making sure Isabella could hear. "Mucha pendeja! I told her I wanted to be left alone."

"Well, clearly, she doesn't understand English," Denny added.

"Clearly," Agatha huffed.

"Hassan pay for her room too?"

"Yeah, what about it?"

"Look, Aggie," Verity continued, "we just wanted to make sure you're alright."

"I'm alive, aren't I?"

"Yes, but we fear you might be in danger."

"How so?" Agatha shot back.

"Well, we have reason to believe Hassan is connected to Annie's murder."

"That's a load of lies, and you know it!" Agatha lashed out.

While Verity kept Agatha distracted, Denny tried to pose as the child with ADHD dragged along with his mother to her friend's house. The flat was what he expected. It was almost as if they came rundown by design, as if one day in 1986 or whenever, the builders slapped the building together and busted out all of the windows, cut electrical lines, and bred rats in the walls before tenants moved in.

And there it was – that cat urine smell again. No sign of a cat either. It was like that titanium plant he'd drive past just near Albany on his trips down to Eugene. No way Agatha was smelting titanium in her flat. Denny found his answer quickly. On one of the end tables was a piece of aluminum foil with a hole clearly burned in it – meth. Just what they needed. Agatha noted Denny looking down at the paraphernalia.

"It's not mine, I promise," she pleaded with the cop.

"We've got bigger fish to fry than your drug use, Aggie," Denny said. "Although, I wouldn't be surprised if there was a connection between the supplier and the killer, eh."

"It's not mine," Agatha obviously lied.

It was strange. The girl was so independent, but Denny could tell she was still just a little girl. But what's this? Among all of the teenage makeup products and cutesy goo-gaws and doilies, there was a pregnancy test. That didn't belong. Denny squinted, trying to not be so obvious. It was positive – two pink lines. Hassan. It had to be, or one of his boys.

"Who's the father?" Denny asked.

"That is private!" Agatha snapped as she covered the positive test with a soiled Watchtower she'd tossed onto the table.

"How far along are you?" Denny pressed. "Three months? Four? Is that why you're wearing a baggy hoodie?"

"Screw you!" Agatha cried.

"How long have you been sixteen, Aggie?" Denny would not back down. "Hassan is the baby daddy, isn't he?"

"Get out of my flat!" she screamed.

"That's all I need to know," said Denny, deadpan. "Thank you for your time."

Denny ushered Verity out and shut the door right as a stiletto heel lodged itself in the wood.

"You didn't have to be so direct," Verity scolded as she climbed into the passenger seat.

"What does she have to hide?" asked Denny, ignoring the tongue lashing.

"What're you on about?"

"Have we given her any reason not to trust us? I mean, if she was abused, wouldn't it not be logical to let people that can handle it handle it?"

"She doesn't trust you, Denny."

"Why not?"

"You've not given her a reason to. How did you get your people to trust you back home?"

"I built a rapport," Denny replied contritely. "You're right. I think I'm just letting it all get to me. I want this case over and done."

"Then you need to show her you care."

"Still convinced Hassan's innocent?"

"Not a prayer," Verity replied. "If I've got my timeline straight, Aggie was fifteen when she got pregnant. Even if it's not Hassan, it was more than likely someone in his gang, and they're all adults."

"He's fried then."

"I was afraid to admit it before, but yes."

"What do you think of Issy?" Denny asked.

"You want the ugly truth?" Verity answered with a question.

"That's what we're trying to get to," Denny replied. He was starting to get tired of people beating around the bush here.

"You ever hear of the grooming gangs?"

"I may have heard a bit about them on some podcasts back home, and Whit mentioned something like that in passing yesterday when we chatted" Denny replied. "Where was it? York? Leeds?"

"Rotherham," Verity confirmed. "But in reality, it's been all over the Midlands and the North. I guess since we're in the safety of your car, I can talk about it freely. These blokes come here and refuse to integrate. You know, women are second-class citizens in countries like that. Put two and two together, and you get grooming gangs. They pass these poor girls around. And then when they're done with them, they kill them. Whenever it's been reported, the victims are sent to jail for offending the migrants. And what's even more stupid about it? Other migrants who do things right and mind their own business get caught up in this. Everyone loses – the English, the immigrants, the police; everyone except the groomers and the politicians who choose to protect them. It's been happening for over forty years, and there's nothing we can do about it. You see, that's why we've been trying to dissuade you from pursuing Hassan. Everyone knows he's in on it. It's Crenshaw's worst-kept secret, but anyone who's tried is shut down."

"Ain't that something," Denny mused. "I'm paid to do something I can't do."

"Nothing would please me more than to see these thugs returned to wherever they came from and our streets cleaned up," Verity growled.

"You better be careful," Denny chuckled. "We might find a white sheet in your house."

"Very funny, but that's why we think you can do it."

"What? Be a sacrificial lamb?"

"Well, you haven't exactly made a lot of friends here with you stomping around like you own the place."

"You willing to go with me to jail when we start hurting feelings?"

"You wish, eagle boy," Verity chuckled.

"Eagle boy?"

"Hey, it was the best I could come up with on the fly."

"Not better than 'Princess'," Denny laughed.

"Get on with it," said Verity. "I'm tired."

"Then I say we've put in a good day's work, and we go confront Hassan tomorrow."

"Good, because you've kept me longer than I want."

Denny put the car in gear and headed back to Preston. The drive was unusually quiet, making Verity quite uncomfortable.

"I didn't know you spoke Spanish," Verity said, breaking the silence.

"I spent my childhood in immersion," Denny replied. "My abuelo wanted to raise American kids, as you may remember. My mom wanted to put her American kids in touch with their Latino roots. Every weekend, it was Don Cheto on the radio and *Sabado Gigante* on the TV. Paid off. Being bilingual gets you ahead in the U.S. Remember how I said my brother pastors a Spanish church in Tillamook?"

"Interesting," said Verity. "I guess I could've assumed since you were half Mexican, you may know."

"Hardly," said Denny. "Unless your parents actually come from the motherland, you barely know any Spanish, and people who are only half are even less likely to learn the language. To be honest, I never thought I'd use it here. Meeting Issy, I guess, was just some crazy stroke of luck"

"Well, color me surprised," Verity replied as the car continued down the road.

Chapter 12
Feelings

Hassan proved a very difficult man to find. For Denny, this seemed to become a recurring theme in this investigation. If someone was just on the periphery, they'd be easy to find. They'd have a chat, maybe get somewhere, and be on their way. Then, when they actually needed to talk to the subject, Denny and Verity would find they'd just vanish.

It had been yet another week in this investigation. It was at the point where the duo was being brought in to help investigate other cases. It was all small stuff – a shoplifting ring here, a pickpocket, or, as Denny refused to even make the arrest, an offensive social media post of a three-year-old saying boys are boys and girls are girls.

"Just make sure to get a VPN or post anonymously," Denny advised the old granny. "Next time, they probably won't send me."

Fervor for finding Annie Love's killer hadn't died down either, and Ian Love was using her loss as fire in his campaign for MP. There was no news, and yet it was all the news was about. Denny often wondered how this was all being reported back home. He hadn't heard any news on the local channels about any murders in the United States lately. Then again, the assumption in Britain was that mass shootings were just a daily occurrence everyone dealt with over in the U.S. Why would they report on the random murder of a Chicago alderman-hopeful's kid?

Denny sat in the passenger seat of one of the squad cars one Wednesday afternoon. (Whit had finally put the kibosh on the Mustang.) The pair had just finished assisting in the bust of a pedo ring in Blackburn. What should have been an honor for Denny to cuff the ringleader had devolved into a petty complaint to the higher-ups. According to the pervert, Denny had been too rough. The ringleader was pulling at Denny like a toddler who doesn't want to be restrained, all the while complaining that he was being treated roughly and deserved dignity. In Denny's defense, the moron was resisting while he was escorting him out. The whining about the roughness actually manifested the roughness, and the boy lover found himself slammed up against the side of a Land Rover.

"Ow!" the pedophile screamed like a sick parody of his victims as he pulled at Denny. "You're hurting me!"

"Stop resisting!" Denny growled.

"I'll write to the Times about this!" he complained

"I hope they cut off your goods and feel them to the warden's dog," Denny hissed into the pedophile's ear as he slammed him against the SUV right before another constable pulled him off.

Now, here he was, sat in the car like a naughty schoolboy about to receive the third degree from his overworked mother. Verity was assigned damage control as the perp was stuffed into the back of another patrol car. Her partner, now her responsibility. With the screaming for mob justice somewhat pacified, she climbed in behind the steering wheel.

"What the everlasting bloody he…"

"'And whosoever shall offend one of these little ones that believe in me, it is better for him that a millstone were hanged about his neck, and he were cast into the sea'," Denny interrupted. "Jail's too good for that piece of crap."

"That's all fine and well," Verity continued, "but because of that, he'll likely walk free."

"You're telling me they're just going to let a known pedophile walk because he was slammed against an SUV?" Denny asked incredulously. "Are you kidding me right now?"

"And you threatened him with castration," Verity added. "You can't threaten them."

"I didn't threaten him," Denny defended himself. "I told him I hope they castrate him. If he's too stupid to tell the difference, that's on him. Maybe he should've thought about that before diddling kids."

"And this is the man they say raped a prostitute," Verity mused out loud. "Do you understand what's going on though?"

"Let me guess," Denny shot back sarcastically before pouring more sarcasm on top of his sarcasm sundae, "I hurt his wittle feelers?"

"In a word, yes. Police brutality. That's what they'll say. He'll claim you hurt him. He'll say he felt threatened. And so, he'll walk."

"Simple as?"

"Simple as. What's gotten into you? You've been a cop for what, eleven years? How does this not register?"

"I hate pedophiles," Denny replied darkly. "Those words of Jesus, I take those to heart. Millstone necklace is too good for those people. To hell with his feelings. I mean it."

"I agree with you," Verity admitted, "but none of us want to see you in jail or worse."

"What's worse? Going to see Jesus?"

"We all like you here," said Verity as she put the cruiser in gear. "You seem like the only man here that can freely speak the truth."

"Well, it's pretty easy," Denny replied. "Just call it like you see it. We're not in the business of protecting people's feelings. If the dignity of one man costs another man his life, he had no real dignity to begin with."

"And you, a foreigner, presume to change the rules?"

"Seems like that's already happened," Denny replied coldly. "There's no way it was always like this. I seem to remember a time in both our countries where sex offenders, rapists, child molesters, were all hanged, no questions asked."

"Yeah, well, that's gone away with burning witches," Verity commented.

"Difference being the so-called witches didn't deserve it. Just a bunch of old grannies that knew how to wash their hands."

"Well, I hope you have that whole speech ready when Whit calls you into his office. You know he will, right?"

"Won't be the first time I've received a shellacking from the old man."

"Old? He's hardly forty-five!"

"Either way, he's going to take my side on this. He knows where I stand."

"Good luck then."

As Verity pulled the squad car into Headquarters, Denny noticed a black Rolls parked right in front of the building in the no-parking zone.

"Someone's going to get a ticket," Denny chuckled.

"Not if that is who I think it is," Verity added as she climbed out of the car.

Denny and Verity walked into the building side-by-side. Gone was the tapping of computer keyboards. Instead, everyone's attention was focused on the racket coming from Whit's office. It wasn't Whit's voice making said racket.

"I have never seen such insolence from a detective, especially one of yours, Whiteaker!" came the shout. "In the time you've brought on that bloody Yank, I have received nine different complaints from my constituents! Do you know how scared they are?"

"Is that?" asked Denny.

"Our local MP," a fellow detective, answered, "the Honourable Michael Lorde."

"I have never received so many complaints about one detective in a lifetime as I have received about DC Lawton!" Lorde continued behind closed doors, but somehow clear enough to where the barrier barely muffled his rant.

"Ooh, he's talking about me!" Denny mocked.

A collective chuckle rose from the gathered crowd of LEOs.

"On top of that, insubordination! He refuses cases, refuses arrests. We have laws for a reason, and he refuses to enforce them. I don't care how he feels about it. And then, I hear just this afternoon he beats one of my constituents! What kind of department are you running here? Are we now allowing police brutality here in Preston?"

"News travels fast," Verity whispered to Denny.

"Look, DC Lawton, he's different," Whit explained. "He may be a bit unorthodox, but he's shown great results."

"Oh? And I hear he's yet to solve the Love murder," Lorde retorted. "Some results from your new best man. DI Whiteaker, you either bring him under control or sack him! Otherwise, we'll have to reconsider your position in this governmental structure."

And with that, he turned and slammed the door behind him, the blinds clinking against the glass. As he stormed out, he made direct eye contact with Denny. Michael Lorde, MP was a tall man in his late 50s. He looked every part the stereotypical politician – coiffed gray hair with just a peppering of black in his beard and temples, he wore a charcoal three-piece suit with a red and blue striped tie, a gold pocket watch chained to his vest. Beneath all of that, Denny had to stifle a laugh at the clicking of his tiny footsteps from his size-8 oxfords. The detective could physically feel the hatred from his frigid blue eyes piercing him like a laser beam. The laser beam carried more than just hatred. It told Denny everything Denny needed to know about that man.

"He doesn't care about anybody," Denny whispered to Verity.

"Politician," Verity commented.

"No, I mean he only cares for people as far as they can benefit him," Denny continued. "Friends, family, may have them on the outside, but his inward life is an island all unto himself."

"Again, politician."

"Let me rephrase that," Denny said. "He's only protecting these people because they vote his way. Look at him. No way he's actually been to the projects. You think he's ever met anyone in Crenshaw besides the few that run the protection rackets?"

"I see what you're saying," said Verity.

"You think he's ever been to Crenshaw?"

"I'd be surprised if he's left the cities save for driving the M-roads," Verity admitted. "Heck, today's probably the first time he's ventured onto any A-road."

"Exactly," Denny replied. "And he's all butthurt because he knows his little isolated world is being challenged. If the reality of what he's caused is brought to light, he's gone come Election Day. You heard who he's protecting. The 'constituents' he's talking about are all the rapists and pedophiles we're putting away."

"DC Lawton," came Whit's stern voice from his office.

"Wish me luck," Denny said to Verity as he entered Whit's domain.

"Shut the door please," Whit instructed as Denny entered. Whit waited for Denny to do so before speaking. "What the actual bloody devil was that today? You slammed a suspect up against a car."

"Look, I know I was a bit rough with the guy," Denny excused himself, "but he was already making it hard on me."

"DC Lawton, I know how you feel about these kinds of people, but you know it's not professional. You and I both know that wouldn't go over well in Portland either."

"It'd probably go worse," Denny chuckled.

"Here," said Whit as he reached inside a deskside refrigerator and tossed a can of Dr. Pepper to Denny, "have a fizzy pop on me. What am I going to do with you?"

"Well, you could always fire me, ship me back to Portland," Denny replied as he popped the tab on his soda.

"Lawton, you know I have to pretend to want that. Saves me from getting me 'ead chewed off whenever some blasted MP or government official comes sniffing around."

"We have them back home too, boss. We had a state representative from our country try and shut our unit down. Joined up with a Hood River guy to push to redirect police funding for vice squads to LGBT education for inmates. Come to find out, I caught both of them with their pants down when we busted a local brothel. Put a big damper on their whole enterprise, and it died in the House. Those guys with those 'Locally Hated' stickers on their clapped-out Civics, I was the real deal, sans the clapped-out Civic and the stickers."

"Look, I know you have nothing to lose, and you don't care what people think," Whit continued, "but when you go home, we still have a job to do. You can't lose your cool on these people, even if all you did was just pin him against a car and tell him what you wished would happen to him. Come on, I'd love to have a go at that guy. I have a little girl at home, and whenever I see her, I fear for how dangerous the world really is for her."

"I'd assume normal people would love it if we beat the ever-loving crap out of a few more pedophiles. Anyway, given the kind of person he was, he probably dug it."

"Lawton, I'm the lead detective here. You're my subordinate. This isn't a human-dog relationship. I don't need to keep you on a leash. I do, however, want this taken care of. We need to make this right so that we can continue to do what we're supposed to do."

"What do I do? Go down to the jail and make nice with the boy lover?"

"My secretary has arranged a meeting at Mister Lorde's house tomorrow. She will provide you the address."

"So, you want us to kiss and make up?" asked Denny.

"Not necessarily. I want you to meet him, let him know you're not a danger to anybody."

"Well, I am a danger to criminals," Denny objected. "Is he a criminal?"

"Do you really want me to answer that?" Whit shot back.

"Politician, got it."

"Yes, but you need to let him know that you're not the type who just goes around accusing people of crime just because they look a certain way."

"Look at me, Whit. I do look that 'certain way'. Does he seriously think I'm a racist?"

"Put your name in the newspaper without a picture," Whit went on to explain, "and they'll all just think you're some rando from Burnley."

"I can already tell you this meeting won't go well," said Denny.

"All I can tell you then is to not make him even madder. He already wants your head."

"I'll do it, but I have a bad feeling about this."

"You'll be fine. Just remember, he can make or break you."

"Either way, I only seek the truth. I don't care about his feelings if they only lead to a falsehood."

"I understand. You just need the pretense so we can carry on our work."

"I hate being fake."

"These politicians don't know the difference."

"Are we done here?" asked Denny.

"One more thing," Whit said in closing. "Any news on the Love case?"

"Hussein Abdul's vanished into thin air."

"Well, hopefully these late distractions might bring him out of hiding if you've spooked him. Keep it up. We all believe in you."

Chapter 13
Michael Lorde, MP

Denny wore his Sunday best to meet with the local Member of Parliament. He hadn't dressed up so well since he had left Oregon, but here he was wearing a black three-piece suit with a forest green shirt and a novelty Portland Timbers FC tie he had received for Father's Day the year before. He added some black shined cowboy boots for good measure as he wanted to make a statement to this high and mighty politician.

Eschewing the police car, Denny drove his Mustang. He wanted to show up in style, but it was also a power play. It was something that said, "Look at me. Do you really want to play me?" Verity rode with him, the expectation being that they go on their normal rounds of the Love case after the meeting with Michael Lorde. There may have also been the fear that things would go sideways with the high and mighty politician, and two people would be better if a hasty escape was warranted.

"I feel like this is a waste of precious time and money," Denny told Verity as he adjusted his tie.

"You'll be fine," Verity comforted Denny. "Just don't say anything that'll offend him."

"What, like the truth?"

"Maybe this is a disaster in the making," Verity admitted.

"Just keep the car running and prepare to peel out of here if things go south," Denny joked as he climbed out of the Mustang.

"You'll do great," Verity reassured Denny like a wife speaking to her husband right before the big interview. "Don't just go swaggering in there like you own the place. Remember, you're still a guest in our country, and he sees you as a party crasher."

Michael Lorde's mansion was impressive to say the least. Denny thought he had seen everything when he met the Loves. He was clearly mistaken. Michael Lorde lived every man's dream. Out front were several exotics parked, several models of each make – Lamborghinis, Ferraris, McLarens, Jags, Koenigseggs, Bugattis, Rolls Royces, and even a Hennessey Venom F5 – all parked around a palatial water fountain with a naked cherub puking up a gout of water from his mouth. There was a full regulation-size football pitch visible from the drive, as if a busy Member of Parliament would ever have time for a soccer match, to watch one or play it. (Apparently, Michael Lorde held a rather sizeable stake in Preston North End, so the field was a practice pitch that allowed him to work and watch his team.) A doorman opened the house to Denny, revealing a spacious foyer with twin staircases wrapping around each side and meeting in the middle on the second floor. If he hadn't known any better, Denny would have thought the King lived here. He marveled that an MP would have such a palace. Then he remembered that most politicians enrich themselves in unscrupulous ways, so the wonder went away as quickly as it came to him.

Once inside, a butler led Denny through the mansion. It all made sense now. As wealthy as Ian Love was, he was still the little guy compared to Michael Lorde. Ian Love was a self-made man. There was no way Michael Lorde made all this kind of money in one lifetime. A fish tank filled with exotic tropical fish that seemed like the size of Keiko's old tank at the Oregon Coast Aquarium? In the middle of the house? For what purpose? Does this guy live just to impress his friends? Was there a Sea-World-style fish show he didn't know about? What was next? A hall of mirrors like at Versailles?

The butler led Denny through double doors into a large room lined with oak and mahogany. It seemed much too big for the single desk and chair, as large as they themselves were. Behind the desk, illuminated by a large floor-to-ceiling window that overlooked the football pitch was Michael Lorde, MP.

"Welcome, please have a seat," the Member of Parliament invited Denny as he gestured at an impressive desk chair opposite him.

The Roundhead was dressed in another three-piece suit, this time a navy color with a blood red tie. He smoked a forty-five-minute cigar, freshly lit. He held the cigar box up to Denny, offering a smoke. Denny grabbed the Cuban out of the box and fiddled around with it as he took a seat. Lorde took his seat in an even-more impressive desk chair and tossed Denny the cigar guillotine. Denny was never a casual smoker, but in the line of duty, he had learned the tricks of the trade as he cut the end of the cigar off and lit the death stick.

"I assume you know why you're here," Michael Lorde started.

"I take it you're not having me here for any commendation," Denny bantered.

"One thing Whit never said you weren't was terrible conversation," Lorde chuckled. "That's not to say commendations can never be in order, depending on how your performance goes in the coming months."

"Well, I guess it's a good thing I don't care what people think about me," Denny replied coldly.

"Right, but the whole country is looking at Lancashire right now," Lorde argued. "You do realize that the murder of my opponent's beloved daughter has made national news? They've even picked up the story in New York and Atlanta, just small snippets on Fox and CNN, though."

"I'd think so," Denny replied. "It was pretty horrific – pretty little thing found floating in the harbor with half her face blown off. That kind of crime doesn't happen every day, especially in a village like Crenshaw."

"Yes, and it has come to my attention that you have been pestering my constituents about it," Lorde continued.

"If by constituents, you mean I've been asking questions of people who may be related and have some information about it, then yes."

"Of course, DC Lawton, but you misunderstand me. I mean, you have pestered, well, a certain segment of my constituency."

"Let me guess. They have a similar melanin content to me, and they have names like 'Mohammed', 'Omar', and 'Aziz'? Those guys, right?"

"Yes, DC Lawton. See, I don't know how they do things in Texas…"

"Oregon," Denny interrupted. "I'm from Oregon, and I can tell you, people don't like it over there either."

"Then you see my predicament? These people come from Third World countries, scared out of their wits, and the last thing they need is some person with a funny accent coming in accusing them of a murder they likely didn't do."

"In my defense, your Lordship," Denny replied, "it was only one, and he's definitely not scared out of his wits. He knows exactly what he's doing."

"Right, but do you know how this looks?"

"I don't know," Denny retorted. "Do you know what a teenaged girl with her face blown off looks like? Do you know what a mother who has lost her baby looks like? Do you know what a father who poured his life into his little girl only to lose her looks like? Do you know, firsthand, what a broken family looks like? I'll tell you it looks a lot worse than one immigrant getting his little feelers hurt. It's gut-wrenching, and people just don't give a crap. Instead of fixing things, we'd just rather leave them broken because doing the right thing makes us feel all icky inside."

"So, it's like that now, is it?"

"Listen," Denny continued, "like I've told everybody and their brother since I got here, I worked the streets in vice for ten years. I watched as politicians threw money at the problem and then turned around and encouraged the problem. And because someone has the wrong melanin count or sounds too local, they're ignored because to bring justice would be seen as racist, and xenophobic, and Islamophobic."

Denny fiddled with the lit cigar as he rested back in his chair. Lorde blew a puff of smoke as he let out a sigh.

"You are a bull in a china shop, DC Lawton," Lorde explained. "We cannot afford to offend these people. And that's another thing. When you are told to investigate a crime, you investigate a crime."

"I had better things to do than to arrest a soccer mom for saying men are men and women are women," Denny grumbled back. "I don't do things for virtue of 'just following orders'. That's how half of Europe got conquered in the 1940s, was just young German kids following orders. So, now we have harmless people going to jail for wrong think while the actual sickos walk. For example, your pedophile friend. I hear he's going free because I scared him. Is this real life?"

"We have to protect the most vulnerable," Lorde excused himself.

"Horse crap!" Denny shouted. "Your 'most vulnerable' are those who victimize our most vulnerable. You can't tell me a pedophile is your most vulnerable. You can't tell me that a man who runs a gang who grooms and rapes young women is among the most vulnerable, even if he's a migrant and has brown skin. Look at me. Am I among those most vulnerable, or does my English name count me out?"

"So obstinate," Lorde sighed.

"You sit here in this mansion in the middle of a big city," Denny began. "You've accumulated wealth beyond imagination. Tell me, how often have you actually left the city, save to drive on the motorway between cities? Have you even been to Crenshaw? Do you know the kind of people I'm dealing with? Have you even met your beloved migrants? I believe not. You see, I know these people. I talk with them. I've built a relationship with them. They are scared, but not of me. They're scared of other migrants. All because you have let people in who don't deserve to be here. You protect the people in power. You're on the side of the pedos. You're on the side of Hassan Abdul. Heard of him? I'd be surprised if you have."

"Have you finished?" Lorde asked, his former boredom simmering into rage.

"Oh, I'm just getting started," Denny chuckled. "You see, I don't have anything to lose here. I'm here because I have no friends back home, so I can talk all day. Throw me in prison, I don't care. Because guys like me, we seek the truth, and then we find the truth, we face it. People like you don't like the ugly truth. And you know what the ugly truth is? You care for number one. You like to call yourself a public servant where you're really a public master. So, I ask you again, have you ever met the everyday constituent outside of Preston or Blackpool? God forbid you step foot in a place like Pendle or Gisburn. Them folk too white fer ye? But no, you sit here high and mighty in your Preston mansion where you can act like the benevolent politician dispensing grace upon all the brown people. Meanwhile, those brown people are scared and oppressed – not by the police and not by the everyday small-town Englishman, but by fellow migrants who refuse to leave the old ways behind. Quick, what's the rate of child marriage in the average British city?"

Lorde stuttered at this.

"You can't tell me, can you," Denny continued. "What's your next order of business after you kick me out of here? Are you going to a fundraiser? Gonna look good for the cameras? Maybe put a little Pakistani baby on your knee in solidarity with the oppressed migrants?"

Denny took a breath here. He stared Lorde down. The MP was clearly more than agitated. He had death in his eyes. Denny cleared his throat before he continued.

"You see, Mister Lorde, I don't like you. You're just like every other big-city politician who would rather country folk don't exist except to feed them. I've dealt with people like you all my life. I've stepped from one Portland to another, just with funny accents, funny money, and people driving on the wrong side of the road. You don't scare me."

By now, about a quarter of Denny's cigar had burnt away without a single hit. To punctuate his point, the detective planted the stogie into the ashtray set out in front of him, extinguishing the expensive smoke. Michael Lorde was beet red.

"Mister Lorde, I don't know what you set out to accomplish today," Denny continued without missing a beat, "but if it was to

124

intimidate me into towing whatever line you were leaving out for me, you're clearly mistaken. I do what I do because it's the right thing to do. My job is to serve and protect, not squander and neglect. A brown migrant is just as human as a white Briton. He is just as capable of evil and culpable as his fellow man. To think anything less is dehumanizing. To think them incapable of evil is to think them incapable of forming their own opinions and making their own decisions. Do you think brown people are stupid, Mister Lorde?"

"So, you mean to tell me you plan to continue in the way you've been carrying on?" Michael Lorde trembled when he finally found pause.

"The short answer," Denny replied measuredly, "is yes."

"Then you know this will not end well for you," Lorde said holding back the tirade that was bound to be loosed at the slightest drop of a hat.

"I've said it before, and I'll say it again," Denny answered, "I've lost everything that means anything to me. Now I have nothing to lose. Do your worst. Throw whatever you've got at me. Wanna kill me? I'm even prepared for that possibility. I'm still going to do right by the people of this county, even if it means hurting the feelings of those you clearly hold dear."

Michael Lorde was a barrel of gun powder with a lit fuse. The only thing that could stop the explosion was for the hero to swoop in with a second to spare and snuff it out. Denny could read the room the whole time. This was his intent. No, he never wanted to make nice with Michael Lorde. There was no way of doing that honestly. No, he wanted to put Michael Lorde on notice that he was going to be exposed for the fraud he was.

"Now, if you'll excuse me, sir," Denny continued politely, "I need to get to work."

And with that, he stood up and extended his hand. Lorde ignored the gesture. Denny turned about and headed out. The house was deathly quiet. The door was opened for him as he walked out, a butler stationed outside to see him out. As he jogged down the steps, he heard a set of swift, tiny footsteps. Denny jogged faster and darted for his car. He leaped up over the top and slid across the hood like Tom Wopat.

Michael Lorde was too slow for Denny, his tiny feet unable to keep up with Denny's athletic clodhoppers, bursting out of his house as the cop climbed into his muscle car. The last thing Denny heard before he shut the door was a word that started with the letter "F" followed by some garbled noises that sounded somewhat like English.

"I take it he took it well," Verity chuckled.

"About as good as one can," Denny replied, beaming at his partner.

Chapter 14
Untouchable

That had gone as well as expected. Anyone who had worked with Denny for any length of time and possessed half a brain knew that he wouldn't budge an inch from Michael Lorde's demands. It was clear that Hell itself couldn't move Denny Lawton.

Denny and Verity completed their rounds as normal and with the same results as expected. There were no leads on Hassan Abdul's whereabouts. Wasn't like that would change anytime soon if Michael Lorde had anything to say about that. It was clear to even Stevie Wonder that Michael Lorde was more concerned with making sure any and all migrants were clear in the sight of the law, even at the expense of those who were truly in the clear.

"I got the reports," Verity told Denny as they walked into the police station.

"What are you gonna do?" Denny chuckled, "Copy and paste?"

"If it's all the same to you," replied Verity.

"Have at it," said Denny. "I'm going to go to my desk and wait for hellfire and brimstone to come down from Whit."

"Good luck," Verity wished to Denny.

Verity sat down at her computer and opened up the file from the previous day. It was as if they were spinning in circles. It was all the same conversation from the last several weeks. From time to time, she would glance over toward Denny's desk. He sat there, staring at his computer intently. There was still no sign of Whit. Perhaps the old man already knew what was going to happen and just decided to let it go until someone else complained. That would make the most sense. Still, she marveled at how her partner could stay so calm, cool, and collected despite having everyone come down against him. Sure, there was the whole thing about him not having anything worth taking, but could it really be that simple? Was doing the right thing that calming to him?

Verity opened the Thursday folder, the day before, and immediately hit the "Save As" option in the drop-down menu, changing it to Friday. She glanced back over toward Denny's way. Still at his desk, still staring at his computer, still no Whit; but now she noticed he had his Bluetooth headphones in. She clicked "Print" and walked over to Denny's desk.

Denny had Facebook opened on the monitor. Verity walked up behind to watch the video playing on his news feed. It was a group of little children no older than six all dressed in white shirts and blue jeans and denim skirts with bright yellow bandanas. From what it looked like, they were singing. As Verity watched, she noticed two of them bore a passing resemblance to Denny. (They also happened to be the only ones clearly singing their little hearts out.) After a while, she could see the song had ended, at which point, two women ran up to the steps and began to usher the children down. At this point, Denny reached his hand out and touched the monitor where one of the women stood. She had lush golden hair from what Verity could tell. That had to be

Talia, Denny's ex; that was her only conclusion, given the longing gaze he gave the monitor when he placed his hand over her image.

"Why don't you take a picture? It lasts longer," Denny growled.

"How did you know?" asked Verity.

"How couldn't I?" Denny returned as he pulled out his earbuds and closed the browser. "It was all I could do not to turn around and say something about you breathing down my neck for the last three minutes."

"Your kids?" Verity pressed, ignoring Denny's complaint.

"Rickey Haddon and Hudson Voddie," Denny replied with longing in his voice. "Yeah, named my firstborn after the guy who stole my wife."

"They looked like they were having fun," said Verity, trying to distract from the anger Denny was feeling toward Rick.

"Royal Riders," Denny explained. "It's their kid's program they do on Wednesday nights – kind of a cowboy or army cavalry theme. They have singing as part of the program every week, and then every month, they do a song or two on Sunday mornings."

"You miss them all, don't you?"

"Every day," said Denny.

"And yet you keep saying you have nothing to lose," Verity went on. "Do you actually believe you've lost your boys?"

"Princess, I have a kid I haven't even been able to meet, a little baby girl, all because her mother has decided I'm a raging psychopath who uses his power of the badge to rape random women. Yes, I've lost them."

"I don't think you have," Verity encouraged.

"Tell that to the divorce court and the Multnomah County Sheriff's Department. Can't do much with a restraining order."

"You give up too easily."

"Lawton!" came Whit's barking order.

"Duty calls," said Denny, clearly ready to be done with the conversation.

"This isn't over," Verity called to him. "Seven o'clock, my place. Bring some tortillas and dress casual."

Denny was never one to be late. He showed up to Verity's house as instructed at seven on the dot wearing blue jeans and a Diego Chará jersey he'd bought at a Timbers match that summer. He had never been to Verity's place before.

"I honestly thought you wouldn't come," Verity chuckled as she answered the door.

"What a coincidence. That's what I thought," replied Denny, holding up the bag of tortillas, trying to figure out where they should go.

"Just put the tortillas on the counter," Verity instructed. "Hallie's over at a friend's house for the night, so we're just doing dinner for two if you don't mind."

Verity had dressed down into some sweats and a baggy Burnley FC hoodie. To Denny, she had always been some uptight British cop, only letting her hair down one time in front of him, and only that one time out of necessity because all of her hair ties had gone M.I.A. Tonight, her hair was down, and she actually seemed like she would be fun to be around. Even their drinks and lunches together were all in the name of business.

"I brought the tortillas," said Denny, "so, what's dinner?"

"Okay, so I've been doing some searches online," Verity explained excitedly, "and I found a taco recipe I think you'll love."

"Oh, so we're going for cultural appropriation?" Denny jabbed.

"Oh my! Is that what this is?" asked Verity worriedly.

"Maybe, maybe not," Denny chuckled. "I'm just kidding. Come on, you know me. You think I give two craps about cultural appropriation? Anyway, I appreciate the gesture. Let's see what we got."

"Oh, but I wanted to cook for you," Verity pouted.

"Why? Because I got a case of the sads?"

"Fine, I'll let you cook," Verity said defiantly.

"Oh, no, let's see what you can do Ms. Baker," Denny chuckled.

At first glance, it was your standard white people taco fare. Verity had purchased several packets of taco seasoning from ASDA. From there, it was ground beef, mild salsa, sour cream, romaine, and grated cheddar. Marisol Lawton would have thrown a fit had she been there.

Denny chuckled as he watched his partner excitedly toss the seasoning packet into the browned-up ground beef.

This was truly a side of Verity he hadn't seen before. It reminded him of home. At times, it seemed he caught glimpses of Talia, especially that one time she dyed her hair brown – lovingly making him dinner after a long day at work. It was as if he could feel his old life tapping him on the shoulder. That was nonsense, though; the old life was dead and gone, stolen by his best friend.

"So, you cook often?" Denny asked, trying to break the ice.

"All the time," Verity replied. "Even when Elliott was still here, it was always me doing the cooking." She looked down ruefully. "Nine years I was with that tosser, and not once did he ever have a job. Left me to do all t' work and raising Hallie on top of that. Then one day when I finally put t' 'eat on 'im, 'e decides 'e's a bloody poof and buggers off on down t' Brighton."

Denny's chuckle had graduated to a snicker. Verity took notice.

"It's not funny," she moaned. "Elliott's a right tosser, he is."

"I'm sorry, Princess," Denny gulped, "the way you go all Lancashire when you talk about your ex…"

"Well, he is."

"I know," said Denny with a cough as he caught his laughter. "Any man who wouldn't work to provide for his family and then leave when his wife tries to light a fire under his butt isn't a man. I guess, if he's decided he's part of the LGBT community, he might not consider himself a man either."

"You win that one," Verity giggled, trying to hide her bright red face. "Oh, look, dinner's ready."

"Oh, I almost forgot!" Denny exclaimed before rushing out the door, only to return a few moments later with two bottles of Tamarind Jarritos. "I've been saving these since I left home."

"Tamarindo?" Verity read the label.

"It's an acquired taste, kind of like Marmite," Denny joked.

"Well, make up your plate. I'm not waiting," Verity instructed.

Talia's first time making Denny tacos hadn't gone over as well as Verity's. That was partly due to Marisol Lawton breathing down her neck the whole time. Both times, Denny was more than happy to partake of the fruits of their labor. It wasn't anything fancy – not the street tacos his mother made, but it was the heart behind it – Talia's love and Verity's friendship.

"You don't like them. They're rubbish, aren't they?" Verity asked as she nibbled at her fingernails.

"I'd say these are the best tacos I've had since I came to Lancashire," Denny replied in approval. "Better than the Taco Bell up the road from the police station."

"Well, that's something."

"Thanks," said Denny.

"Thanks for what?"

"For trying to make me feel at home. It really means a lot. It's just been a long three or four months. Kind of takes me back."

"I'm glad I met with your approval," Verity chuckled.

"But promise me this," Denny added, "next time, we're doing this at my place; and I promise you, by the time you're done eating dinner, you'll be jamming to Banda music and scarfing down hot Cheetos."

"So, you don't think it was that good?" Verity asked as she stood up to take up the empty plates.

"It was mild, which is still good," Denny defended. "Honestly, reminds me of home.

"So, like Talia's cooking?"

"Didn't want to bring her into this," Denny replied.

"I'm sorry. Did I offend you?"

"Not at all. Just thinking about her today has been very hard."

"You still love her?"

"I never did stop loving her," said Denny. "She stopped loving me. And you know the crazy thing? I should've known it was bound to happen."

"That she'd leave you?"

"That my line of work would land us in this situation. I mean, every other cop working vice was already divorced, sometimes two or three times. It was like they couldn't stay faithful."

"But you were never unfaithful," Verity added.

"It's hard, but I was always faithful. You know, she trusted me at first. I always made sure to never give her a reason not to trust me."

By now, the conversation had moved into the living room. A football match was playing on the television – Burnley was fighting

Everton trying to prove they still belonged in the Premier League. The match was muted, so it was just the conversation.

"She trusted me. Even when I was first accused, Talia trusted me. She didn't just up and leave me. Rick lied to her. He poisoned her mind. She knew how hard it was to stay blameless and faithful in my profession; so, ten years of doing it with one accusation, it didn't follow."

"Rick must've been pretty persuasive then?"

"He fooled us all. That's the sad part about it. He sowed that seed of doubt in her mind until within a week, just a week, she couldn't even look at me."

"I couldn't see just changing my mind about the man I love just like that. I loved Elliott, but it was a series of abuses of my trust over several years that did it for me."

"It makes total sense to me."

"How so?"

"Do you know why I got into vice in the first place?"

"Now that never made sense to me. What does a faithful church man think he's doing going into vice?"

"I saw all these kids who were like me at one point," Denny began.

"Church kids?"

"Church kids, unchurched kids, whatever walk of life," he continued. "They all started out living normal, happy lives. You don't end up on the streets selling your body and shooting up heroin just because you thought it was such a cool idea. You do it because it's the only option you have left."

"What about coming from a loving two-parent household was so stifling?"

"Princess, I'm going to tell you something I haven't told anyone in almost twenty years."

"Say on."

"See, I was the first in my age group to hit puberty. All of my friends were singing the high notes in Royal Riders while I sounded like Barney the Dinosaur under their falsetto. We had this family friend in the church – Jana Crockett. Never thought anything of it at first – sweet lady in her early thirties and all that. She was one of my mom's friends. Remember now, I'm the middle of three boys, and she always paid close attention to me, especially after my voice dropped. Imagine a twelve-year-old with a moustache. I never noticed it at first. She started giving me preferential treatment whenever we went over – extra servings of dinner, little gifts here and there. I don't even think her husband noticed."

"She groomed you?"

"Last person you'd expect, right? It was two years before she actually went through with it. Took a year for her to get me in a room alone with her. It was under the pretense of giving me a gift or needing to talk to me about something spiritually serious. You know, she and her husband were my Sunday School teachers. Then one night when I was fourteen, she called me into a separate room because she had yet another gift for me: her. I had no idea what was happening. It felt so good to be touched in every which way, but it felt so wrong because my parents had a big talk with me when I turned thirteen. In her own mind, she was giving me the gift of manhood, but she took away my innocence."

"Oh my! Denny, I'm so sorry that happened!"

"That was only the first time. When I was fifteen, I finally told my parents what was going on. One would think their own mom and dad would take action. They just laughed it off the notion that such a modest, godly woman would ever rape a teenaged boy. Apparently church mouse women are incapable of evil. It was just me acting out and being rebellious because I was fifteen. Tried my pastor – same result."

"Nobody?" Verity almost whispered.

"I don't, I don't blame them," Denny stuttered with a tear in his eye. "It was almost twenty years ago, and still to this day, we're so ill-equipped to deal with abuse when it happens the other way around. With girls, it's expected because they're naturally weaker than men. It's so easy for a man to force himself on a woman. For a woman to force herself on a man, it's psychological. She has to make it seem like it's the right thing. With someone like that, she already has society on her side, and it's not some evil conspiracy or preconceived notion. It's just logic, and Jana Crockett used that logic to get what she wanted: me in bed and to feel young again or some weird psychobabble like that – I don't know."

"And she's still…"

"Still friends with my mom, still active in my old church, and now my ex-mother-in-law."

"Your what?"

"Oh, yeah, I left that part out. She set me up with Talia to get closer to me. Dumb broad thought that would keep me imprisoned."

"But you got out."

"In some ways, yes. In others, no. Talia is the spitting image of her mother. I fell in love with her because she's different, actually walked the talk her mother spoke. She actually loved me and would have never hurt our children like that. Princess, she's beautiful, but I found myself having to shut my eyes at times with her because it took me back to those moments when I was just a fifteen-year-old boy. I couldn't even…"

Denny broke down, convulsing and sobbing. It was raw. For Verity, Denny was no longer Denny. Gone was the confident detective who didn't care what anyone thought – who just did what he wanted and would ask forgiveness later.

"I sometimes think," Denny continued as if the wind had been knocked out of him. "I sometimes think if I had actually given Talia all of me, had I been able to tell her what her mother did to me and not just the goody two-shoes polished part that she knew, I'd still be there. I'd be right there by her side, raising our children. It would still be us against the world. Instead, I ran and hid inside myself. She never knew what her mom is. That witch thought she could keep me, but the moment I said 'I do' to Talia, we packed up the car and moved to Portland. Left that church and found a new one. Created a new life. I applied to PPB and eventually became a vice cop. I saw a lot of kids who went through what I went through, being groomed by the people they should've loved and trusted, and wanted them to know there was hope – that just because their lives started out bad, it didn't have to end bad."

Denny had almost completely collapsed into Verity's arms. That was never his intent. It just all sort of happened by accident. He couldn't remember how he had gotten there – the little cry session had blacked out some of that. She felt warm. He missed that. Talia had that same warmth, and here was a woman with whom he had shared his

135

deepest darkest secret. He had shared with her the last bit of his broken heart. She never laughed it off. She believed the whole thing. The last piece of his heart now belonged to Verity Baker.

It all just happened as naturally as putting on his shoes in the morning. He felt her hands on his. That had happened inadvertently several times before, similarly just a natural occurrence that was quickly remedied. But this time, it wasn't remedied. He kept his hand there. He noticed how soft and womanly Verity's hands were. The next thing Denny noticed, his lips were locked with Verity's. There it was again — that old warmth he had been missing for months now. There were no words, just thoughts of "I shouldn't" and "I should" racing through Denny's mind. He wondered if Verity was thinking that too. No, she was enthralled. He could see it on her face. She was soft. That's what he was feeling. That's what he was missing.

Anyway, what bad would it do? He wasn't married anymore. He had no commitment to Talia. Wasn't his fault anyway. And here Verity was, just as single and divorced as he was — left abandoned by a man who was almost certainly not coming back. Here she was now, practically throwing herself at him. What would this one little moment hurt? Anyway, he had already revisited the past tonight, so why not just take one small memento back from it?

Part 3
The Impossible

There was no way this was happening. Maybe nothing would come of it. Like, who would take these clowns seriously? A hooker and a known pimp? Who would take them at their word? Then again, that hooker was a trusted police informant. If they took her word when she was to testify against the pimp, what would stop them from taking her word when she testified against the cop? What would make the juicier story? Oh, he knew it. Pimps always go down, but a cop who doesn't walk the talk is too hard to pass up. They'd take the cop story over the pimp story in a heartbeat.

Denny breathed heavily as he shut the door behind him. They couldn't touch him here. That was the idea. Home – so different from out there.

He walked into the living room, trying to hide his fear. What was he feeling? TV static? Was that the way to describe the empty pit that had opened up in his heart? Were there camera's watching him suddenly from every nook and cranny of his house like some sick reality show?

Then there was Talia, sweet Talia, cleaning up after Rickey and Hudson's impromptu pizza party, going above and beyond his request because she loved being a wife, mother, and homemaker so much. Denny rushed in and hugged her as tight as he could without hurting the baby. Home, that's what this felt like now, home — so far from the desiccated, putrid living corpse that was Michaela Roberts. He could smell her conditioner, feel her softness in his hands.

"What's gotten into you?" she asked excitedly. "You've only been gone an hour and a half. I figured you got caught up with work and had to stay a little later than usual. It's alright. I just thought it would be best to get lunch cleaned up before it all got out of hand."

Right, he was never this touchy with her. Sure, he had loads of affection for her and loved her more than life itself, but he was never one to just up and show great overzealous affection out of nowhere, not even after a long day at work.

"I just missed you," Denny excused himself.

"After an hour and a half? What's really going on?" Talia pressed.

"Nothing, I just wanted to spend the day with you, not go into work on my day off."

"Denny, don't lie to me. I'm not stupid. You were more than fine with me sleeping the afternoon away. Tell me the truth."

For as little as she knew about the profession, Talia could sure tell when Denny wasn't entirely truthful about work. She knew he went to dark places. She also knew there were things he kept back about those dark places, because it was too dark for any sane person to begin with.

"There might be trouble soon," Denny confessed.

"Wait, for our family? Do we need to move?"

"See, I didn't want to worry you."

"Denny, you need to tell me what's going on."

"Okay, we don't need to move. I don't know. Some things may be said about me in the next few days. I just need to prepare you for it."

"What are they going to say?"

"There may be some accusations. I didn't do anything, but I was set up. There's some bad people out there that want me off the streets."

"But that's ridiculous. Not you. Not my Denny. You would never do anything to anyone."

138

"I know, but not everybody gets that. I'm just going to be up front and honest. I won't bore you with all the details, but an informant turned on me."

"Listen, I don't care who said what, I know you. You're the last person who would hurt anyone."

"Your vote of confidence is very reassuring," Denny scoffed.

"Denny, look at me," Talia ordered defiantly. "No, seriously, look at me."

Denny turned back to his wife, his eyes everywhere but meeting with hers. But there she was — the love of his life, the whole of her, as much as his diverted eyes could see. So much hurt had brought her to him. His pain had been turned into the brightest spot in his life. She was there, open for him and whatever he had to say.

"Denny, I love you. If you say you didn't do it, you didn't do it."

Chapter 15
Everything I Am

Denny held Verity's soft form against his body. All the while, the memory played in his mind – the lead-up, the very act, the shower afterwards, falling asleep with her cradled in his arms. He remembered every second of the simultaneous pleasure and guilt as Verity let him have his way with her. This time was different. This time, he didn't have to close his eyes. This time, the pain of what had happened to him was absent. This time, he didn't see Jana Crockett as he looked into Verity's eyes. It was all Verity all night. The first time it was just him and the woman, not him, the woman, and somehow Jana. For the first time in his life, Jana Crockett hadn't even entered his mind as he made love.

The quiet granted him a moment of reflection as Verity drifted in and out of subconsciousness, a tiny snore followed by a stir. He ran his fingers through her caramel hair as he thought about the ramifications. This wasn't his wife or his girlfriend. This was his coworker. He barely knew her, barely even thought about a life with her. Sure, there were signs that maybe she was interested in him before, but going from accidentally touching hands to giving up the most secret parts of each other within a matter of hours was unnatural.

It was all wrong, all of it. Sleep didn't come as easy for him as it did for her. When he woke up on Saturday morning, it wasn't the first time his eyes had shot open in realization of what he had done and was doing since actually doing it. He kept his eyes on Verity, too afraid or unwilling to make a move until she was conscious and lucid enough to have a talk. When Verity finally did wake up, he was still, a blank expression on his face as if he were frozen there as a statue the whole night long.

"Good morning," Verity said happily as she turned to face him, a sweet smile on her face.

"We should not have done that," Denny said blankly, the stony expression remaining.

"Maybe not," Verity replied sleepily, "but it was enrapturing all the same."

Denny sat up. He looked into Verity's eyes. Of course, she didn't understand that she wasn't his to take. She wasn't a part of his world – the world he came from, the world where sex was a sacred bond between man and wife; anything outside of that was just a man unable to control his appetites. It didn't matter how bad he or she wanted it. It didn't matter how much they needed the release. It didn't matter that there would be no spouse for either of them to hurt. He saw. He lusted. He took. The fruit was taken. Death followed.

"I had no right," Denny continued. "I feel like I just used you, like I needed comfort, and I grabbed the first human I could find with two X chromosomes."

"I let you," Verity countered.

"It doesn't matter, Princess. I violated everything I am last night. I didn't do this because I loved you. I did it because I miss my ex-wife. I did it to fill a hole in my heart that will never be filled again."

141

"So?" she pressed. "You got what you needed. It was a fling. You felt good. I felt good. We were mutually respectful and didn't physically abuse each other. Who did we hurt? Who did we so offend last night?"

"Would you like me to make a list? First, I hate to even say it because it makes me sound like a freaking boy scout, but we violated workplace guidelines."

"Who has to know? I'm not going to say something."

"Second," he ignored her, "I offended God."

"There it is," she mocked. "You're afraid Sky Daddy's going to zap you."

"Yes and no," Denny replied, audibly hurt. "Anyway, that was very offensive. You mock everything I am. Verity, I love God. You know this about me. I'm very open with that faith."

"Denny, the time for fairy tales is over. Anyway, it's offensive and hurtful to me that you'd even think to infantilize me. You don't think I know what you're doing?"

"Verity, you knew exactly who I am."

"You are a very moral and upright man who seeks nothing but truth."

"At least I thought I was."

"So, what, that's all gone out the window now that we've had a moment?"

Denny sighed deep in thought. He couldn't expect Verity to understand. For her, there was no world where there was peace and forgiveness. For her, it was a world of no moral absolutes. Do that which is right in your own eyes. After all, what's it going to hurt? Only a one-night stand. Then it's two nights. One thing follows another, and you find yourself raising a child with someone you ultimately hate but are attached to until that person decides they need to find themselves. And then what's left? More broken homes, a child growing up confused by two parental standards, more than enough anger and bitterness to go around.

"Do you know why we have sex?" he asked.

"If you're going to give me the talk, my parents already gave it to me when I was twelve," Verity replied in annoyance.

"Let me rephrase that. Do you know the spiritual significance of it?"

"Again with the spirituality."

"It's called 'making love' for a reason, Princess. You're supposed to love the person you're sharing a bed with, and sometimes, you love that person so much that it creates another human being."

Verity laid back in bed, almost dejected. Denny had made a very good point.

"Then if it's all the same to you," Verity started, trying to hold back tears, "I thought there was something between us."

Denny stood up out of the bed and started to dress himself.

"Are you seriously leaving me after I just told you my feelings?"

"No, I just…"

"Well, screw you then! You led me on, and I gave you me, body and soul!"

"So, now we're getting it. But then you made a mockery of everything I am," Denny shot back, "so I guess we're even."

"I can't believe you're doing this," she cried.

"Does this not sear your conscience even a little?"

"I don't understand," Verity sniffled.

Denny sat back down next to her.

"Is there not something inside of you that tells you this is all wrong?" he asked her. "Even just for a second, is there not a little voice that tells you that even when this feels so right that it's all just so wrong?"

"Okay, so I hurt your feelings," Verity whispered as she swatted Denny away.

"You didn't hurt my feelings, Princess. I mean, the whole attacking my faith, convictions, and morals was a little uncalled for, but you didn't hurt my feelings. You gave me exactly what I wanted in the moment. Let me rephrase that. You gave me what I've always wanted in the moment. You gave me instant gratification. I can't sit here and lie and tell you that I hated it. You know this isn't my first time going outside of marriage."

"But why are you so bothered by it? No Jesus answers. Just tell me what was so wrong with it?"

"I will never be able to give my heart to a woman fully. Jana took that from me. I couldn't even fully give myself to my wife because she

143

had a piece of Jana always with her, and I can't give it to you. Either way, conversation's going back to Jesus."

Verity leaned up against Denny. Denny wrapped his arm around her shoulders. Tears began to well up in his eyes. He tried to hold them back, but some of the salt water leaked out. Verity scooted in even closer to Denny, his body heat warming her from the chill of the room.

"My whole life, since I was twelve, I've just wanted to love someone completely and not be afraid of them knowing what happened to me or what their reaction would be. What would Talia think, knowing her mother is an abuser? Then I come here after I've lost everything, and I meet you. You're someone who's been hurt just like me. You've been cast aside and left to fend for yourself. We've worked together so well, and crap…" he trailed off.

Verity could see Denny breathing, actually see the rise and fall of his diaphragm.

"I don't know if it's because you're not connected to Jana or what, but I am attracted to you. I'll admit that. You're a beautiful, intelligent woman, and Elliott was an idiot to dump someone like you. Not just that, but you believed me when nobody else did. You looked beyond the accusations and saw the character. I would love to have a woman like you."

"Then what's stopping you? I'm right here."

"We're colleagues, and I still barely know you. Do you see where I'm coming from? What? We work together for a month, and then the first time I come over to your place, we have sex? That's no way to start a relationship. It's backwards, upside down."

"But do you love me then?" Verity asked with a tinge of hope and fear.

Denny rested back against the wall. No, this was all wrong. She was his colleague, maybe a friend off the clock. So, what? Some subpar tacos, and he spills his guts to her? That's enough to start a whole new life with this, let's face it, random woman?

But then on the other hand, they had just shared the most intimate moment a couple could ever have with each other. The archaic term for sex, "to know", is not so far off. Call it an ancient double entendre, but there is power behind the meaning. In a sense, he did know her. If a man like Denny showed enough interest, she would open herself up to him completely. Denny, for all his foibles, knew that it was easy to fake being like him. True character is easy to hide, by the way.

"What were you expecting from me last night?" he asked.

"What do you mean?"

"I told you my deepest, darkest secret that not even my ex-wife knew. Were you trying to get me into your bedroom, or was it just spontaneous?"

Verity buried her head in her hands. She was trembling, no, convulsing.

"I, I don't know," she confessed through her tears. "I've thought about how lucky a woman was to have had you as a husband this whole time and wished Elliott was like that, but I don't know. When you told me what had happened to you and how brave you truly are, I guess I wanted someone like you, and you were right there in front of me. It was just so easy to get it, to live the life I always dreamed of."

"The human condition," Denny said. "We see, we want, we take. It's how the original sin happened in the garden. It's how it all happens now. Look, I know you can't fully understand how I feel about this, but I need to apologize for everything."

Denny stared deeply into Verity's eyes. He put his hand to her cheek to wipe her tears.

"Princess, you are a beautiful and smart woman who didn't deserve the hand you were dealt. You're brave and strong, raising your daughter while working full-time. Any man would be lucky to have you as a wife."

Verity sat up and hugged Denny. His spirit and brain were fighting flesh and body.

"I'm not mad at you for any of this," he went on. "I know you were trying to make me happy. Honestly, I'm flattered by everything you've said about me, and it seems like you meant it. That being said, if it so bothered me in the moment, I could have said 'no' at any time. I failed in that respect. That's what I tell those kids. It's a battle, saying 'no' to something that feels so good in the moment. I feel like crap, but not because of you. I went against my own advice. I could have said no."

"This doesn't have to go on," Verity said.

"I'm going to be honest here," Denny replied, "but it's going to be very hard working with you from now on, because there is something between us. There's no denying that."

Verity placed her hand on Denny's and leaned back against his shoulder.

"There's so many things that could come of this, good and bad," he continued. "What if you get pregnant? You know I'm going to say 'no' to an abortion, right?"

"If that happens," Verity replied, "we'll cross that bridge when we come to it, and I'll always be able to carry a piece of you with me."

"That sounds very sweet, Princess, but I'm serious. I am going to struggle, because I do feel an attraction to you," Denny confessed.

"Do you want me or not?"

"Only if you come to church with me tomorrow."

"Deal."

Chapter 16
Hiding in Plain Sight

This was not working out. Denny could feel it every time Verity climbed into the car with him. This was now becoming routine. He would leave home early and pick Verity up at her place. On occasion, Hallie would squeeze into the back seat of the Mustang and make them late to the station.

Every minute he was alone with Verity, Denny could feel himself gravitating to her past the professional or even friendly level. The agreement was to keep the relationship, if it could even be called that, on the downlow. Nobody, not even Hallie that knew Denny and Verity were seeing each other in a way. To her, they were just very good friends. There were no official dates, just the carpooling and occasional hangouts, but there was something else. When Hallie was gone and

147

nobody was looking, Verity would rest her right hand on Denny's left as he rowed through the gears. Denny never tried to stop it either.

Denny's bank account was taking a hit too. Lunch was on him every day. He would even buy the drinks at the pub, Fat Terry himself being the only one on the outside who had any suspicion of anything between the two; but it didn't concern him, so he happily took Denny's money, even more so when it came to giving the two cops information on Crenshaw's lowest of the low.

Denny was now in that phase where he was no longer the new guy, but he wasn't one of "the" guys. A new rookie had joined, and he was just Denny now. Gone was the fresh excitement of a new job, but mixed with the new job inexperience was the everyday ho-hum of going to work – a now-established routine.

The Love murder was still the primary thought on his mind. Every day he came in, he would check his emails and the reports. There was nothing. Without Hassan Abdul, there were no more leads. Nobody knew where he was, not even Fat Terry. No amount of cash could draw Hassan out either, or convince anyone to give up the location as to his whereabouts.

It was one of these days as the weather grew colder that Denny decided to go pay a visit to Agatha Love at her flat. He was working alone today, for Verity had called him and told him not to come get her. Apparently, she was up the better part of the wee hours of the morning vomiting up the entire contents of her stomach. Denny had shared supper with Verity and prayed he wouldn't blow chunks in the middle of the workday. However, Denny reasoned that it would be the perfect day to brush up on his social skills. There were many choices to choose from, but who better than to practice on the last person he had scared half to death?

Denny pulled in front of the rundown flats. It was all the same people staring at him like he was the first white Christian missionary in 18th-Century Africa. He waved at the lady at the front desk as he passed her by – same old Indian lady who waved him on, now recognizing him as a legitimate visitor. Same smells as he exited the lift onto Agatha's floor – cat urine and cigarette smoke.

"Nope, go away," was Agatha's immediate reaction as she tried to slam the door in Denny's face.

Denny winced as his size 4E foot was crushed between the door and the frame.

"You know more than you're letting on, Aggie," he told her. "Just let me in."

"Go away, or I'll start screaming," she threatened.

"Aggie, I have a badge and reasonable cause," Denny threatened right back. "You know I can come in there and arrest you for anything illegal I find in there, and you know I'll find something."

Agatha grunted angrily as she opened the door for Denny.

"I hate you so much," she said as she ushered him in.

"I suppose you know why I'm here," Denny guessed out loud.

"I take it you haven't figured out who killed me sister," Agatha replied as she started clearing a pile of clothes off of the sofa, clearly tired and sick.

Denny could see she was starting to show. She tried to hide it, pulling her t-shirt down, but it was all too obvious.

"See, that's just the thing," Denny started, "I am ninety percent sure I know. It's just a matter of finding him."

"How do you know it was a 'him'?" she asked, gesturing to the spot she had just cleared.

Denny took a seat on the sofa. Agatha grabbed a Preston North End tumbler and sat down on a broken-down recliner.

"If it's a ninety-percent guarantee of who it is, I know whether or not it's a him or a her. And I think you know who it is, Aggie."

"Guess again, Taco Boy."

"Taco Boy," Denny marveled, "that's a good one. Is it because of the..." He gestured to himself as if to point out the obvious fact that he was Latino. "Look, I am almost convinced you know. You won't get into trouble if you tell me."

"That's the last thing I'll hear before you cuff me," Verity shot back.

"I ain't about that," said Denny as he reached to the back of his belt and pulled out his cuffs. He tossed them onto the mess that was already on the coffee table. "I'm not in the mood to do any arresting today, unless it's this one man; and I really want to know where this piece of crap is."

"I don't know where he is," she fired back.

149

"Do you even know who 'he' is?" Denny asked.

"You and I both know who you're talking about, Detective Lawton. I'm not some stupid little girl you get to baby around."

Denny chuckled at that. In his eyes, she actually was still a stupid little girl that needed to be babied around. Here she was, all alone, cut off from everyone who truly loved her, carrying the child of a murderous psychopath who only liked her for the power he held over her. The way Ian had talked about her all those weeks ago, that she was still his little girl, he would welcome her home with open arms. He would take that baby of hers up on his knee and love it no matter whose it was. He would be grandpa to that child, not some distant grandfather off somewhere that happens to exist. That was the kind of parent Ian Love was. That was the life Agatha was throwing away for what? Freedom? Fear?

"Hassan doesn't really love you, does he?" Denny asked.

"Of course, he does. How could you say that?"

Denny glanced down again. Now, Agatha's hand was on her belly, clearly protecting the life that was growing inside of her. So grown up, but still so little. Denny knew this situation. His informants, some even younger than Agatha, were all like this. They were so independent in their own eyes, but deep down, they were crying for Mommy and Daddy.

"Let's just say I've been around the sun about fifteen or twenty more times than you have," Denny replied. "If a man can help it, he would never leave his woman. He'd stick with her, be faithful, no matter what life throws at them. So what, he pays for your flat. Does he come by to see you? Does he care about how you feel? So, he provides monetarily as he does for every other one of his baby mamas. That's not love, Aggie. Trust me, I've lived it. I was married for eleven years. If you aren't his world, Aggie, he doesn't love you. Polygamy? Don't get me started on that. Sorry, not sorry for getting religious on you here, but there's a reason God created the first marriage to be between one man and one woman. No man can serve two masters. Either he'll hate the one and love the other. Aggie, there's plenty of people who truly love you and want the best for you, and Hassan isn't in that number."

"He scares me, Detective Lawton," Agatha trembled through her tears. "He pays for our flats to keep us quiet."

"And he rapes you?" asked Denny.

Agatha was visibly frightened.

"Can they hear us?" he asked. "I mean, is the place bugged?"

"I don't think so, but the walls are thin."

"Noted. Let's just whisper then. Hassan does rape you, doesn't he?"

"Not just Hassan."

"His whole gang?"

"Every one of them."

"Explains why his body guards looked so hungry whenever they did the pat down on Detective Baker."

"And it's all the time," Agatha continued.

"This may sound stupid, but hear me out," said Denny, "when was the last time he assaulted you?"

"Two weeks ago," she responded quickly.

Denny mouthed "Two weeks" with an expression of shock.

"And it was Hassan?" asked Denny.

"Habib and one of the body guards held me down while Hassan…" she trailed off before doubling over in pain and tears. "It hurt so bad," she cried. "I wanted it to stop, but he just kept at it. I couldn't say anything. Every time I did, he just hit me. And my baby…"

"Was it just you?" Denny asked, his temperature starting to boil. "Was it just you they hit?"

"After, after he had finished with me, he let Habib go do what he wanted, and he went after Issy."

Despite his swarthy complexion, Denny was red hot now. It had to be Hassan. Here it was – the open secret: Hassan was at the lead of a rape gang, and nobody was brave enough to call it for what it was. Everybody knew what he was doing, but anyone who could do anything had their hands tied. Anyone who was brave enough to speak out was silenced, if not by the gangs, then by the very people who were supposed to be protecting them.

Denny felt sick. It wasn't last night's dinner. No, it was the full realization that he was potentially on the wrong side. Oh, he knew that they arrested people for frivolous reasons, but he still held out faith that maybe, just maybe, the whole constabulary wasn't actively kowtowing to the man and covering up a massive grooming gang.

"Go home," Denny instructed.

"What?"

"Leave this flat. You don't have to be Hassan's concubine or whatever you are to him. Go see your mum and dad. They love you. They want you."

"But I can't go back," she cried as she pointed at her stomach. "They'll kill me. They'll kill my baby."

"'But when he was yet a great way off, his father saw him, and had compassion, and ran, and fell on his neck, and kissed him. And the son said unto him, Father, I have sinned against heaven, and in thy sight, and am no more worthy to be called thy son. But the father said to his servants, Bring forth the best robe, and put *it* on him; and put a ring on his hand, and shoes on *his* feet: And bring hither the fatted calf, and kill *it;* and let us eat, and be merry: For this my son was dead, and is alive again; he was lost, and is found. And they began to be merry'," Denny quoted. "That's a story about a young man who didn't even have a right to his father's money until he died, but the old man gave it to him anyway. He went and blew it all on booze and women until he ended up broke and starving and wanting to eat pig slop because his job feeding the pigs couldn't even afford him a bite to eat. So, one day, he decides he'll go home and just ask to be a servant, because they have it better than him. Instead of greeting him with anger or even obliging his request to be a servant, the dad calls him his 'son' and dresses him in fine clothing, even going so far as to throw a party for him, killing their prize calf and serving it up for dinner. Aggie, your dad loves you. Annie may have been the golden child, but you are still his little girl. To your mum, you will always be her baby. There is no hatred from them. There is no animosity. You know what the last thing your dad told me was when I set out to find you? He told me to bring you home, because you're still their baby. You may feel like you're rejected and garbage to them, but they will love you no matter what."

By this time, Agatha had risen from her recliner and slowly walked over to the sofa. She plopped down next to Denny and leaned on his shoulder, crying like a little girl. That's still all she was to Denny.

"Pack up what you need," said Denny. "Get out of here. Forget Hassan. He can find something else to play with. Just pack up and go home."

Agatha, through a slow process of starting and stopping, dried her tears.

"If you need, I can drive you over to their place."

"Give me ten minutes," she said, smiling through the remaining tears the streamed from her eyes.

"I'll be downstairs," said Denny.

No closer to finding Hassan Abdul, Denny still felt accomplished as he walked through the lobby. That was one objective from the first day he had finally achieved. He had removed Agatha from this situation and confirmed that Hassan had been in the area. He still felt as if he were playing with fire. With one of his sidepieces gone, he would be on the hunt. Agatha could talk. She would be taken seriously. Her father had political connections. Denny could more easily draw Hassan out now, but he would be even more dangerous. There was no telling what Hassan would do to get Agatha back in his orbit.

As if by luck, Denny didn't need to draw Hassan out. As Denny walked out to his car, who should pull up to the apartment building but Hassan Abdul himself, gliding along in his personal Bentley Continental GT. He was clearly coming by to get his kicks. Denny wouldn't offer him that satisfaction. Hassan knew it. He saw the cop and mashed the accelerator.

"Not today," Denny said as he rushed for his Mustang.

He slid across the hood and climbed in. Hassan already had some distance, so he was at a disadvantage. He had seen the Bentley disappear around the corner, so he gave chase. The exhaust and whistle of the twin-turbo V8 echoed throughout the block of apartment flats. Soon, it was joined by the rumble of the Five-Oh Coyote V8 of Denny's Dark Horse.

Hassan knew the village like the back of his hand. Pretty soon, the exhaust note bounced off the walls of every building to become a cacophony of sound, the listener unable to place where it was coming from. Denny was lost. It was as if Hassan was everywhere and nowhere all at once. There was no finding him now.

Feeling somewhat defeated, Denny pulled back in front of the apartment flats. Agatha was waiting with a small duffel bag in hand. She climbed in, and buckled up.

"I'm going to see about finding some protection for you guys," said Denny as he put the car in gear.

"How come?" asked Agatha.

"If I knew where you lived, and I was looking for you, and if I was someone like Hassan Abdul, I would stop at nothing until I had you back," Denny replied. "I promise, you'll be safe, and I will make sure Hassan Abdul is brought to justice, whether it be the rape or the murder. He will be brought down. You have my word."

Chapter 17
Any Way You Can

Denny angrily pounded his fist on his desk as he read the complaint made out to him. This wasn't the first time it had happened, but this time, it hit close to home. All for doing his job and protecting people, and this was the thanks he was getting.

"Of all the namby-pamby things to complain about," he raged. "Causing them distress by my presence. Like, what even does that mean?"

"Well, you can be a scary bloke sometimes," Verity put in before tossing a potato crisp in her pie hole.

"Princess, all I did was go up to Agatha's. She let me in and left the flat willingly. I didn't say a word to anyone else. I was welcomed into the building by the receptionist. Seriously, there's no reason for this stupid complaint."

Denny was still sour over losing Hassan the previous day. The fact that he fled proved the gangster knew Denny had something on him, and it was almost a guarantee that he had influenced the anonymous complaint, if he wasn't the one who made it in the first place.

"Huh, did you know these guys are based right where you're from?" Verity said, ignoring Denny's explanation as she gestured at her bag of Kettle Brand Chips.

"I'm telling you Princess, this has Hassan written all over it. Sometimes, I just want to play an *Uno reverse* on these clowns and write up a complaint on them about them stressing me out."

"That might make him more dangerous then," Verity added. "If he's as cross as I think he'll be about losing one of his girls, don't be afraid if he becomes an actual threat."

"Agatha told me what he is," Denny went on. "The things she said he and his buddies did to her, and Issy, and all of the other girls that live there make me want to find him even more. Like, at my very core, I don't want the justice system to even have a chance to find him. If I had my way, I'd bring a short piece of rope and find the tallest tree in the county. Don't write that down either."

"Aren't we thankful, then, that you aren't in charge?"

"Princess, I just know that by the way things are going, he will never see justice. For good reason, Aggie will get cold feet, or the jury will be intimidated into silence. He'll walk free and live on to terrorize even more people, create his own personal caliphate right in the middle of Crenshaw."

"More likely," Verity replied, "it won't even go to a trial."

"Right, they'll arrest her for even deigning to report it. I mean, we're in the business of prosecuting victims now, right?"

"Well, I won't."

"I know you wouldn't, Princess. But there's so many people that are 'just doing their job'. You and I both know that Whit can only do so much. They only find out too late that they are actually the baddies," Denny chuckled bitterly.

"I take it our friendly neighborhood MP would make the ultimate decision," said Verity.

"Well, given the fact that Michael Lorde hates me, it wouldn't surprise me if he did every last thing he could to subvert this whole thing."

"That makes things harder," Verity replied. "Honestly, I'm surprised he hasn't made any moves to get Whit fired."

"Who says he hasn't? Speaking of, who can we trust? It's you, me, Whit, who else?"

"Yes, us three," Verity counted, "and the Loves. And maybe Josh, but he's a beat cop, but he hates a lot of the stuff he has to do. By the way, good job getting Aggie home. Her mother called me this morning before you picked me up. I forgot to tell you."

"It seemed like a happy reunion," Denny explained, "but she didn't say much. I still think she knows Hassan pulled the trigger. In fact, I think she was there and saw it."

"But why not tell us now?" asked Verity.

"I still don't think she trusts that she's safe. Like I said, I'd wager Hassan's got everybody out there looking for her, especially if she starts telling the right people that he raped her."

"What are the odds he hasn't even thought about looking at her place?"

"With all of the security they've got," Denny concluded, "I wouldn't show my face there. If I were a scumbag, I'd exhaust every other resource before coming to the obvious conclusion."

"And then when you get to that conclusion?"

"Lawton, Baker," came Whit's call before the conversation could continue.

"Ready for today's caning?" asked Denny as he stood up from his desk.

"Have a seat," Whit instructed the two detectives as he closed the door behind them.

"If this is about the complaint," Denny started, "I just want to say that I'm starting to stick them to my refrigerator like my kids' school drawings. It's quite the collection, I'm not gonna lie, but I'm running out of space up there."

"It's a start," said Whit, as if Denny's new refrigerator decorations were an actual formal subject. "First, I want to congratulate you, DC Lawton, on getting Agatha Love home safely. Her family commends

157

you. That being said, you did have the complaint against you by an anonymous source. I guess you've already figured out who it is, or at least who it's connected to. As per usual, it will go on your record. I'm sorry about that."

"Whit," Denny chuckled, "just slap me on the wrist already and tell me what a naughty boy I've been."

"Anyway, Ian Love rang me this morning," Whit continued, ignoring Denny's overly-bright mood. "Says they've had threats."

"Threats?" Verity blurted out in confusion. "What kind of threats?"

"Strange vehicles driving by," Whit replied, "people walking along the sidewalk and just stopping to stare at the house. It's enough to give them the creeps."

"So, he does know," Denny whispered to Verity.

"Who knows?" asked Whit.

"Denny and I were talking about the odds of Hassan Abdul finding out where Agatha is before you called us in," Verity beat Denny to the reply.

"It's an idea, and highly likely," said Whit. "However, we don't have any confirmation of who is actually hanging around there, or even if it's threatening. For all we know, the Loves might just be hypervigilant and noticing things more."

"Am I to get a complaint against me for this?" asked Denny.

"No, but the Loves will be getting a full-time police detail until this is all resolved. Now, you have a witness against Hassan Abdul. You may not get him on the murder, but if you get more of his girls to talk, we can build up a solid case."

"What of an arrest warrant for Hassan?" Denny pressed. "Any luck there?"

"I've been trying to get a hold of our highly esteemed justice of the peace," Whit explained. "No such luck. The problem is we don't have anything definitive on him. In the eyes of the law, the sicko is still squeaky clean."

"You mean to tell me that in a country where there's a security camera on every street corner and in every house, there's not one video of Hassan doing anything? Not one?"

"That's the problem, Lawton," Whit went on, "just merely driving in front of somebody's house isn't exactly a crime. We drive in front of people's houses every day."

"Intimidation!" Denny exclaimed.

"See, we can't prove anything," Whit excused the poor judicial process.

"That is a crock of B.S., and you know it, Whit!" Denny exploded. "How many times have we been sent to arrest some poor schmuck because he posted the wrong thing on social media and offended the sensibilities of some namby-pamby white chick named Kynsleigh projecting her privileged standards onto some poor brown migrants who actually agree with what's been said? Are we going for intent here? We have all the evidence for intent to nab this guy. I say we do it. What have we to lose?"

"Sit down, Lawton!" Whit shouted, as if he was having Royal Navy flashbacks. "While I tend to agree with you, you may not raise your voice in my office. Is that clear, officer?"

"Yes, sir," said Denny as he slumped back down into his desk chair.

"Now, I don't make the judicial system in this country work any more than you do. We are bound by what our magistrates allow. It is up to us to provide the burden of proof. What is so obvious to us will not suffice when you have a presuppositional bias. So, my original suggestion remains, Detective Lawton: go interview the other girls. You say he and his gang raped more? Get their testimony. Get enough, and they can't ignore us."

"So, that's all?" asked Denny.

"That's all we can do," replied Whit. "I'm sorry it's not so cut and dry like it is back in the States." Whit stood up from his chair and pivoted to face the wall. Side by side, mounted on the wall behind his desk, were a Union Jack and St. George's Cross, the symbols of his homeland. The old detective pondered over them pensively before he spoke again. "It used to be. I fear those days are behind us now. They even want me to take these down," he gestured at the flags. "It's my own silent protest. See, we can all do the right thing, but the courts and magistrates hold the true power. Do the right thing here it seems, and it's like spinning tires and deep mud. You get nowhere, and you just get yourself dirtier. But you can take down Hassan Abdul. I know you can, but it won't be cut and dry. Just because it's obvious doesn't mean it's admissible. You get that son of a... pardon me, I got carried away. You get him off the street any way you can."

"And you'll have my back?" asked Denny humbly.

"You make sure it's all on the up and up as far as regulations go, and I swear, I will see that they know that you're the hero we all know you are."

Denny sat back in his chair, resigned to the reality that it was nearly impossible to do any basic police work here.

"Somehow, I feel like getting these people to talk won't even be enough," he told Whit. "You may very well have my back, but what happens when they blow you off? Do we gather a mob and storm the Magistrates Court, push the evidence right in their faces, make them listen to us?"

"That's above my paygrade," replied Whit. "I don't suggest you do something stupid."

"Then I guess we head out to Issy's and see if we can't rustle up some info from her," Denny concluded, slapping his thighs before standing up.

"Good man," Whit replied. "And before you two go, I meant what I said. You give me something I can use, and I will have your back one hundred percent."

"Yes sir," Denny replied as he slipped out the door behind Verity.

Denny was ready to end this. It's a funny thing when you know someone is guilty as sin, but they're still innocent in the eyes of the law because of a myriad of technicalities. A cop should have good instincts, but instincts don't convict criminals.

"My car or the county's?" Denny asked as he and Verity walked out to the parking lot.

"You know the rules," Verity said, rolling her eyes at him.

"Right, what's the worst they could do? Fire me?" Denny chuckled as he hit the unlock button on his remote.

"Now, why would he ever do such a thing?" Verity mused.

As was custom, Denny opened the door for Verity and then ran over to the other side to climb behind the wheel.

"Ey up, Verity!" came a friendly cry.

160

"Oi, Josh!" Verity exclaimed. "Welcome back!"

Josh had tied the knot with Louisa and recently returned from his honeymoon. There was not a happier man at that police station in Preston that morning than Josh.

"Good morning, Detective Lawton," the cheery uniform addressed Denny.

"Good morning, Josh. Just get back from vacation?" Denny asked.

"It was amazing! Oh, and Louisa! You wouldn't believe how amazing that woman is! I wish I could spend a whole other week with her in Nice, but, you know, duty calls. Didn't realize there'd still be such a buzz still around the Annie Love murder."

"Well, we're still trying to find the bugger that did it," said Denny. "We got Aggie home, but the people that hurt her are still at large."

"Well, it looks like I'm patrolling that area today," Josh said. "Apparently, there's been some suspicious activity around their place."

"It's a long story," said Verity.

"Well, it is your case, so I won't go too deep into it. I'll just make sure it's all safe over there."

"Just let us know if you see anything suspicious and give us a call," Denny instructed.

"Will do," Josh replied as he went on his happy way.

"I've never seen anyone happier than that kid apart from my toddlers," Denny chuckled as he slid behind the wheel. "How he does it, I don't know."

"Oh, hush, he's in love," Verity reprimanded before placing her right hand on top of Denny's left, a gesture that was all-too common between them nowadays.

"Princess, what are we doing here?"

"What d'you mean?"

"I feel like we're playing with fire. I mean, I feel like I'm going up against the most powerful people in this country, magistrates, MPs, and for what? A girl was murdered, and her killer is likely the wrong race? How often does this happen? How long has it been happening here?"

"What do you have to lose?" asked Verity. "It's what you've been telling me this entire time, Denny. Why the sudden change of heart? Why are you now so afraid to do what needs done?"

161

"It's all changing."

"What's changing?"

"A few months ago, I would've said I had nothing to lose, because that was the truth, but now," Denny looked directly into Verity's eyes, "I don't think that's so true anymore."

Chapter 18
Do Your Worst

It would take more than the word of a drug-addled pregnant teen to convince any magistrate that Hassan Abdul was a monster. In fact, it would take a whole army, it seemed. The mission seemed clear: get enough dirt on Hassan Abdul to take him down for the rape gangs, and maybe someone would be brave enough to come forward and admit that he was the one who pulled the trigger to end Annie Love's life or at least had a hand in it.

"You ready to end this?" asked Denny as he pulled up in front of the apartment building.

"More ready than I've been in a long time," Verity replied.

The same people were there as always – all brown faces, not an Anglo-Saxon in sight, not a word of English spoken among the

163

multitude. Approaching the apartment building from down the street, all had seemed normal. Children were playing, women in burqas, niqabs, and hijabs were seated on the benches supervising their young charges, and men of all ages were puffing on cigarettes while cutting up with one another. That all changed when the gray Mustang pulled up to the curb. The play stopped, the women's attention to their children intensified, and the men stopped talking and crushed their cigarettes. They were all staring at Denny. The last time Denny visited, which was just one day before, he had seemed to go unnoticed. True, until he opened his mouth, one could be forgiven for confusing Denny with one of these poor migrants, but these people now seemed terrified of his presence. Something was terribly wrong with this picture. Before, if they paid him any mind, it was all out of curiosity. Today? It seemed like there was genuine fear.

"Look at them," Verity noted. "What's gotten into them?"

"I have an inkling," Denny replied, "and I don't like it."

As they entered the lobby, it was the same story. Even the old Indian lady at the front desk hid herself in a back room, occupying herself with some menial task until the cops left the lobby.

"It's like they all know what's about to go down," Denny said as they approached the elevator.

The two detectives breathed a collective sigh of relief as they entered the elevator. Neither had noticed the suffocating atmosphere of the residents. It was as if their gloom had descended down upon the whole place like a thick blanket and trapped all of the air inside, slowly replacing the life-giving oxygen with toxic carbon dioxide with nothing to change it back to oxygen. As the door to the lift opened on Issy's floor, that same nauseating feeling, along with the cocktail of cat urine and cigarette smoke returned.

It smelled awful up here. In truth, the whole building smelt of body odor, tobacco, and excrement, but this was different. It smelt of life, but not in the strangely beautiful way it normally smells. No, this was life corrupted, as if life wasn't the intended result. The scent worsened when the two detectives approached Issy's door and knocked.

"Isabella Mendes," Denny called out as he rapped on the door. "Policia. ¿Está ahí?"

There was no verbal answer. That made sense. If that murk from downstairs had made it up here, Issy might as well have joined that number.

Denny was about to pound on the door again when he heard a groan. There was pain behind it. He shot a knowing glance at Verity. Without a word, he backed up to the wall on the other side of the hallway.

"Watch yourself," he instructed Verity as he started kicking at the door.

In reality, it wouldn't have taken that much effort to kick the door down. Everything in this building was slapped together so cheaply that Denny could have probably just smacked at the door with the palm of his hand and brought the whole thing down, frame and all.

Once inside, Denny listened again for the groaning. There were tears behind that groan. He and Verity split up to find the girl. Stepping over the garbage left by the two tenants, Denny was afraid she was hidden and would step on her.

"Issy!" he called.

"Denny, in here!" Verity called from the door Issy's room.

Without hesitation, Denny barged in. The scene that met him was horrific.

"Call an ambulance!" he yelled to Verity.

Issy was there, barely clinging to life. She was beaten, bloodied, and barely recognizable as a human. What was left of her clothing had been ripped to shreds, barely hanging off of her fragile form. The poor girl was curled up in the fetal position clutching her midsection.

"Mi crío!" Issy cried. "My crío!"

"Mira," Denny said as he took off his jacket and covered her up, an attempt to preserve a shred of her dignity.

"Pajarito que cantas en la laguna
No despiertes al niño que está en la cuna.
Ea la nana, ea la nana
Duérmete lucerito de la mañana.
A dormir va la rosa de los rosales
A dormir va mi niño por que ya es tarde.
Ea la nana, ea la nana
Duérmete lucerito de la mañana.

Pajarito que cantas junto a la fuente
Cállate que mi niño no se despierte.
Ea la nana, ea la nana
Duérmete lucerito de la mañana."

Denny sang her a lullaby; one his mother sang to him often when he was little. It was the first thing that popped into his head as he watched over the poor girl. She couldn't be any older than sixteen or seventeen – almost a full woman, but still just an innocent little girl in his aging eyes.

"Little bird that sings in the lagoon
Don't awaken the baby that's in the crib
Oh, the lullaby Oh, the lullaby
Sleep little morning star
The rose of the rose garden is going to sleep
My baby is going to sleep because it's late
Oh, the lullaby Oh, the lullaby
Sleep little morning star
Little bird that sings in the spring
Hush so that my baby will not wake up.
Oh, the lullaby Oh, the lullaby
Sleep little morning star"

He translated the words in his head the same way his mother had to him when she wanted him to learn what the song actually meant to her. He brushed Issy's black hair as he did his sons when he would put them down to sleep. In a way, what Denny was witnessing right here was an attack on innocence. He remained that way until the medics showed up.

"How is she?" one of them asked as the remainder of the paramedics barged in behind him.

"She's been beaten," Denny replied. "It looks like she's gone into premature labor as well. She was crying out for her baby."

"Bloody Nora!" the medic exclaimed. "Isabella, can you hear us?"

The girl didn't open her eyes.

"She doesn't speak English," Denny said. "¿Isabella, te despierta?"

There was no answer as the medics began to lift her onto their stretcher, one on either end. She was alive – that was clearly visible;

166

she was breathing heavily. Either unconscious or in no mood to talk, it was a good sign though.

A crowd had gathered in the hallway, obviously beckoned by the sound of the paramedics' sirens. This proved difficult for the medics as they rolled Issy out toward the elevator.

"Get out of the way!" Denny barked as he held up his badge. "Y'all better move!"

That helped only a little. Some of the crowd parted. Denny found he had to shove a couple men who were getting a bit too close.

"Stay there and wait for the uniforms," Denny instructed Verity as he entered the elevator with Issy and the medics. "I'll be back up in a minute."

"Please be careful, and hurry back," she replied as she stood guard over the door, her own petite frame barely enough to hold back the swarming mob.

With the elevator doors closed, there was finally some peace and quiet. As if a part of the building's built-in trashiness, the elevator moved at a snail's pace. This gave Denny the window of opportunity he needed.

"Issy," he spoke in the girl's ear. "¿Puedes oír mí?"

Issy opened one of her eyes as far as it could, both of them swelled shut.

"Sí," she groaned out.

"Bien," Denny replied. He had one question for her. One word that would confirm all that he needed to know. One word, and he would have his man. Denny took Isabella's hand. The poor girl gripped his hand tight, as if he were her own father. She trusted him fully. "¿Hassan?"

"Sí," she replied again as tears began welling up in her swollen eyelids. "Sí, Hassan."

"Gracias, Issy. Dormir ahora."

Denny stayed on the elevator as they wheeled Issy out to the ambulance. He had Issy's word. Hassan had raped her. That was two witnesses now. He wondered how many more would be sufficient to sway the courts on his way back up to the flat. By now, uniforms were arriving on scene. Poor Verity was doing her best to quell the crowd, but they were beginning to overwhelm her.

"Move it!" Denny ordered as he made his way back to the flat, pushing through the crowds, even having to get rough with a couple of the men at times.

It didn't take long for the uniforms to show up to the flat with Whit in tow. The old man was visibly distressed. This was big, but still complicated things further.

"This evidence enough for you?" Denny asked.

"For me, yes," Whit replied as he covered his nose.

"She was raped, Whit," Verity told the supervisor.

"And she told me who it was," Denny added.

"You have it in writing?" asked Whit.

"Just her word on the elevator," Denny replied.

Whit was forlorn. He knew the reaction he would get from Denny, so he prepared himself with his own angry reaction, starting with a four-letter interjection. That seemed to stop any tirade Denny would spew right in its tracks.

"That won't work!" Whit explained. "We need that in writing with someone who is with it."

"We have witness who heard the confession," Denny explained.

"Do they speak Spanish?" Whit shot back.

"Well, no, I don't think so."

"Then it's no good. No telling what you two actually said in your conversation."

"So, what? Do I visit Issy in the hospital once they get her stable?" asked Denny. "Do we take a translator or something?"

"If you get her to talk," Whit replied.

"What if we talk to some people around here?" Verity chipped in.

"What makes you think they'd talk?" Denny threw back. "You saw how they looked at us. They're scared. They know we're trouble because we're going to attract Hassan's attention."

"Yes, but now that there's a big police presence, they may feel safer."

"Could go either way," Whit added.

"I guess it's worth a shot," Denny admitted.

"But you let me do the talking," Verity admonished with a half grin. "You tend to scare people."

"Only when they have a reason," Denny retorted.

The crowds were dispersing by the time Denny and Verity made their way out to the hallway. With the assault victim gone, police activity was confined to the flat, which was closed for business.

Verity's feminine touch seemed to work on the first try. A soft knock and her gentle voice was enough to convince the resident to open. The first person was a middle-aged woman in a black hijab – not the type who would strike one as Hassan's type; at least, they didn't think the young, enterprising gangster was into older women. She stared at Verity with a strange expression of calm and disquiet, as if being a female and a cop were two totally different things, impossible to mix.

"Uh, yes, we're from the Lancashire Constabulary," Verity introduced herself. "DC Baker and DC Lawton. We were just wondering if we could ask some questions."

The woman leaned out into the hallway. It seemed as if there must have been someone watching. She ducked back in.

"Come in," she beckoned with haste.

The two detectives followed her in.

"Please, sit," she rigidly gestured to an old sofa.

Denny and Verity took their places on the couch, sinking down into the broken-down furniture. The old woman sat in an old armchair facing them.

"So, I guess you know why we're here, Missus?" Verity began.

"Please, not so loud," the woman said. "The walls are very thin. And my name is Lobna Mohammed."

"What do you know of Hassan Abdul?" Verity asked, her voice barely above a whisper.

The woman's expression of calm and disquiet shed the calm and mixed disgust with the disquiet.

"That bad?" Verity commented.

"My only daughter, Rashida," Lobna began, "that monster, he had her. All of his men took turns on her. Fourteen years old, and they took her innocence from her."

"May we speak to her?" asked Verity.

"No," Lobna replied curtly.

"No?"

"She is in hiding," Lobna explained.

169

"Is she in that much danger?" Verity pressed.

Lobna paused a moment to compose herself.

"Under Sharia, Rashida is to be executed for being raped," the woman replied.

"That's BS," Denny broke in. "England isn't under Sharia."

"No," replied the woman, "but Hassan Abdul's world is under Sharia, and anyone under his power can be put to death at his command. That is the reality for us here."

"Which would explain why his baby mamas are still alive," Denny concluded.

"I do not understand this 'baby mama'," the woman said.

"It's an Americanism," Verity explained. "He's referring to the women he's impregnated – the mothers of his children, for lack of a better term."

"Yes, he keeps them alive, and perhaps, he will keep my Rashida alive, but I cannot risk it."

"What of her father?" asked Verity. "Is he anywhere in the picture at all?"

"His work takes him far away, out on the oil rigs in the North Sea. We hope that one day, we may be able to pursue the life we once dreamed of, and he'll be able to come home to Crenshaw full-time and be with our family here."

It was hard to take in. Here was a family that did everything the right way, but they were forced to live in these squalid conditions and under the rule of a lawless thug who imposed his own medieval third-world law.

"How many women are there in this flat that Hassan and his gang use"? Verity asked.

"Countless many."

"Think they'd be willing to make accusations and help bring this guy to justice?" Denny put in.

"Detective Lawton, we are deathly afraid of Hassan Abdul. You saw what he did to that poor Spanish girl next door. We hear it all the time, at all hours whenever he comes by, hoping that we're not next – girls being hit, raped, tortured. The men, they laugh. Oh, and all the other sounds they make. It's so, so… so inhuman."

170

"What if we could make sure we get this monster off the streets?" Verity chimed back in.

"You could do that?"

'Give us names and flat numbers of every girl you know that Hassan or his crew have hurt," Verity said, "and we'll get a whole list. Please, Missus Mohammed, help us save Rashida."

Chapter 19
A Dream Ablaze

Denny was more of a father to Hallie than Elliott ever was. Hallie was the daughter Denny never had. The open secret of the Denny-Verity power couple was becoming more open and less of a secret by the day. As much as he was falling for Verity, he doted on her daughter just the same. From outings to even the smallest treats, Denny loved on Hallie as if she were his own. He would often joke with Verity that he couldn't tell if she saw him as her new dad, or was just there for the beach and unlimited streaming apps, or both.

Christmas Eve was no different. Tonight, the *Nutcracker* ballet was showing in Blackpool, and Hallie had always wanted to go. Every year, Verity was too tired and stressed from work, and Elliott made the same excuses he would always make, which usually just translated to him being lazy. This year, though, this year was different. Denny was here to take an active interest, not only in the life of Verity, but in the life of her daughter. This year, he wasn't just taking them out to see a ballet; he was making a night of it.

It had been dark for several hours by the time Denny showed up at Verity's at 6 in his Mustang. Hallie loved riding in the muscle car, more viewing it as a rollercoaster than a means of transportation. Denny driving like he was in the Daytona 500 didn't help the situation much. The little girl was jumping up and down with glee as Denny revved the motor before shutting it down. Hallie practically leapt into Denny's arms as he stepped out of the car, still small enough to be held.

"Shall we get going?" he asked as he put her back down.

Denny opened the passenger door and scooted the seat forward to allow Hallie into the cramped back seat, still small enough for a child her size.

Verity looked at Denny like she had never looked at any man before, not even Elliott. Was this actually happening? Was she not just moving on, but starting a new and better life? She wondered where Denny had been all her life. She gladly slid into the car after Denny put the seat back.

It was a cold and wet evening. Denny was struck at how it was so similar to Oregon, even with the drastic change in latitude. Even with the conditions, the Mustang stayed planted to the road. He was not taking any risks, even with Hallie prodding him to push the "tickle button", her name for the accelerator. Driving the speed limit would get them to Blackpool in more than enough time.

Verity's house, a townhouse a few blocks from the beach, was on the far northwestern edge of the Crenshaw Peninsula, not too far from Denny's beachside cottage. This necessitated a drive south through the entirety of the peninsula to get anywhere. Most people traveling out of the village stuck to the road straddling the Irish Sea, preferring the luxurious beach houses to the immigrant slums.

"Denny, what's your favorite *Nutcracker* character?" Hallie asked, still bouncing up and down in her seat, though restrained by the seatbelt.

Denny pondered it for a moment. All of his years living in a big city where shows like this were easily accessible, and he hadn't taken the chance to go see the *Nutcracker*.

"The Mouse King?" he guessed. He at least figured he could come up with some random character he'd heard of.

"The bad guy?" Hallie jeered.

"Hey, cut me some slack. It's the first time I get to see it too," Denny chuckled.

Verity just sat in silence, staring proudly at Denny. She wanted him. She wanted to tell him he was becoming her world. She wanted him to be hers, all hers. How she dreamed Elliott would have been even a fraction of what Denny was. She had never felt so safe and secure with a man, never been able to trust a man to just do the bare minimum; but here was a guy whose bare minimum was going above and beyond and then even further than that.

"Hold up, what's this?" Denny's inflection had suddenly changed.

"Oh, my!" Verity exclaimed.

Denny brought the car to a stop. They were nearing the southwestern edge of the peninsula. Right here was the Love Mansion. That was to be expected. What wasn't to be expected was the raging inferno consuming the house.

"Call the fire brigade!" Denny barked to Verity as he leapt out of the car.

Fire was rapidly moving throughout the place. The palm trees were already ablaze, quickly consumed by the flames. Falling fronds dropped from the trees onto the pavement, flaming all the way down. Without hesitation, Denny bolted through the front door. Immediately, smoke filled his vision.

"Ian!" he called. "Harriet! Aggie!"

Out of the darkness and smoke, a pair of silhouettes appeared. It was a butler dragging Harriet Love on his shoulder.

"Missus Love, where's your husband and daughter?" Denny pressed.

"Ian's looking for Aggie," she coughed.

"Get her out of here," he instructed the butler. "Is there anyone else in here?"

"I'm the last staff member to leave for the day," the butler replied. "Just them."

Denny was already on the move. He continued calling for Ian and Agatha. There was no answer. The furniture in the great room was now being consumed.

"Ian Love!" Denny cried. There was still no answer.

Denny started down the hallway that he assumed led to the bedrooms. He cursed himself for not having gotten more familiar with the mansion's layout. That didn't matter much. He found Ian Love passed out on the floor. Denny knelt down beside the man. He was breathing.

"Ian, wake up!" Denny shouted.

"I need to save... Aggie," he croaked.

"Yes, you're doing great," Denny encouraged the old man, "but you need to save yourself. Get out of here. I'll find her."

Ian Love stood up, wobbling back and forth.

"Do you know your way?" Denny asked urgently.

"Save Aggie," was all Ian Love could say.

"Just get out of here!" Denny shouted.

Ian Love finally turned and headed for the only exit confirmed still safe. Denny continued on, again, cursing himself for not figuring out where Agatha was staying. By this time, the hallway was thick with smoke. Denny knelt down and crawled on his hands and knees to stay below it.

"Aggie!" he shouted. "Where are you?"

He peered in the rooms that were opened. No luck.

"Aggie!"

"In here!" came a faint cry.

There was one more door. It was closed. Denny tried for the door handle, only to burn his hand.

"Stand back!" he shouted, ignoring the searing pain in the palm of his right hand, "I'm breaking the door in!"

Denny charged for the door and shouldered it with all his might. It was like hitting a brick wall. There must have been something collapsed blocking it.

"Detective Lawton!" Agatha cried. "Please hurry!"

Denny continued his futile attempt to break into the room.

"Please!" she continued with a cough. "I can't breathe!"

"Jesus, help me!" Denny cried out as he slammed the door again, not even thinking about the pain in his shoulder. "I'm coming, Aggie! I got you! Hold on!"

"Please! I don't want to die!" she cried weakly.

"Freaking move!" he yelled as he slammed his entire weight into the door yet again.

Just then, a firefighter grabbed him by the shoulder.

"Help her!" Denny shouted.

Before the firefighter could begin chopping at the door, an ominous rumble emanated throughout the hallway. Its source came from behind the door. The ground shook as the unthinkable began to unfold. An ungodly shriek from Agatha was heard before it was cut off by the sound of falling rubble.

"Aggie! No!" Denny shouted.

Denny sat on the curb in front of the smoldering heap that was once a mansion, a blanket over his shoulders and a bottle of ice water in his hands. He stayed there, catatonic, not making eye contact or saying a word for nearly an hour.

A second-floor storage room right above Agatha's had begun to blaze hot. Part of the room had already collapsed, blocking off the window exit and her door. It didn't take much eventually for the weight of the rest of that room to collapse on Agatha's, killing the girl instantly. That was the only solace Denny could take in the girl's death, was that she was killed pretty much instantly. As much as she felt fear and knowledge of her coming demise in that final second, the crushing blow had knocked her unconscious before her brain could even register that she was being crushed.

Agatha's cries still played in Denny's mind even as Harriet Love's gut-wrenching wails at losing yet another child echoed throughout the village. He couldn't even look at them. What could he say to them? He had promised to find their daughter's killer, and now their only other child was dead. He had failed Ian and Harriet Love. What now? What was to happen to the broken family being made whole again? No more family dinners. No grandchildren to bounce on granddad's knee. No mother-daughter tea. It was all gone. The future was dead.

Denny was unaware of the company that had joined him. Verity had sat down next to him on the curb. She put her arm around him and rested her head on his shoulder. For a while, she said nothing, only keeping him company.

"I took Hallie home in your car, if you don't mind," she finally said meekly.

Denny brushed her comment off. Anything besides this was an afterthought. So what? There'd be other plays, other outings. Same couldn't be said for Agatha.

"I really don't know what to say, Denny. You did what you could."

The echoes of Agatha's plea played in his mind once again, like a cry from the dead. "I don't want to die".

"She depended on me, and I let her down," Denny finally broke the silence.

"You didn't let anybody down," Verity tried to comfort him. "There was nothing you could do to save her."

"There had to be another way. I promised."

"There was no way. They said any possible exit was blocked. Aggie was essentially dead before you even found her, you just didn't know it yet."

Denny looked up at Verity for the first time. It was obvious that she had spent some time crying too, likely in the car on the way back to the Love Mansion after dropping Hallie off.

"What do I tell them, Princess? What would you expect me to tell you if it were Hallie?"

"The same thing I'm telling you. You did what you could. Beyond the supernatural – and let's be honest, it'd have to be a big miracle – there's nothing else that could have been done. You were very brave, that's for certain. They know what you did. They know you charged into that home and risked your life to save Aggie. That's more than any parent could ask for from a complete stranger. So, you didn't save the girl. You're still a hero." Verity straightened up, almost ready to change the subject. "Anyway, Whit's on his way. They've found some petrol cans near where they think the fire started. They're suspecting it's arson."

177

"They wouldn't be so stupid," Denny whispered. "There's cameras everywhere."

"They're already digging through the rubble," Verity explained. "They found a camera that had been broken. Not melted, broken, as if someone had hit it with a blunt force object."

Denny's eyes lit up at this piece of news. Perhaps, there was a small silver lining in this tragedy. Perhaps, this would lead to some arrests. Perhaps, the Annie Love murder was actually making steps toward being solved.

"Is there a database where these cameras send their video to?" Denny asked.

"I don't know," Verity replied, "but Whit's just arriving."

Denny and Verity stood up to greet Whit. It was obvious he had been pulled away from a nice family dinner, still wearing his ugly Christmas sweater.

"Whit!" Denny called.

"Lawton, you absolute blithering idiot! What did you think you were doing running in there like that? You could've been killed!"

"Never mind that," said Denny. "The security cameras, is there a way we can access the files?"

"What for?"

"They found a camera that's been smashed. If it's arson, we may be able to find footage of them breaking the cameras," Denny explained.

"Well, no duh," Whit chuckled. "I'll see about getting access from the Loves. It shouldn't be a problem."

Several hours of footage were stored in the cloud, and yet there was no luck. These guys knew what they were doing. It was the same stuff. Several suspicious cars would drive by. Several people would stop and stare at the house. Then, around a quarter to six, the cameras would stop recording one by one, but there would be no sign of the perpetrator. The camera would just go to static, occasionally shaking a bit right before – a sign of sabotage from being hit with something. Whoever was doing this was great at staying off-camera.

"What time is it?" Denny asked as he selected the last file.

"Almost midnight," Verity replied.

"You sure Hallie's okay with you being gone like this?" Denny asked.

"She's a smart girl. You know that. Just this last video, and we're done here."

"Shame. I really thought we were onto something here, but this guy stays out of the camera masterfully. I was really hoping we were dealing with a complete simpleton here."

Denny clicked play on the footage, fast-forwarding to around half past five. This camera was placed high above the ground in a discreet place, right above Agatha's room and the storage closet. It was pointed at the ground in front of the windows, a wide angle that captured from the flower bed at the base of the house, across the lawn, and into the street. A quarter to six came and went. The camera stayed rolling. Out of the corner of the frame, a figure appeared. He looked familiar. Another much larger figure appeared next to him. It was clear both of them were wearing gloves. Made sense. The heat from the flames would make sure their prints were left.

The large man with a long black beard, wearing a three-piece suit and a Taqiya began dousing the siding of the mansion with gasoline. He finished that off by tossing another full can of gasoline up, breaking through the glass of a window right underneath where the camera was mounted – the storage room.

With this accomplished, the first figure, a smaller man wearing a Man United hoodie, jeans, and a beanie, flicked open a lighter. He pulled out a wad of paper from his pocket and lit that ablaze, tossing it with expert aim into the upstairs window. The frame suddenly lit up with the flame underneath the camera. The smaller man then tossed the still-flaming lighter next to the base of the house, immediately setting it ablaze.

All of this was done quickly and with quiet precision. Soon, the house was a raging inferno, and the camera went fuzzy before melting and then to static.

"Go back," Denny instructed.

Verity rewound the video.

"Stop there," said Denny.

Verity stopped the video on the frame where both men looked up toward their handiwork. It was obvious who the culprits were just by looking at their descriptions. The freeze frame just went to prove beyond the shadow of a doubt that Hassan Abdul and Habib Ibrahim were now guilty of homicide.

Chapter 20
Finished

It was a bittersweet morning when Denny showed up bearing gifts. Verity was barely awake as she opened the door to let him in early. Hallie was still asleep as Denny began setting out gifts underneath the Christmas tree. His task complete, he collapsed on the sofa.

"Coffee?" Verity offered as cheerfully as she could.

"Cafecito if you don't mind," Denny half-joked. "A big mixing bowl of it if you got it."

"If only I could make it that strong," Verity chuckled before disappearing into the kitchen.

Denny felt he could doze off on this couch. The events of the previous night still played over and over in his mind. The terror in Agatha's voice never left him for a second. Her screams kept him awake, as if an accusation of "Why didn't you save me? Was I that unimportant?" – a terrible, terrible echo for him as he tried to at least fall asleep. Even in his own comfortable bed, even with his eyes closed, the ghost of Agatha Love would not let him sleep. He had promised her that she would be safe, so where had that gotten her? What was she now? Was she just a pawn in Denny's ceaseless campaign to bring the gang lord down? Had he put her in harm's way by encouraging her to leave that cesspool and speak the truth?

And where was that all going? The gang lord takedown. Is that what this murder investigation had turned into? This had all started out of a suspicion that maybe, just maybe, Hassan Abdul had pulled the trigger and ended Annie Love's life. That enough made him a monster. Was it good enough to bring him down for raping underaged girls? Last night was his answer. The monster was still free, the Love sisters were dead, a family was permanently broken, and many more women and girls were scarred for life and living in fear for the day the next hammer would drop. And on top of that? Their own leaders refused to lift a finger to help them, instead, slowing down those who would fight tooth and nail to rectify the problem.

"What time did you get to bed?" Verity asked, breaking Denny out of his stupor as she handed him a mug of black coffee.

"Around three."

Verity looked at the time on her phone.

"Denny, that's only three hours of sleep!"

"Sleep? I thought you asked what time I got to bed."

"Did you?"

"Not a wink."

"Denny, you shouldn't have. You need your rest."

"Princess, I'm not going to miss Christmas," Denny replied with determination, "especially after having to cancel last night's outing."

"Oh, I know, but Hallie understands. It's happened all her life."

"Well, not anymore."

"Really, Denny, if ever there was a good reason for canceling a family outing, trying to save the life of an innocent girl is good enough. It sure beats whatever excuse Elliott has, and Hallie knows. You should've heard how excited she was about how brave you were when

I drove her home. Elliott? He'd wet himself and cry himself to sleep if he were faced with sommat like that."

"Well, at least let me make it up to her," Denny said, hands outspread in a pleading gesture.

"Fine," Verity said," but if you fall asleep while she's opening presents, I'm hitting you with a pillow. You've been warned."

"Then, refill my mug," Denny chuckled. "I'm not missing this for the world."

"You really do miss them, don't you?" Verity asked. "Your family, I mean."

"Is it that obvious?"

"Sometimes, I fear we're just a surrogate for what you've lost."

"I won't lie. I miss my boys and my little girl. I mean, how can you miss someone you've never met?"

Verity screwed up her face for a second before remembering how Talia had filed the restraining order against Denny before she had given birth.

"Talia," Denny continued, "I find myself coming closer and closer to the realization every day that there's no going back. I had hoped that even after the divorce we could reconcile and maybe even start over, but that chance ended when another man put a ring on her finger. Heck, I'd even thought at times that maybe she'd see the light, dump Rick, and come back to me."

"And where does that leave us?" Verity asked, taking her spot next to him on the couch and resting her head on his shoulder.

"Better off than our exes," Denny replied, wrapping his arm around her.

Before they could continue their time any further, Hallie burst into the living room. Denny chalked it up to an intervention from the Almighty. He had feared that he would allow himself to get caught up in the moment and take things too far again. He could feel that temptation growing inside him.

"It's Christmas!" Hallie shouted as she bounded over to the tree.

"Okay, Hallie, let's not lose our heads," Verity admonished.

"I want Daddy to open his gift first," Hallie declared.

Verity was taken aback. Had this little girl lost her mind? Daddy? Her father was probably alone in some rundown flat in Brighton, reeling from a one-night stand with a drag queen.

"Hallie," Verity tried to break the news to her daughter softly, "Daddy isn't home for Christmas."

Hallie turned her gaze form Verity to Denny. She had already grabbed a small flat box from under the tree. Verity didn't recognize it. She took the present to Denny.

"It's for you," she told him meekly.

Denny glanced nervously at Verity. He cautiously tore at the wrapping paper. After what seemed like an eternity, the remainder of the paper slid off to reveal a framed photo of Denny and Hallie at the Blackpool Tower Eye – Denny with a fatherly grin posing next to Hallie with an even cheesier grin overlooking the Irish Sea. On the bottom of the frame was a molded plastic text: "**Dad and Me**" in Comic Sans. He sat there speechless.

"Do you like it?" asked Hallie.

Verity eyed Denny nervously.

"I think it'll be the centerpiece of my desk down at the precinct," Denny declared.

Hallie ran up and hugged Denny. He was surprised such a small girl could choke him out. He embraced her back. It couldn't be helped. In his mind, though, he could still see and hear the ghost of Agatha Love accusing him, watching him enjoy Christmas with his surrogate daughter while her parents were spending their Christmas mourning theirs.

His mind drifted from the sweetness of the moment. In this messed-up fantasy playing on some messed-up stage in the back of his messed-up mind, Hallie was now in the place of Agatha Love. This little girl that now saw him as the only real dad she ever knew was scared and alone. A whole new nightmare scenario played out, something he knew he would see when his head hit the pillow later. One day, he could picture Hallie in a similar position – in need of help while he helplessly rushed to her aid, only for him to fail and for her to lose her life. He shook it off.

"Why don't you open your gifts?" he suggested to the little girl.

Without a word, Hallie darted for the tree, grabbing every box she could find with her name on it. In the meantime, Verity brought another round of coffee in for Denny, conspicuously displaying a pillow for him in her other hand.

Denny had thoroughly spoiled Hallie. She would be kept busy for hours unchecked. The last gift was a small box, no bigger than nine square inches. Denny fished it out from under the tree and handed it to Verity. She looked up at him, her blue eyes big and full of anticipation. As she unstrung the bow, her heart began to pound harder. There was trepidation mixed with the anticipation. What if it was too soon? What would people say. Verity opened the box. It was a ring.

"Is this..." Verity began to ask.

"So, in my culture," Denny began to explain, "not the American culture or the Mexican culture, Baptist culture... some circles, we have this thing called a 'promise ring'. It's not exactly an engagement ring. What it means, at least to me, is that you're the only one I have eyes for. I know, it's kind of weird. I'll admit that. It's just..."

Verity reached out, grabbed Denny by the chin, and kissed him.

"Say no more," Verity tenderly said.

She placed the ring on her finger. Through all the hurt and broken promises, this ring was better than anything she had been given. There was meaning, actual meaning, not ceremony, behind this ring.

"I'm ready to move on," Denny declared quietly so that little ears wouldn't hear. "You're the only one for me."

Verity, already right in his face, pulled Denny closer and embraced him. If Hallie could choke him, Verity could have easily snapped his neck.

"So, Hallie," Denny spoke up as the girl was fiddling around with a Barbie dollhouse, "Christmas is 'Anything Can Happen Day'. Do you know what that means?"

Hallie paused her little project and turned her wordless attention to Denny.

"It means," Denny continued, "that we have a whole afternoon to ourselves, just the three of us. Also, seeing that our plans were botched for last night, we are giving you the opportunity to pick what we're going to do this afternoon."

Hallie considered it for a second. It was very tempting to just sit around, veg, and play with whatever toys she got for Christmas. It was a tough decision.

"Can we go see people at the hospital?" Hallie asked.

"Hallie, I don't think…" Verity started to advise before Denny cut her off.

"Why do you want to go to the hospital?" asked Denny.

"Aseefa told me her sister, Malia, was in hospital," Hallie replied. "I thought that we could go to the hospital with some 'get well' cards and give them to people for Christmas."

"You sure that's what you want?" asked Denny.

"Not everybody gets to enjoy Christmas at home," Hallie answered back.

Boy, that hit Denny hard, even out of the mouth of babes. The logic there was sound too. And this little Hallie Baker, even she had the wherewithal to know that there were people worse off than her.

"Then let's get ready to go to the hospital then," Denny replied tenderly.

Hallie had purchased three packs of Christmas greeting cards with some money she had saved up from her birthday. On the drive to the hospital, she wrote wishes of a merry Christmas and a speedy recovery for each and every one.

Malia's ward was on the third floor. Here were many people, mostly women, recovering from trauma. Bruised and battered, an even greater percentage of the women here were victims of domestic violence and rape. That picture of a broken Isabella lying on the floor curled up in the fetal position crying for her lost baby returned to Denny. This was the ugly face of crime allowed to run free. How often would any of these women show up on the brink of death only to willingly go back to the filth and slime that did this to them in the first place?

Verity escorted Hallie around to each bed, making sure the little angel didn't needlessly wake any resting patients. The girl was beaming, as if she had seen just the hinder parts of God's glory and returned from Mount Sinai to declare the good news to the unwashed masses. A few of the women, though in great physical pain, actually tried rising from their beds to hug Hallie. For them, Hallie was the only person in the world who actually cared.

Meanwhile, Denny walked around the ward, still reeling from the previous night's events. Even through all of the good this morning had brought, those pained dying words of Agatha Love, her shriek of fear cut off by her death, echoed in his brain. So many of these poor women were in her exact position at one time. How many of them were Hassan's victims? How many more would join them until the powers that be stopped infantilizing people like Hassan just because they have the correct amount of melanin? Then, the sight of Isabella played back like a GIF in his mind.

He could barely take it. He turned tail to leave when he caught someone out of the corner of his eye. The last bed in the ward was occupied by none other than Isabella Mendes. It broke Denny's heart to see her. She was hooked up to the various machines around her bed, but she was awake. She had been cleaned, but she was still a sight. Her face was still swollen, her skin black and blue with bruising.

"Issy! Bueno," he greeted her quietly. "Feliz Navidad! Como estas?"

"Me siento como basura," Issy croaked with great effort.

Denny sat down on the chair by her bed.

"Doctors y enfermeras?" Denny asked casually.

"La major," she replied.

"¿El crío?"

"Ausente," Issy replied flatly.

"Oh, Isabella, lo siento."

Isabella winced in pain and pressed a button on a remote she kept with her. One of the machines shot some morphine into her bloodstream. Immediately, she relaxed back in her bed.

"Hassan?" Isabella asked.

That was new. Of course, she'd want to know. It was he who had impregnated her, only to abuse her so badly as to kill their child. She, above many other people, would want Hassan taken off the streets and brought to justice.

"Casi ahí," was all Denny could say.

Isabella made direct eye contact with Denny. There was determination there and longing for this all to end. No, it was dependence. Isabella, in fact, all of the girls here and in the slums of Crenshaw, depended now on Denny to finally bring this piece of trash down once and for all.

"He is a very bad man," Isabella struggled to tell Denny in English.

"Si, si," Denny agreed. "Descansar ahora."

"No, no," she protested. "He kills."

"Who? Who kills. Hassan?"

Well, that was obvious. In addition to the proof of him torching the Love mansion, he had been the cause of Isabella losing her baby.

"Hassan y Miguel."

"Miguel? Who's this Miguel."

"Hassan… amigo," Isabella struggled out.

"¡Órale!" Denny exclaimed in silence, trying to remain discreet.

"Yo sierra," Isabella tried to explain.

"¿Tu sierra qué?"

"El asesinato."

The nurses had left a notepad with a pen on the little table next to Isabella's bed. Denny handed it to Isabella.

"Guardar tu voz," Denny instructed her to save her voice in Spanish. "Yo necisitar una declaración."

This investigation was finished.

Chapter 21
Read It and Weep

Michael Lorde sat at the wide desk in his constituency office. He had just returned from a New Years ball. Well, the ball, at least he thought there was a ball – it was all just a blur after a few rounds of brandy – was a day or so ago, but his hangover lasted longer. It was a Friday, one day before the weekend, but apparently, duty calls. No rest for the weary. So, here he was, returning to work from probably the worst hangover of his life. And the funny thing? It satisfied him. Oh, there would probably be some compromising photos and videos of him debasing himself in public. There was sure to be some misdirecting and saving face, but that's what PR was for. Michael Lorde, MP could sit pretty in his office, ruling over his tiny kingdom of plebs (however much he was granted from the Crown and whatever lord actually owned the land).

The MP had just opened up his emails for the day. He sighed at what he saw as he scrolled down through the mailbox. Apparently, his opponents were losing steam already. That what happens when people have the wrong ideas. They eventually either lose steam or end up behind bars. Either way, it's a win-win. With the new year starting, campaigning would be ramping up for the summertime elections. Lorde didn't worry about it. He'd won by a landslide in every election for the last twenty-five years or so, so this one shouldn't be so different. This constituency was firmly in his grasp, if only for one thorn in his flesh.

That Ian Love, that was his one worry – the one thing that kept him up at night. Everything Michael Lorde had spent twenty-five years fighting for – a Bright New Glorious Lancashire, as he called it – would be so easily reversed and torn apart if the likes of Ian Love were somehow elected to Parliament. Even so, he didn't worry. If Ian Love were to push his campaign too far, he could join the rest of those who so offended the sensibilities of the high-born in jail. If that didn't work, there were other ways of keeping him quiet, perhaps forever. Lorde worried, though, whether or not that would even quiet him down. It seemed like no matter what was thrown at Ian Love, he'd just stand back up even stronger, like the Roadrunner and Wile E. Coyote.

News of the second tragedy for the Love family was still making the media rounds – a Christmas Eve tragedy. He couldn't remember, but Michael Lorde was pretty sure one of his assistants had rattled off some sappy pre-written condolences for Ian love and his wife and then posted it up on his socials to show how benevolent and caring he pretended to be. In truth, it made his glad. Maybe if the fool would have focused more on his family and not on trying to shake the world, his daughters would still be alive. Well, should've thought about that before spewing such a wrong and hateful opinion.

Michael Lorde spun away from his desk toward his big picture window that overlooked his football pitch and reclined back in his chair. The sun was shining on the bright green turf outside – a pleasant start to a day that promised storms later in the afternoon. This campaign was going to be easy. All he had to do was take down Ian

Love, or let Ian Love himself self-destruct, and he would be sitting pretty for another five years. No worries here, just good times and a good cigar.

The door to Lorde's offices slammed open violently. He leapt out of his seat in shock, nearly soiling himself. He turned around only to be met by the dark brown eyes of one Detective Constable Dennis Lawton. There was fire in those eyes. Michael Lorde glanced to his right. In Lawton's left hand was a manila envelope.

"Read it and weep," Denny barked forcefully.

Denny slammed the envelope down on Michael Lorde's desk. Oh, Lorde knew what it was. He felt that knot, that drop in his heart – the kind you feel when you've gone on for so long, covering up every sin imaginable, only for the hammer to drop years later, when you least expect it. There would be no easy win. In fact, there would be no win at all. The trajectory of Michael Lorde's life had changed in an instant. There would be no sitting pretty in Parliament, not now, not ever.

"It's all there notarized," Denny told the MP coldly. "Everything – names, witnesses, accomplices. We're just waiting on the magistrates to issue the warrants. I'm giving this to you only as a courtesy so you can give it to your lawyers to build up your defense. You're gonna need it. Don't think I'm not charitable. Everyone, even the worst, vilest creature, deserves a fair trial, even you."

Michael Lorde was beet red, one heartbeat short of a panic attack. He gawked at the envelope.

"Soon, the whole county will know what you did," Denny went on. "We're not afraid of you anymore. People are speaking up. You don't control us. This is free, Lorde. See, I don't like people who prey on impressionable little girls. Going through Hassan was pretty sneaky."

Denny whipped out his phone. He snapped a photo of an old Winchester Pump proudly mounted on the wall.

"I believe if we run a ballistics test, we can safely say that that's the murder weapon. I understand not wanting to get caught, but why did it have to cost little Annie Love her life? Was it really worth five more years in Parliament? Was it worth that poor girl's life just so you could have some modicum of control? Did you actually think it would end like this?"

Michael Lorde clenched his fists in rage.

"You know, I'd keep those fists right where they are," Denny noted, "unless you want to add assault on a police officer to that list of charges. Then again, what's another year or two added to a life sentence?"

Michael Lorde went on clenching, his fists so white you'd be convinced his bones would burst forth from them.

"Anyway, Mister Lorde, if I were you, I'd get my affairs in order. I hear prison isn't fun, especially the kind they'll send you to. Godspeed."

And with that, Denny turned and walked out of the office and to his car. He didn't hurry this time. His pace was steady and nonchalant. Michael Lorde hesitated for a moment before giving chase. What could he actually do? Kill him? Grab that shotgun off the rack and blow his head off? He could, but then that would take away even the glimmer of hope he'd have in a fair trial. No, in the end, all Michael Lorde had were words, meaningless words. Denny could hear the slurs hurled at him as he walked to his Mustang.

"You bloody wetback!" Lorde shouted. "Think you're so tough because you're a dirty brown Mexican! Let me gut you, I bet dirt would come out. You brown cucks are all the same! You just wait! You haven't heard the last of me!"

And so, the true contents of the man's heart were spilled out for all the world to hear. None of it touched Denny. None of it surprised him. He knew Michael Lorde never truly cared for anyone with a skin tone any darker than sour cream. It was all just a façade, and Denny pulled the mask off of this monster.

Denny took one last look at the crazy scene – a man smartly dressed in a three-piece suit seemingly shouting curses at the sky and pontificating like a tweaker on the side of the road. It was a sad scene, but he put that sadness out of his mind when he remembered who it was.

"Another round for our hero!" Fat Terry shouted as he filled every last stein of every last pub patron with ginger beer. It had become a running joke that had turned into appreciation for the teetotalling cop from Oregon. Any other day, it would be ale after ale, pint after pint, poured in those cups, but today was different. It seemed as if the very air they breathed was freer.

The warrant had come down from the local magistrate only twenty minutes after Denny had left Michael Lorde's office. The second Whit had the order in his hand, he led a team of uniformed officers who swarmed the local constituency office. There, they frog marched the disgraced MP out and into a squad car in front of every camera in Lancashire, from the lowly news blogger to the BBC. News of the arrest spread faster than wildfire in a dry, unmanaged forest. Video footage and pictures were splashed all over social media. The general applause would be deafening were it an actual applause. The objections from the few were weak and meaningless. Politicians were put on notice: shape up or you too will be frog marched out of your office in disgrace and shoved into a marked patrol car.

Whit read the charges emotionlessly, as if he were just a text-to-speech program spitting out some pre-programmed script, "Michael Lorde, you are under arrest for murder, conspiracy to commit murder, rape, statutory rape, assault, assault with a deadly weapon, and failure to report a crime. You do not have to say anything, but it may harm your defense if you do not mention when questioned something which you later rely on in court. Anything you do say may be given in evidence." Any one of those charges, if successful, would put Michael Lorde away for at least the rest of his working life, if not until death, which might come sooner rather than later given the crimes of which he was accused.

"You know, they still have to convict him," Denny chuckled as Fat Terry filled his mug.

"Come on," Terry jokingly whined, "don't ruin all the fun."

"I'm just saying, this fight isn't over. You still have Hassan out there roaming free."

"Not for long," a patron added. "You know the next guy what sees him is gonna kill him."

"Hey, we may be rid of Michael Lorde," Denny explained, "but he's just one of many who would have you arrested for offending the wrong person. To truly be free, you have to change the laws and enforce the good ones already on the books, and for that, you need new local magistrates."

"I know, we'll 'ave Fat Terry run," another patron shouted.

Terry pondered that, seriously considered it.

"I dunno, boys," he said, "you really want me all stuffy in a magistrate's office."

"If it means free beer, then yes," yet another patron said.

"Well, ya got me then," Terry chuckled.

"Next round's on me!" the patron shouted. "House ale for us and ginger beer for our two teetotalers."

Verity had eschewed alcohol, even off the clock as of recent. Her explanation was that she wanted to be a good support for Denny. All the same, everyone was suspicious because Denny had no desire or temptation to even touch the stuff.

"You're getting a taste for spicy food, Princess," Denny chuckled as he sipped yet another pint of spicy ginger beer.

"That she is," Fat Terry added. "This stuff will burn ye up worse than whiskey if ye let it."

"Just think, Terry, in three months' time, she'll be putting away ghost peppers like they're candy."

"Oi, can't I just enjoy my ginger beer judgment-free?" Verity finally shot back.

Verity sipped her soda defiantly.

"So," Terry continued, "any news on another investigation, seein' that ye've been initiated, Yank?"

"I'm sure we'll find out on Monday when we go in," Denny replied. "For now, I think I'll just gladly enjoy the small 'W'."

"More like a big 'W'," Verity cut in. "Don't sell yourself short. Hardly anybody busts sommat open like this, not on their first go either. Now that you've taken down an MP and the biggest gang lord in all of Lancashire, you've put any and all corrupt politicians on notice."

"You know what that means though, right?" Denny replied. "It means that I have a big target painted on my back. Don't laugh. I know it's all melodramatic here, but the fact remains that I've made enemies."

"But you've told me before that you have nothing to lose," Verity reasoned, "so why worry about it?"

"Do I though?" Denny asked, placing his hand over Verity's.

"I won't tell Whit," Fat Terry said with a chuckle, giving a knowing glance at the couple.

"I'm not joking though," Denny went on. "I had them on my back the whole time in PDX. You can push, and push, and push, but you poke the wrong person who's just powerful enough, you will be forced back. Ten years in vice taught me that. The root of the problem wasn't that people needed drugs or that people wanted to make money off of the drugs. That'll always be a problem. The root was the powerful politicians, like Michael Lorde, who ignored it and even pushed for it. They'd gaslight you and tell you how clean and beautiful the city was, even bringing the freaking governor in to show you all the nice parts of town they'd curated for social media. They wouldn't dare show the actual filth that resides there. They wouldn't show the actual despair people are in. Throw money at a problem, make it worse, lie about it, rinse, and repeat."

Denny was now fired up. The whole pub, who had gone back to their drinks initially, were now engaged in Denny's conversation with Verity and Terry.

"There was this one guy – mental as all get-out. His mind was freaked out on acid. He'd been known by PPB to randomly mug people, raped a few women, countless acts of public indecency on top of that. My first year as a patrol officer, we arrested him too many times to count – so many complaints; and every time, the city and county just let him walk. Then, one day, I don't know, had to have been my third year on vice, he got on a MAX train and stabbed two men who were trying to pull him off of a woman he was in the middle of raping. They bled out there in the aisle while he defiled an innocent woman who was just trying to get home to her baby girl and husband. Now, tell me, who had the power to stop a man who was clearly out of control? Would've been us had the mayor and our feckless chief let us do our jobs. Had he been held indefinitely, those women would still have their chastity, their husbands would have the satisfaction of knowing that they were the only ones that intimacy with them, and those men would still be alive. No, I don't blame criminals when they're allowed to roam the streets unpunished. That's their nature. It's like blaming a dog that's been bred to kill when it mauls a toddler to death. We blame the owner, right? For not restraining or training it

195

properly. I blame the politicians and people in power who choose to let them walk. If you're given the power to make a positive difference, you do it. Plain and simple."

"Another round for Denny!" Terry shouted, and he began filling steins with ginger beer.

"Maybe you should run for MP someday," Verity told Denny, scooting closer to him.

"You actually think I'd have a shot here?" Denny chuckled.

"Who here would want to see Denny Lawton serve as our MP, give us a big 'aye'!" Terry shouted out.

"Aye!" a collective cry rang out.

"Alright, lads, then let's sing it out for 'im!" Terry bellowed. "Come on, you know the words!"

For he's a jolly good fellow
For he's a jolly good fellow
For he's a jolly good fellow
And so, say all of us

"Okay," Denny conceded with a wheezing laugh, "maybe in about five to ten years after Ian Love has had his time in the spotlight."

"Maybe by then, you'll 'ave a missus and a few tots of yer own," Terry said, eyeing both Denny and Verity. "Always a good look when the candidate has a pretty wife and family."

"We may have to work on that," Verity chuckled nervously, gripping Denny's hand harder.

Terry turned around and started cleaning empty mugs.

"Classy guy," Denny commented, almost whispering, to Verity.

"Classy guy," Verity repeated back to him.

The pub was back to its rowdy self again. Everyone had gone back to their drinks and conversation. Into the party stepped Whit. He was drenched from the pouring rain that was falling outside.

"Brandon Whiteaker!" Terry shouted. "Oi, 'ave an ale on me."

"Thanks, Terry," Whit said as he took a seat next to Denny.

"Hey, boss, what's the news?" Denny greeted Whit excitedly.

The expression on Whit's face was anything but. Long and stern, Denny immediately detected trouble. Whit pulled a piece of folded paper out of his pocket. He slid it over to Denny. He unfolded it. At the top was the Seal of the State of Oregon – a gold heart with a setting sun, sailing barks, wheat with a plow, and an ox-pulled covered wagon around a banner that said "The Union" and surrounded by thirty-three stars and concentric circles of navy blue and gold.

"Extradition orders," Whit explained. "Oregon DoC sent them over as soon as we dumped Lorde off at the jail."

Denny could not speak.

"What for?" Verity nearly shouted in confusion.

"The state has concluded their investigation, Denny," Whit continued his explanation, "and they're charging you with assault and attempted rape on your informant."

"That's a load of poppycock!" Verity spat. "You and I both know Denny would never do that!"

"I know, I know," Whit admitted.

"I told you this would happen," Denny replied to both of them. "And you know the funny thing, I thought it would happen sooner. But Michael Lorde said he wasn't done with me."

"Wouldn't surprise me if he tickled the ears of the magistrates across the pond last thing he did before we came for him," Whit admitted with a sigh. "Anyway, it's Friday. I'm off."

Denny held up his hands in surrender, ready to be cuffed and stuffed..

"Not here, not now," Whit told him. "I'm holding this over until Monday. You turn yourself in first thing, and this will be a whole lot easier. I'm sorry, Denny."

"No, don't be."

Part 4
The World v Dennis Lawton

Annabelle Love's blindfold was removed violently. The darkness removed only revealed more darkness. But no, there were stars. Her eyes were adjusting. The ground was moving. Wait a sec, it was rocking. A pale moonglow revealed the water underneath the ground. Not the ground, some kind of platform – a boat. Her hands were still tied behind her back, so she found balancing herself even more difficult as the deck pitched up and down and back and forth. She took some solace in the fact that the ropes weren't too tight, so they weren't digging into her wrists.

There were men all around, men with dark skin, all except one. She recognized him – clearly an Englishman, and he was holding a shotgun in his hand.

"Mister Lorde!" she exclaimed excitedly, only for the familiar excitement to wear off. Michael Lorde did not share her enthusiasm. He just glared at her coldly.

Annabelle looked to her right. Agatha was there, clearly drugged out of her mind. Two of the thugs were holding Agatha back. Two more girls stood against the rail of the boat, also drugged and barely holding on.

"Aggie, what're they going to do?" she asked nervously. "What's going on here?"

Even through her drug-filled haze, Agatha turned her head in shame. Annabelle's face wrinkled and contorted in fear, as if it was all too obvious what was going to happen.

"Look, there's been a terrible misunderstanding!" she pleaded. "I was just trying to find my sister!"

"You may have been," said one of the thugs, the leader, "but she would rather stay with us."

"No, Aggie," Annabelle pleaded, "please, come home. Mummy misses you. She cries herself to sleep every night. Daddy didn't mean what he said. He's just so concerned for you. You don't have to live like this."

"Oh, but she does," the thug leader countered. "You see, I own her now. And you know what? Looks like I own you as well. Well, what do ya know! I have me the whole set."

As if to punctuate his point, he went around behind Agatha and placed his hands around Agatha's belly, like an expectant father. Only there was not the warmth and love you would expect from an expectant father. Agatha was his, and that baby was his – a human owning other human beings..

"Mister Lorde," the thug addressed the MP, "it's your call. I say we take her, make her one of our..."

Annabelle couldn't hear the rest of the thug king's plan, but the grin from both of them told her all she needed to know.

"No!" Annabelle cried. "You can't! Just wait till my father hears about this!"

"Your father is just a loudmouth politician who will disappear into the ether, just like every other politician who decides he needs to run his mouth around here," Michael Lorde spat. "He's weak and powerless. I'm not worried about anything he'll do to me."

"He'll stop at nothing to save me."

"Really, little girl," Lorde shot back with an evil chuckle. "Does he even know you're here? Does he know you followed Aggie out to her rendezvous with Hassan? You'll be long gone, little miss, before he even wakes up."

And with that, Michael Lorde turned to go to his cabin.

"She's yours, Hassan," Lorde told the gang lord emotionlessly. "Do what you want with her. Just make sure she disappears. Whatever it takes to distract Ian Love from his campaign."

The thugs turned to her. Before Annebelle weren't men, but ravening animals. They looked hungry — hungry for meat, or at least they looked like they wanted meat. One of the thugs even licked his chops. Was that how low they thought of her? She was just another hunk of meat?

Annabelle looked around for an escape. There had to be a way out of this. She could see the lights of Crenshaw afar off. She could make a swim for the peninsula and alert her father who would no doubt alert the police. She was a good swimmer; it wouldn't be all that hard.

For some reason, be it to have more fun in overpowering her, one of the thugs, pulled the ropes from her hands. She was free. She had her opening. Annabelle elbowed one of the thugs in the stomach and kicked another between the legs. Then, she grabbed a knife one of them was carrying on his person. She darted forth. Michael Lorde, still holding the shotgun, was still sauntering toward his cabin. He turned about to see the commotion and Annabelle running toward him, screaming like a lunatic whilst wielding a knife.

Michael Lorde shot Annabelle Love with his shotgun. One second, there was a pretty face contorted in fear and rage. The next second, half of that face was replaced by a void, her brain, skull, and viscera exposed, a cloud of blood, brain matter, and disintegrated bone filling the air around her head. Michael Lorde couldn't tell if she lost consciousness the second the side of her face exploded, or if she had mercifully lost consciousness before her brain registered the fact that she had been fatally wounded. To him, it seemed that she lingered for a second, the right side of her face coming to the realization that this was it. Life was over. There was no saving Agatha. It had all come to this on a boat in the harbor.

"Throw her over," Michael Lorde coldly ordered Hassan's thugs. "There's bleach in the supply closet. Clean up this mess."

Hassan's men picked up Annabelle's corpse and threw it overboard — no pity, no remorse, just business as usual. They didn't even have the decency to watch her remains descend into the depths. They just tossed her in and returned to their former tasks.

"If anyone asks, you don't know what happened to Annie Love," Lorde told Hassan.

"What about them?" Hassan gestured to Agatha and a couple of the other girls he had with him.

"Make sure they don't talk."

"And if they do?"

"What do you think?" Michael Lorde asked, as if it were obvious. He turned his attention to the thugs throwing the lifeless body of Annabelle Love over the side of the boat.

Chapter 22
Until It's Over

Denny had decided that weekend that he would not be dragged in like a common criminal. He would present himself as an innocent man with nothing to lose. He would surrender himself with his head held high.

Denny had picked out his clothes just for the occasion. He was to be the picture of dignity, so everyday street clothes would not do, even for the long flight. The night before, he had shined his black oxfords to a mirror finish. He ironed and starched a light blue button-up and black slacks. To finish off the ensemble, he set out a gray and blue argyle sweater and a navy tie. He packed an overnight bag, reasoning that it would be a swift trial, as was guaranteed in the Constitution, and he would be released and sent back here. If not, he wouldn't need any of the items as he would be wearing government-issued threads: the State of Oregon's official prison uniform of blue jeans and t-shirt stamped with the State Seal.

He tried to sleep the night before, but sleep would not come to him. He was going home, but home was no longer home. He had left that all behind and built a new life here in England. He tried praying. Even with that comfort his faith brought him, he could not drift off to sleep.

Around four in the morning, he decided that this whole sleeping affair was overrated, so he took an ice-cold shower. It felt like a thousand needles burrowing deep into his skin all at once, but at the same time, it felt oddly therapeutic, as if it cleared his mind.

And so, instead of lying in bed thinking, Denny stood in the shower thinking. He thought about everything that had brought him to this moment – every decision he and others had made. After all, he was an abused kid who so wanted to be able to connect with other abused kids and encourage them that their abuse did not define them – that they could live a happy life with a family. And where did that get him? Accused of a crime that any sensible person would know he did not commit.

Denny turned the heat up in the shower near the end and nearly scalded his face. He stepped out and wrapped himself in a towel. He let the water in the sink run hot and started wetting down a brush. He stropped his straight razor and then lathered some shaving cream with the brush. If he was to be dignified, he wanted the closest shave possible. His thoughts still played out the story of his life, nearing the episode where he went to England to solve the mysterious case of the fishing village harbor murder.

Denny started his shave with the grain of his beard. The scrape of the blade against his rough face sounded like butter being spread on toast. That's all that filled his hearing. He lathered his face again for the next pass, this time up against the grain to get any remaining hairs still standing.

Denny paused a second and looked in the mirror as he began that second pass. The blade of his razor was right over his jugular. It would have been so easy to apply just a little more pressure and end this nightmare. He would bleed out, maybe not even feel much if he passed out in shock; then, when he didn't turn himself in, Whit would send one of his uniforms there with a warrant and find him dead. It would no longer be his problem.

That was the old Denny thinking – the one who didn't have anything to lose, and the thought only lasted roughly five seconds. He looked at a picture of he, Verity, and Hallie at a Christmas carnival in Lancaster. What if Whit sent Verity as a gesture of goodwill? He couldn't stand the thought of Verity walking in only to find his naked corpse with a gash in his neck. He kept normal pressure on the blade and shaved up, getting the last of his beard. He passed his hand over his cheek – smoother than a baby's bottom.

Shaken by the mere thought of considering suicide, Denny applied some cooling aftershave and got dressed. He fried some eggs in the kitchen and brewed a pot of coffee. Six cups of coffee later, the sun was beginning to rise. It was time to face the music.

Denny grabbed his bag, making sure he had his wallet, phone, and passport on him. He had decided to let Verity take the Mustang for the duration of his time away. Even with the threat of prison time, he rationalized that there was nothing substantial or realistic on him and that he would be home in a day or two.

Denny tossed his overnight bag in the trunk of his Mustang and was about to climb in behind the wheel. That's when he noticed something. He had seen it out of the corner of his eye when he walked out, but now, it was clear as day. Sitting on the corner diagonal from his house was a British Racing Green Bentley Continental GT, the same one Hassan drove. Denny squinted his eyes to see who was driving. It was Hassan.

He decided to play it cool. For all he knew, Hassan may have just been cruising around. People cruise around. At least, he tried to have a positive outlook on the situation, but he knew it all too well. Hassan was out to kill him. He slid in behind the wheel and discreetly switched on his dash cams, one front-facing, one rear-facing out the back window, and one facing Denny himself.

Denny started the car and pulled away from the curb as if nothing was going to happen. He drove down the street, keeping his eye on his rearview. The green Bentley kept on his tail. He made a left onto a side street in the north part of Crenshaw. The Bentley made the left too.

He made another left. The Bentley made another left. He repeated this twice, both with the same results. Now he had visual confirmation preserved on three hard drives that Hassan was, in fact, tailing him.

As he made a right past an old inn, another Bentley – this time another Continental, a sleek black job – joined in the slow pursuit. Denny glanced back. This one was driven by Habib, Hassan's gorilla of a body guard.

He knew it. He was falling into their trap, and they were reeling him in. They knew where he was going, so it was inevitable that he would encounter even more of them or that they'd box him in. It would be a miracle if he could double back or something to outsmart them.

There is a small rise in the middle of the Crenshaw Peninsula. It is the only part of the village that isn't covered in buildings. Instead, there is an ancient tree-covered patch of land surrounded by an ancient stone fence, a relic of a previous age before civilization came to Crenshaw-on-Ribble. Here, one can either take the road straight or make a right and go up over the rise. Denny passed the turn-off. He reasoned that he could give Hassan and Habib just one more chance to back down now before things got ugly. If they wanted him, they'd have to show him how badly they actually wanted him.

As if on cue, another Bentley – a purple Bentayga SUV with gigantic outdated gold spinner rims – stopped across the road in front of him. He had not anticipated this so soon; not here. The Bentayga was blocking the road. Denny looked behind him. The two Continentals were closing in fast. This was definitely an ambush. No question about it now. Out of the Bentayga stepped Hassan's two door guards, the pigs who liked to get handsy with Verity. They were definitely packing. They thought they could kill him so easlily.

Denny pushed in the clutch, as if he were going to put the car in neutral and park it. He had to time this perfectly as to not give any idea as to his escape plan. Hassan and Habib were closing in, but they hadn't cleared the distance to the turn-off; the door guards were going to beat them there. He kept his left foot on the clutch, right on the brake, slowly shifting his right heel over the accelerator.

The second the first door guard reached the driver's side door handle, Denny threw the car into reverse, dumped the clutch, and mashed the accelerator with all of his might, as if pushing the pedal harder would unlock some extra horsepower he didn't know about. The thugs were instantly blinded and choked by tire smoke as Denny fled backwards toward Hassan, Habib, and the turn-off. The two men in the Continentals slammed the brakes for fear of being plowed over by the Mustang.

As soon as Denny reached the turn-off, he threw the car into first and disappeared up the turn-off casting powdered rubber and tire smoke behind him. Even by this time, the two door guards had still not recovered their dropped jaws from off of the ground. As soon as they realized what was happening, they rushed back to the SUV and back toward the turn-off where Hassan and Habib were already giving chase.

Denny knew he had to head to somewhere on the mainland, if not Preston. There were barely any patrols out right now, being still somewhat early in the morning, but the higher population density of the mainland settlements could afford him some protection. He slid through a corner and into the newer brutalist section of the village.

The chase sped through the warehouse district, Hassan narrowly missing a little migrant child on a bike. Denny slid around a corner and flew by Hassan's apartment building. Bystanders gawked at the scene of an American muscle car flying by in this crumbling neighborhood pursued by the three luxury British autos.

Denny wanted to shake these guys if anything. He barreled onto the west drive, the road lined with mansions, including the burnt-out corpse of Ian and Harriet Love's mansion. He narrowly missed a Rolls Royce backing out of one of the driveways, the angry driver blaring the horn at him.

Denny drifted onto the road leading to the causeway. Hassan followed close behind, and was in turn followed closely by Habib. The two thugs in the Bentayga were beginning to catch up to the chase. They tried the same stunt getting onto the causeway as the three cars before them, but they had overestimated the handling capabilities of their whip.

Before the causeway, there was a small fuel station. It was the only fuel station in all of Crenshaw, until it wasn't. As the thug driving the Bentayga cranked the steering wheel hard left to enter the causeway behind the pursuit, he didn't brake. The momentum, first, caused him to not be able to complete the turn, sliding the SUV into the curb. The impact with the curb then blew out the driver's-side tires and threw the Bentayga into a roll, straight into the fuel pumps. A poor man just trying to fuel his trusty Mondeo had only seconds to spare as to make a break for it as the luxury SUV rolled into his only means of transportation before impacting the pump itself. Both the Bentayga and the Mondeo were instantly incinerated, along with the two thugs inside the Bentley.

Denny, Hassan, and Habib all caught this in their rearview mirrors, but the chase didn't let up. They were speeding across the causeway, Denny at a severe disadvantage. Not only was Denny's Mustang naturally aspirated, but the twin-turbocharged V8 mills of the two Bentleys had nearly twice the horsepower. Hassan and Habib were right on his tail.

On the mainland, the chase only gained speed. In the early morning, other cars were starting to appear. Denny tried to go down a side road, veering away from the A-road that led into Preston. The unexpected turn gave him a little bit more space between him and his pursuers as they had to brake hard and lose all of their forward momentum.

Denny was at full throttle down this road, as were the two thugs. Hassan was right on Denny's tail. Denny looked in his rearview. Hassan sneered at him.

The chase passed a little farm house. There, a long-haul lorry with a flatbed trailer was pulling out into the road. It had to swing wide to clear the bollards of the yard it was departing from. Denny barely made it over into the other lane, skidding and barely putting the car in the ditch. Hassan missed the lorry by millimeters, kicking up mud and grass as he slid through the shoulder.

Habib was not so lucky. At his excessive speed, he barely had time to react, barely enough time to register that his life was at an end. He didn't even lift, didn't even brake. It would have been futile. His last words were not words at all. Instead, they were an ungodly scream of terror, cut off suddenly and abruptly as the top of his Bentley made contact with the bottom of the trailer at over 150 miles per hour. The roof was left behind as the Continental continued on under its own power, Habib's right foot still mashed to the accelerator. Habib's battered and broken head, still somehow wearing that same expression of terror, landed safely in the back seat of his Bentley which finally rammed itself into a stone wall on a curve in the road, tumbling over and over several times into a field where it eventually came to rest on its side.

Hassan was not giving up on the chase. He still kept on Denny. This was war. This was to end today. If he was going down, the least he could do was take this cop down with him. Hassan bumped Denny. He pulled up next to the left-hand side of the cop. He rolled down the window. He pointed a gun, a Glock 19, straight at Denny. Denny caught it right out of the corner of his eye and slammed his brakes just as Hassan fired. The bullet flew harmlessly into a roadside tree trunk. Hassan slowed back down to take aim again. Denny slammed into the side of Hassan's Bentley. Hassan lost grip on his handgun, and it tumbled harmlessly into the road.

Without his piece, Hassan turned to the only real weapon he had left: his two-and-a-half-ton missile. He returned the body slam to Denny. The cop would not go down. Denny slammed Hassan back. One of them was going to lose their car today, and neither of them were convinced that it would be themselves. For about a half a minute, they continued down the road virtually glued together, Hassan's eyes white with rage as he glared and sneered at Denny.

The road turned hard left suddenly. Hassan had his chance. He braked early and fell in behind Denny. At the curve, he found a way inside the rear of Denny's Mustang and tapped it precisely enough for the cop to lose grip. Denny tried regain control of his car, but there was no saving it at this speed. The Mustang spun, caught the shoulder, and went into a roll, over a stone fence and into a gnarled old tree, resting partially on its roof near the ancient arbor.

Hassan brought his Bentley to a stop. It had cost him three of his best men, including his personal body guard, but that was sure to silence Dennis Lawton. He looked over at the hunk of metal that was once a £71,000 muscle car. Denny hung inside, limp. Red blood poured down off of him and all over the interior. Something must have been very wrong with the car to cause bleeding like that. No way could any man lose that much blood and live. He was a goner, and Hassan had won.

Satisfied, Hassan turned back toward Crenshaw and left behind for his friends the ruin of the man who tried to ruin him.

Chapter 23
On the Hook

The blinding light was the worst part about waking up. That and the smell. It was that sterile smell all hospitals had, like someone without a sense of smell decided that the antiseptic smelled like lemons and just went with it. Denny knew exactly where he was the second he came to. His eyes tried to focus, ever keeping vigilant for a small Filipina with an attitude to come in and rebuke him for not sleeping. That Filipina never came, and at that, he felt a little dismay. Those Filipina nurses always did that from a place of care and love. There was a slight discomfort in the crook of his right arm, the kind that doesn't hurt, but you know there's something there that shouldn't be. He looked down at his right arm. Through, the haze, he saw a giant IV needle sticking out. He recoiled at the sight of it and nearly blacked out again. He tried not to gag as he looked away. Things should not be sticking out of there.

It wasn't all bad though. The second his eyes completely flitted open, Verity was on top of him, embracing him as if he wasn't connected to an IV.

"Holy crap, woman!" Denny exclaimed as he reached to make sure the IV needle was still properly stuck in his arm, as much as he hated the fact that an IV needle was still properly stuck in his arm. "What happened?"

Verity was now kissing him all over, not leaving one square inch of his face, neck, arms, or hands untouched by her lips – puckering and pecking rapid-fire before Denny could even think.

"Yes, yes, I'm alive, Princess," he tried to comfort her. "I'm right here."

"A farmer found your car on its roof against a tree," Verity started. "They thought…" she began to get emotional, nearly breaking into tears. "They thought you were dead because there was so much blood." Here, she started to giggle at something as if it were all complete nonsense. "Turns out, the transmission was punctured and leaked out fluid all inside the car."

Denny gave himself a once-over. He couldn't feel any pain, just a slight headache.

"I'm not a vegetable, right?" he asked, wiggling his fingers and moving his free arm around.

"They say you blacked out from all of the blood rushing to your head," Verity explained. "You were out for a while. Oh, bugger! I forgot!"

Verity grabbed the remote set next to Denny's bed and pushed a call button. The nurse must have been waiting right outside the door because her arrival was immediate. Denny sighed with somewhat veiled dismay. It wasn't that Filipina with an attitude he was still expecting.

"I'm so sorry," Verity apologized. "I just got so excited you were awake and okay that I spaced on calling your nurse."

She stepped out of the nurse's way, who immediately went about inspecting the detective.

211

"You, sir, were right lucky," the nurse commented as she looked him over.

The nurse was a short, stalky woman in her forties with dirty blonde hair and dark eyes named Sybil. Her eyes betrayed the countenance of a woman who had seen and heard everything and more than her forty-some-odd-years could fit – as if she were really an ancient grandma who had miraculously slapped a young face on herself. But were there not a ten-to-fifteen-year age difference between them, Denny thought he may have even been somewhat attracted to her.

As Sybil continued checking his numbers, in walked Whit. It seemed as if he had entered Terry's on Friday night with one face and had not changed it since then. It was the same melancholy expression Denny had seen when his superior handed him the extradition orders.

Whit stood by the wall, sternly observing the nurse's work. For some reason, there was nothing more terrifying to Denny in that moment that Whit's silence – not the gangsters, not the threat of arrest, not even losing everything he loved. Whit waited there until Sybil had finished checking on Denny and left with a promise that the doctor would see him.

"You were a smart one to keep a dashcam in your car," Whit expressed to Denny as Sybil closed the door behind her.

"Hassan?" Denny asked. He knew exactly who it was. He had seen the thug's mug in his rearview. All the same, he wanted some reassurance that he hadn't gone crazy.

"They're close on his trail now," Whit explained. "Habib Ibrahim, Ali Reza, and Muhammed Zarif, the other three gang members involved in the pursuit, are all dead. Our coroners are scraping up their remains right now. We watched the footage. You handled the car pretty well, if I might say so."

"Then, it's over?" Denny asked.

"If by 'over', you mean that the people directly responsible for the deaths of Annabelle and Agatha Love and the enslavement and abuse of them and more than a hundred women have been taken off the streets and are facing justice, then yes, it is over."

Denny closed his eyes in a silent prayer of thanksgiving. When he opened his eyes, he searched for the remote so he could adjust his bed.

"I honestly meant to come in," Denny explained as he sat up. "They accosted me on my way to Preston pretty much the second I left my house."

"That was obvious," Whit replied drolly.

"I take it this doesn't let me off the hook," Denny chuckled.

"We have a couple men from the Oregon State Police at the office right now waiting to take you into custody."

"You tell them the second they discharge me, I will be on my way over there," Denny replied. "I don't have anything to hide from them. There's no need to prolong the inevitable. I want this done and overwith."

"As would anyone," Whit replied.

Verity had prudently thought to pack Denny a new change of clothes. Not just that, she actually packed a larger duffel bag for him, apart from his overnight bag, anticipating a longer stay.

"Please hurry back," she bade him as one of the State Troopers cuffed him in Whit's office.

"Hey, I still have tons left over from my stocks and bonds," Denny replied. "When I get home, I'm going to hire a good lawyer and be back here within a week. They've got nothing on me."

Tears started to well up in Verity's deep blue eyes. She tried to hold them back, but she couldn't. Here was a man she initially couldn't stand, and in the course of a few weeks, he had become the husband she had always dreamed of. And now, they were taking him away, uncertain if he would ever come back. Sure, he could reassure her all he wanted, but even she seemed to know that the people that hated Denny's guts would drag this on as long as possible.

"Please write to me," she said through her tears. "I want to know everything so I can make sure we're all ready for you to come back. We'll throw you a big 'welcome home' party and everything at Terry's."

"I'll write every day," Denny promised.

Verity pinned Denny with a look of sorrow and anguish. Her face contorted in grief as she watched the Trooper pull at him to take him outside. She finally broke down and ran to him. Verity embraced

Denny – a one-sided embrace as Denny's arms were pinned behind his back.

"Please, don't let them believe the lies about you," she pleaded through the tears.

"I won't," was Denny's stoic reply.

"Denny," her words were filled with love, more love than Denny had ever heard from anyone spoken – not from his mother, not from Talia. These words were spoken from a woman who had given her heart completely to him. There was nothing that could change that. They could completely assassinate his character. He could be publicly remembered long after his death as the Christian cop who didn't live up to the Christian ideals he preached, somehow doing what as expected of someone like him – manipulating and raping a hooker. Verity would continue to believe in him and love him. He was the man she had always wished for. He was the father she had always wished Hallie had.

Mascara cascaded down her cheeks as Verity embraced Denny with all of her might. The Trooper stood there awkwardly, obviously done with this farce and ready to move on. Denny looked back at him. They made eye contact.

"You know I won't run," he whispered to the Trooper.

The Trooper hesitantly unlocked the cuffs. Denny threw his arms around Verity. He kissed her forehead and brushed her side-parted bangs back from her eyes.

"I promise I'll be back," he told her for the umpteenth time as he ran his fingers through her caramel brown locks. "You and Hallie have given me every reason to carry on. Before I came here, I was angry and hurt. I didn't care anymore. I had nothing to lose."

Verity pressed her head hard into Denny's chest. His tie was soaked with her tears.

"I'm afraid," he admitted with a quiver of his lip. "I'm now truly afraid of this stupid trial because I know if I lose this, I lose everything I have ever loved and ever will love. I can take what they'll do to me, but I cannot stand losing everything again."

"Then you need to speak truth and fight," Verity responded through deep heaves. "You let them all know that you're the man that you proved you were to me."

Denny chuckled. For some weird reason, he chuckled.

"What's so funny?" Verity asked, almost indignant at this sudden ignorance of grieving protocol.

"I was just thinking," Denny replied, "your name."

"Um, yeah, what about it? Verity Baker, so what? It's not a funny name. It's practically a normal one."

"Verity. It means truth. It all just hit me. When a man has lost everything he holds dear, even his morals, what's he left with? Verity, truth. It's just, I never thought about it. All this time, I've been looking for truth, and she's right here, standing right in front of me."

Verity embraced Denny even tighter. He thought back to the last time he had truly felt connected to Talia, as connected as he could be with her, before everything had gone completely crazy. It was almost like this. She had embraced him, promising to believe everything he said. She reassured him that everything would be alright, and yet within a week, he was out on his butt. He thought of the bitterness he felt when even she began to believe the lie. Somehow, he felt safe with Verity, safer than he had ever felt. It seemed that even as he was about to be cuffed that everything would be alright, for when he bore his heart to Verity, he bore the whole thing – every ugly bit of it, not just the clean, sanitized bits acceptable for a Sunday morning crowd. And she loved him, every last bit of his dirty, rotten soul. Verity, for her part, knew what Denny was capable of, yet she knew he could control himself. He trusted the truth.

"Now, you take care of that little girl for me while I'm gone, okay," he instructed Verity, wiping a tear from her face. "Tell her I'll be back soon."

Denny put his hands behind his back once more, and the State Trooper cuffed him. Denny didn't resist.

The Trooper began to lead Denny out of Whit's office and into the main workspace. It seemed like they were parading him through for a perp walk. Verity struggled to follow him out. She began to break down in ugly tears. Whit put his arm around her back and guided her out to the main floor, like a minister guiding a grieving widow to her husband's funeral.

Were there any protest against this great travesty going on, it was silent. Those who knew Denny knew he was innocent. Even those on

215

the periphery knew he was one heck of a cop. They knew that none of this added up in the slightest. Those who were glad to see him go were in the miniscule minority; they kept their heads down and their mouths shut. Everyone knew that protest was futile. Instead, they lined the walkway to pay their respects to their newly incarcerated colleague, as if he was being carried away to his grave. Behind them followed Verity, weeping and leaning on Whit's shoulder like a grieving wife. So, yes, it was almost like a funeral.

The Trooper led Denny outside to a patrol car where the other Trooper and a Lancashire beat cop were waiting to take him to Manchester.

Denny turned around one more time before being stuffed into the car. He wanted to catch one more glimpse of Verity. He wanted one more memory of her face before being shipped off to an uncertain fate. There she was, leaning on Whit and still crying. It was bittersweet. While at once he knew her grief, he also knew there was grief because he knew how much she loved him, and that somehow made him feel a little better. He turned back to the car and climbed in unassisted. With the door closed, the Trooper climbed in on the other side, and they sped off south to Manchester.

Verity stayed out there as long as she could, watching her love drive away. She waited until the squad car had turned into a tiny dot before disappearing down the road. This was it. Everyone else had returned to the humdrum of everyday work life. She still couldn't believe it had actually happened. He was gone. For good? Quite possibly.

Verity returned back inside and sat down at her desk. She took a look at a newspaper clipping she had kept framed on her desk since she met Denny. It was from their first day – just a candid of them talking with Ian and Harriet Love at the marina, her all business and he reassuring Harriet Love that they would find the killer. Mission accomplished. She remembered how angry she was at his careless attitude that day. Had things changed so much since then? She took her hair tie out and placed it next to the picture, letting her locks hang loose, just like that first day.

"Go home, Baker," she suddenly heard Whit say from behind her.

"How long have you been there? You made me jump."

"Long enough to know you're not in any place mentally to be able to do any meaningful work today," Whit replied, "and I don't blame you. I know how you felt about him. He's a good man, Verity. He's the perfect man for you, much better than Elliott ever was."

"I'm sorry we didn't tell you," she told him.

"I don't blame you," Whit said. He paused for a second before asking, "Does he know?"

"I was planning on telling him tomorrow."

Chapter 24
The Cogs of Justice

D enny kicked himself in the shins as he sat in his cell. He had been so overly optimistic about the whole thing that he had forgotten that the whole process to even bring a trial to court was long and arduous; apparently, the term "speedy" in the Constitution was a very loose interpretation to the Multnomah County judicial system. Even so, to him, the case seemed so cut and dry.

He had been housed at the Multnomah County Justice Center for a week now with very little word on the proceedings. He had hired a lawyer from a firm that represents churches Christians in ministry, mainly of the Independent Fundamental Baptist variety. If anybody could at least get him off the hook, that's all he would ask for; though his biggest wish was for full vindication.

Denny's reputation had already been dragged through the mud, curb stomped, and then defecated on among the residents of the State of Oregon, as well as many in his old church community. There was no saving that.

Julian Bernie was a sleazeball, though a look at him wouldn't say that immediately. At first glance, he looked like any kindly pastor. He could hang with the best of them. Always dressed in his Sunday best of a Hickey Freeman suit, Johnston & Murphy wingtips, and any combination of button-up shirts and ties, one would think he had just stepped out of his pastoral study, ready to preach what the Lord had laid upon his heart with a big red-letter King James Bible in his hand. He gave fiery oratory as he stood behind the pulpit. That was all well and good, but underneath, he was rotten to the core; Denny could smell it, and this was the unrepentant reprobate the Baptist Legal Partners had sent out to defend him. Julian Bernie had represented a pastor in a case a couple years back that had gathered national attention. It seemed pretty cut and dry: megachurch pastor transports an underage girl across state lines for sex in a state with a lower age of consent, gets caught and arrested. Bernie had somehow convinced a jury to acquit this pastor who was obviously guilty. While a few people left the church (A couple hundred is a drop in the bucket compared to a membership that nears ten thousand.), that pastor was able to return to a hero's welcome and resume his ministry. All the while, that poor girl and her family were shunned and labeled as opportunists. That pastor then turned around and brazenly sued the girl and her family for defamation and somehow won. In another case, Bernie defended a couple who ran a Christian children's home. Cases of abuse, physical, sexual, and mental, had all been reported. Bernie, again, somehow convinced a jury that this was all Christophobic nonsense spouted by some anti-Christian leftwing nutjob. They walked free. The children were left scarred for life with no recourse. Oh, and they also had to pay legal fees for defamation.

And so, here Denny was, an actual innocent man in the hands of the slimiest lawyer the BLP could find. If his reputation as a man who actually followed the words of Christ couldn't be tanked any further, the Baptist Legal Partners had certainly found a way to do it. It was like handing the naysayers victory on a silver platter – Denny's head in a charger.

"Look, Jules," Denny said upon their first meeting, "can I call you Jules? Look here, I'm going to make your job very easy for you. No spin, no lies. I didn't do it. It's plain and simple. In the course of doing my job and checking in on an informant, she conspired with her pimp to accuse me of rape. She fell into my arms, and the pimp took a picture of it at the opportune moment."

"Look, Brother Lawton," Julian replied with an unnerving pastoral tone, "I get that you want to get out of here as quickly as possible, but you know how these things are."

"Oh, how are these things?"

"Well, you know," Julian hemmed and hawed, "they twist facts and make you look like the bad guy."

"Jules, that's what they're doing now!" Denny burst out angrily. "No spin. Just tell them the full truth as I wrote down in my deposition. There's nothing else to tell them other than gathering character witnesses."

"Just let me handle it," Julian replied calmly in that same gentle pastoral, fatherly tone.

"Mira," Denny said, slipping briefly into Spanglish, "I'm a cop. I know how this works. Do you know how many trials I've been to of people I've arrested?"

"And do you know how many people I've gotten off the hook?" Julian asked.

"'Off the hook' implies they were guilty," Denny protested. "I'm far from guilty. Ask anyone who knows me that doesn't have an agenda."

"Do you have any character witnesses?" Julian asked.

"Have you not asked my supervisor?" Denny shot back.

"I did have a brief conversation with him," Julian replied. "Said he'd love to speak on your behalf."

"Is that all?"

"The folks at your church didn't really want to talk. Your ex and her husband had some pretty strong words to say about you. I don't think you or our Heavenly Father would want me to repeat them."

Denny sat back in his chair defeated.

"Look, Brother Bernie," Denny started, "my church has supported you for how many years?"

"Since long before you were born," Julian replied humbly.

"Give me your honest opinion. Compared to all of the cases you've won, even among the majority where you knew the accused was guilty as sin, what do you see in me? Am I guilty or innocent?"

Julian sat back in his chair for a while and breathed heavily. He then sat up and took a long, cold stare into Denny's eyes.

"Not what I want to hear," Denny added, feely antsy, "but the truth. Just flat out truth, even if it hurts."

Julian breathed out and said, "I see a man who has strived his whole life to be blameless. For the first time in my career, I feel like I am looking into the eyes of a man who is completely and unfairly judged."

"And that's your honest answer? No Christianese spin on it? Not something you're getting paid to say?"

"I may be a lying, unscrupulous, bloodsucking lawyer, but I see nothing but an innocent man sitting across the table from me."

Julian was never a good actor. Any intelligent person could see through his over-the-top overtures during his defenses. And yet, today, Denny could see the truth in the man's eyes.

"Then you put together the best defense you got," Denny replied with determination.

That was a week ago. Denny had not spoken to Julian since then. In the meantime, he sat in his cell thinking the day away. He was always looking over his shoulder any time he was out. If he could, he kept his back to a wall. Rapists were frowned upon, cops even more frowned upon. To get at someone who was both would turn you into a legend.

Denny could take solace in the fact that he didn't share his cell with anybody. When he was locked up, he stayed locked up – alone with his thoughts. He prayed. He did pushups. He prayed and did pushups at the same time. When he finally wrangled a pen and paper from a guard, he wrote to Verity.

Another week passed. Two weeks. Three weeks. A month. He heard nothing from Julian. He was getting antsy again.

On Valentine's Day, a letter from Verity finally made it to him. The scent of her perfume filled his cell as he opened the letter. As he unfolded it, he found a few letters smudged and slightly wrinkled in a few spots. She had been crying when she wrote it.

Verity told him how much she missed him. She had a new partner. Josh Young had made detective. She lamented about how lax she had gotten working with Denny and how Josh always asked questions about procedures. Apparently, they hadn't been doing things by the book for a while.

Hallie had been missing Denny and kept asking when he was coming home. The kid was resilient, but giving her a taste of what it was like to have an actual involved father made her long for that kind of affection. Verity included some stick figure art from the girl of the three of them at the beach.

Verity and Josh had finally caught up to Hassan Abdul hiding out somewhere in the Pennines and put him behind bars. Now, he and Michael Lorde were in jail together pending trial. She talked about what a relief it was to have that monkey off of their shoulders. Now, they were going after pedophiles, and there were plenty of them to go around. Lorde was putting up quite the fight too, but it seemed as if the people were now making their voices heard. The worst the magistrates could do was to arrest some of the people making a stink about his crimes. But then, those same magistrates would just let them go due to public pressure. The migrants, too, once afraid of Hassan Abdul and what he would do, were now speaking out on the cruelty of Abdul and the allowance of the crimes by Michael Lorde.

Denny held the letter to his chest. He then grabbed the envelope to store it. When he grabbed the envelope, another piece of paper fell out onto the floor. He picked it up. It was a selfie of him, Verity, and Hallie at the Blackpool Illuminations. He stroked the picture with his hand, as if it were Verity's cheek. Denny crawled back into his bed and began to write another letter.

One day, later in February, Denny was able to make good use of his workout regimen. In the cafeteria, he had turned his face toward the wall for just a split second. It was enough time for another inmate to grab him by the neck. Though he couldn't see it, he could feel the flex of his attacker's muscles as he brought his other arm around to plunge the shank into his neck. His arms still free, he threw his elbows back into the assailant, confusing him for just enough time to grab at the inmate's wrists and cry out for help.

The other prisoners stood back as the guards rushed the two inmates locked in battle. Denny's vision began to blur as he began to choke. The last thing he saw were three guards rushing at him.

When he came to, he found himself in the infirmary. After a week, he was back in his cell. There was another letter on his bed.

Verity told Denny how Elliott was trying to insert himself back into her and Hallie's lives. She mentioned the fact that he had given up everything in the divorce, including parental rights. Elliott was now a broken man. His lover in Brighton had left him for another man. He was sick too. Verity had tried to play it cold with him, but she also struggled with her compassionate side.

"*Please tell me what to do,*" she pleaded with Denny in her letter.

In other news, Michael Lorde and Hassan Abdul were being brought to trial. The walls were closing in so fast on the two crooks that it looked like that one scene from *Star Wars*. Witnesses were coming out of the woodwork. DNA samples from children they had fathered were turning up in the hands of prosecutors on the daily – proof that many of the mothers were underage, and many more were unwilling participants. As he read, Denny mused at how quickly they were able to bring Lorde and Abdul to justice while he was sitting here, rotting away in jail, on a case that should have been cut and dry.

One day in mid-March, Julian Bernie finally paid Denny a visit.

"The heck have you been?" Denny asked angrily.

"You really don't have a lot of friends, do you?" Julian shot back.

"None that aren't gullible," Denny replied with a sigh.

"So I've gathered. Anyway, your trial is set for March 30."

"Did it really take almost three whole months to gather evidence they could've easily found in the last year?" Denny questioned.

"I hired a private investigator," Bernie went on, ignoring Denny's angry question. "He's been looking into this Sticky you've been talking about. Pretty elusive."

"Yeah, so he was," Denny replied. "I didn't meet him until the day he snapped that picture of me and Michaela Roberts."

"Yeah, and we owe that PI big time. He had to get his hands a little dirty," Bernie responded.

"I don't even want to know," Denny huffed.

"Anyway, I've got it on good authority that Sticky bragged to one of his walkers that he faked it."

"So, there's the confession right there!" Denny nearly shouted.

"Keep it down," Bernie hushed him. "Here's the problem: the words of a PI won't hold in court, so we somehow gotta bring in those walkers."

"Can't do that," said Denny. "Do you know what would happen to them if they snitched on Sticky and he found out?"

"Same thing that happened to Michaela," Bernie replied mournfully.

Nothing more needed to be said. Denny knew exactly what had happened. Sticky had planned to kill two birds with one stone, and Michaela had played perfectly into that plan. Of course, the girl was just foolish enough to fall for whatever Sticky had promised her, ignoring the glaring fact that if he found out she was snitching on him to the cops, he would end her. That was, in fact, what had happened. Sticky was notorious for what he did to walkers who angered him, especially when his anger was kindled by their betrayal. As soon as he had had his way with them, they would end up in the Willamette, sometimes the Columbia. Occasionally, they would just disappear entirely, likely washed out downriver and over the bar out in the Pacific. So, while she had initially pressed the charges, Multnomah County still sought to pursue the case – to send a message, to tell anyone in authority underneath the mayor himself that they had eyes on them. Look at someone wrong, and that was another slash in the police budget.

"So, we're sunk?" Denny concluded.

"PPB won't send one of their guys in to actually investigate," Bernie replied. "Heck they won't even send a brother officer from another department. In conclusion, they are hell-bent on putting you behind bars for the rest of your natural life."

Denny sat back and sighed.

"And they couldn't produce a body?" Denny asked. "They never found Michaela Roberts?"

"She's gone, Brother Lawton. She's nowhere to be found, and the prosecution has this Cephas "Sticky" McFarland guy testifying."

"Got any questions on him?" Denny asked.

"I've been looking into him," Bernie replied. "You say he's a pimp? They're saying he was Michaela Roberts' boyfriend. I'm going to be honest, it's very hard to find any evidence he was a pimp."

"Without any of his street walkers coming forward," Denny added.

"That is about the size of it."

"And are you sure nobody could speak on my behalf," Denny asked. "Not even my parents or my brothers? What about my pastor?"

"I'm gonna level with you," Bernie started. "I have gotten some of the worst people off from crimes I a hundred percent knew they did, as you are very well aware of. It was never a question of if they did it, rather how I could make it look like they didn't. I have yet to have a case where said crime was caught on camera."

"Caught and edited to look like a crime," Denny corrected. "They subpoenaed my phone. They have the texts between me and Michaela Roberts. That had to count for something."

"It could be admissible; but it doesn't exactly mean anything."

"Come on, Bernie," Denny pleaded. "I know you're a piece of garbage, sorry, not sorry; but it's the only reason I hired you. I'm desperate here. I'll be honest. Ten years on vice with no problems or real complaints and a faithful marriage should count for something, right?"

"Look, I know you hired me because you knew who I've gotten off, but I have to reiterate that this is new territory."

"Being that I'm innocent, but also have the visual receipts that I apparently did the crime?"

"That about sums it up," Bernie replied.

"Anything I should expect for the trial?" Denny asked with just the slightest gleam of hope.

"You've been accused in the most liberal county with the most liberal judge presiding over the most liberal prosecution and a jury made up of the most liberal people they could drag up off the streets of Portland," Bernie replied hopelessly. "You might get some sympathy points for being part Latino, but I'm going to be honest, convincing these women and girly men that you're innocent is going to be an uphill battle."

Denny leaned back in his chair and sighed heavily, his hands over his face. He brought his hands down, dragging them over his skin so that his face contorted, before slapping them down on his thighs with a jingle from his cuffs.

"Then let the Lord be my Judge," Denny replied plainly.

Chapter 25
All Rise

The sky was dark and gloomy as Denny was loaded into the police van and driven the two blocks from the jail to the courthouse. He had been afforded the opportunity to change back into his civilian clothes for transportation to court, at least some dignity among the humiliation of being paraded out in public like some wild animal.

Verity, his miracle woman, had thought wisely to pack him a couple of his sweaters, in addition to his blazer. Even as cold as late March could get, it was unseasonably cold today, in the low forties, in fact. If the sweater was any help, Denny couldn't tell. The unseasonal wind chill cut right through it.

Cameras flashed and blinded him as he was led up the shallow front steps at street level and into the Multnomah County Courthouse.

All of the local news stations and papers had shown up to report on this trial; even a few regional and national outlets picked up the story. Apparently, news of the corrupt cop who claims to be a faithful husband and a Christian to boot but manipulates and rapes poor, impressionable prostitutes had made the rounds, and everybody wanted a piece of the action.

In the months leading up, the press had already provided their own spin to the story, but the conclusion to their front-page news story had always been the same: "A traditionalist right-wing Christian cop raped a poor prostitute who was just trying to make a living while her heroic friend, a 'real' man, finally got the photographic evidence, thus dismantling the narrative of his perfect moralizing, holier-than-thou Christian life and exposing the true, dark core at the heart of Christianity". The point of the story, as it is every other time it's told, is to shock the people who already wholeheartedly believe it to be true due to their presuppositional bias. Perhaps, a few would protest that it's "not every Christian" or that Denny was "just a bad apple", but the effect was the same: to solidify the popular narrative. And even if proven innocent, the popular narrative would remain unchanged – the truth printed as a retraction buried on page 37 of the New York Times. Forever, innocent or guilty, Denny would be the traditionalist right-wing Christian cop raped a poor prostitute who was just trying to make a living while her heroic friend, a "real" man, finally got the photographic evidence, thus dismantling the narrative of his perfect moralizing, holier-than-thou Christian life and exposing the true, dark core at the heart of Christianity.

Along with the reporters lining the queue poles erected in front of the courthouse, a large gaggle of protestors had gathered, holding up signs saying "JUSTICE FOR MICHAELA" or "HANG EM HIGH". Denny's personal favorite was F*** THE PIGS" with the written f-bomb tastefully self-censored with three asterisks, just to make sure none of the kids were offended, as if anyone in their right mind would have brought a kid anywhere near here.

For a county that liked to spare no expense, Denny found it odd that they decided to keep the courtroom cold, as if they were afraid of running up the heating bill. He could have sworn they were running the A/C, making it even colder in there than outside. Denny was thankful Verity had packed him that extra sweater, even if it did little to stop the cold.

As Denny entered, he looked out toward the gallery. His heart stopped. Talia was in attendance, along with Rick. She had cut her hair shorter, her formerly flowing golden waves now recently styled in neat blonde curls, more like Julia, as if Rick had not only taken Talia from him, but recreated her in Julia's image. She was also visibly carrying his child. Couldn't even be divorced from him a year and remarried, and they already got busy. The flood of anger, hurt, resentment, loss, sorrow, and whatever other negative emotion Denny could feel all hit at once, but he never let it out. Instead, he bottled it up, allowing it to build inside like a whole sleeve of Mentos in a sealed two-liter of Diet Coke. The time to remove the bottle cap would come later when he was alone.

Next to the new Johnson couple were Denny's parents, Brian and Marisol Lawton. Disapproval was plastered on his father's face. Marisol remained stoic, though deep inside, Denny could read her heartbreak that one of her sons, even the one that may have been seen as the prodigal, would be brought before a tribunal such as this.

Denny took his seat in front next to Julian Bernie. To their left sat the district attorney, Curtis Ford. Curtis Ford was the type of weakling poindexter who had been bullied all through childhood, only to become a bully himself once he tasted a bit of power. Reedy and a little flamboyant, Denny could tell at once how he got the job. Ford had ticked off at least one check box of the ongoing Oppression Olympics of the county; it was all too obvious with the heart-shaped lapel pin painted with the Pride/Progress flag. This trial wasn't Denny's first run-in with the DA. Getting him to actually prosecute actual criminals was harder than anything he had experienced in Lancashire. He would have as much put a poor granny away for the crime of being one dollar off of her property taxes as he would have let a bloodthirsty murderer go because he checked off one of the Oppression Olympics boxes he was so fond of. As such, Denny knew that Curtis Ford had it out for him. When Curtis Ford wanted to put someone behind bars, he never held back; and today, it was clear that Ford was bound and determined to make sure Denny was to spend as much time as possible behind bars. He doubted Julian would be up to the fight.

What was worse? The jury was made up of every oppressed group the county could find: women, men who thought they were women, women who thought they were men, androgens with more piercings than skin, African-Americans, Asian-Americans, Arab-Americans, Indian-Americans, Native Americans, a gay Muslim polyamorous paraplegic Mongolian nose flute artist and part-time Gambian horticulturist named Fong; oddly, no Latinos – perhaps, out of fear someone would have sympathy for their primo and hold up the jury in their final deliberation.

"All rise," the green-clad bailiff shouted. "The Honorable Judge Kristin Jessop presiding."

As if Denny's heart didn't already sink when he saw Curtis Ford as his accuser, he knew he was sunk the moment he heard the judge's name. His knees began to buckle as the woman walked up to her throne. First off, she was one of those androgens mentioned before – strangely feminine but strangely masculine. She had white, butch-cut hair, thick-rimmed glasses, and a square jaw. She spoke in a low, guttural tone, as if she were mocking the men in her life or trying to make herself sound even more masculine for her more feminine wife.

"Court is now in session," Judge Jessop announced with a bang of her gavel. "Please be seated. Defendant has pled not guilty. We will now hear his case."

"Ladies and gentlemen of the jury," Bernie began his oratory. Denny could already see the sneers as his lawyer had already made an enemy of many jury members by misgendering at least half of them.

"Objection!" Curtis Ford shouted.

"Sustained," Judge Jessop replied coldly.

"Defense must use the term 'people of the jury' as there are more than just men and women," Curtis explained.

"Way to go," Denny sarcastically mumbled to himself.

"I apologize, people of the jury," Bernie corrected himself. "Anyway, people of the jury, I would like to introduce you to Detective Constable Dennis Lawton of the Lancashire Constabulary, formerly of the Portland Police Bureau. Now, I've gotten to take a little time and get to know my friend, Denny Lawton. Denny is an upstanding citizen, a family man, and a peace officer of outstanding integrity. People of the jury, I want to introduce you to this man and show you that he is

230

not only innocent of the charges brought against him, but that he is above board and blameless of any accusation you can throw at him. I am going to show you the real Dennis Lawton, not the sick, twisted piece of human filth that the media or our worthy prosecutors would like to paint a picture of, but a man who will go above and beyond to protect, not only those he loves, but complete strangers. You will see that this whole accusation is nothing but an elaborate scheme by Portland's shadiest characters in her underworld and her government to bring down their finest officer."

Denny was awed by Bernie's audacity. What he said was true, if not a little embellished. Denny had a sneaking suspicion, though, that it was not near enough.

"I would like to call the accused to the stand," Bernie continued.

Denny stood up and took the witness stand. The bailiff brought a Bible, a big King James. Denny was quite surprised they'd actually bring a Bible and not some other weird book, like a Koran or even the *Communist Manifesto*, which to him seemed more appropriate in this setting.

"Put your left hand on the Bible and raise your right hand," the bailiff instructed. "Do you swear to tell the truth, the whole truth, and nothing but the truth, so help you, God?"

"I do."

Denny took his seat in the witness stand.

"Detective Constable Dennis Lawton," Bernie began his cross-examination, "Denny, can I call you? Denny Lawton. Please state your occupation."

"Current or former?" Denny asked.

"For clarification, it might behoove you to state both," Bernie replied in a fatherly tone.

"Well," Denny began, "for about eleven years, I was with the Portland Police Bureau – one year on patrol and ten in vice. For the three months leading up to my arrest in January, I was a detective with the Lancashire Constabulary in Preston, England."

"Can you state to me what happened, in your own words, on the afternoon of Sunday, August 10?"

Denny took a deep breath. He looked out at the gallery. Talia was already sitting on the edge of her seat, Rick beside her sternly resting

231

with his arms crossed. Brian and Marisol stared blankly at him. It was as if they were all judging him — as if what he was about to say didn't align with whatever lie they had told themselves, that they themselves would carry out the condemnation.

"I had just gotten home from church," Denny began. He then went on to describe exactly what he had told Verity all those months ago. In the end, he rested his own accusation solely on Sticky McFarland. "Sticky pushed me into Michaela. He then took the video and screen cap to make it look like I was assaulting her."

It was all the same statement he had given in August. It had been written down. Nothing had changed. A consistent story was a good mark, but not exactly a sure mark, of his innocence. That was still at least one point to Dennis Lawton.

"Good, DC Lawton," Bernie congratulated his client, "you may return."

Denny went back to the bench.

"Does the defense have any more to say?" asked Judge Jessop.

"Nothing more, your honor," Bernie replied.

"The court will now hear from the prosecution," the judge announced.

Curtis Ford stood up and brushed his suit down, as if he could magically iron it by the heat of his hands. He walked smugly up to the front of the courtroom, or at least, that's how Denny read it. And why not? They had never gotten along, and he knew that Curtis Ford would love nothing more than to bring down an adversary.

"People of the jury," Curtis Ford announced, "you've heard Detective Lawton's story. I'll admit, it sounds pretty convincing, but don't be deceived. In the next few moments, you will hear the truth of how this seemingly upstanding, moral citizen is a cold and calculating opportunist and rapist. You will hear how this so-called peace officer used his position to take advantage of one of his informants. You will hear of the bravery of Cephas McFarland bringing to light this nefarious abuse of power. People of the jury, I will prove to you, beyond the shadow of a doubt, that that man, if he were even worthy to be called a man, is guilty and should be put away for as long as the law allows, and not a second of time less, if not longer!"

Denny shuddered in his seat. Those words, lies, all lies. Sure, he had seen it many times. The stinging words of the prosecution always sounded satisfying when spoken against the actual guilty. But for Denny, he who was innocent, they cut deep. Like, who did this shill think he was? Denny wanted to cry out, to make it stop, tell this lying piece of crap where he could put his lies, to ask him where he thought he was getting off with all these lies. Lies! All lies, and he could do nothing about it but sit in his little chair in this little courtroom of this little courthouse of this little county and listen to his name be smeared and dragged through the mud.

Curtis Ford didn't even bother bringing Denny up. He had banked on the possibility that, due to his existence as a Christian man, the handpicked jury would have already decided his guilt and that the rest was just procedural. It would make for good press and only go and prove their point: right-wing Christian men are the devil.

"State your name," Curtis instructed a well-dressed man in the stand.

"Yo, my name is Sticky," the man replied.

"Your given name for the court," Curtis corrected.

"Yeah, it's Aloysius Cephas McFarland," Sticky returned.

"So, tell me, in your exact words what happened on Sunday, August 10."

"Yeah, so I was just walkin' around, and I heard a scream from inside the old Hotel Stumptown. You know, that old firetrap in the Pearl District?"

"Continue," Ford persuaded Sticky.

"Yeah, so I hear this scream, and I run in. Definitely some poor girl is in danger. I whipped out my phone flashlight because it's all dark in there. That's when I found the source of the screaming. Detective Lawton was in the process of sexually assaulting Michaela Robetrts. I snapped the picture for evidence. Luckily, for Lawton, he got off of her before I had to rock his world. But yeah, what you see in my photo is what happened."

"That'll be all, Mister McFarland," Curtis said as Sticky exited the stand. He turned back to the jury. "So, you see, we have an eye witness, a photograph even, of this terrible crime."

Curtis took his seat, defiantly straightening his lapels. This was going to be a cake walk for him. To have every scenario in this court case set out like every primetime court drama was a gift.

"I'd like to call Cephas McFarland to the stand," Bernie announced. Cephas returned to the witness stand. "So, you say you just happened to be walking around when you heard the screaming?"

"Yes," was Cephas' annoyed one-word reply.

"Okay, I can buy that. I mean, it is a bit different from the version of events my client has given. You say you had your cell phone. In fact, you say you took a picture with that cell phone."

"Well, I had to get evidence. Black man like me, they won't believe me. In fact, they'd probably blame it on me."

"Blame what?"

"The rape."

"I can see that."

"Objection!" Curtis shouted. "Leading questions."

"Sustained."

"Look, I'm just trying to get a better picture of this situation. I'm sure you understand that my job here is to defend DC Lawton through all means legally. That being said, I have one more question: where's the phone?"

"Objection!"

"Overruled."

Finally, a break for once.

"You said it was a screen capture," Bernie pressed. "You know, we could actually prove this whole thing if we were able to see the whole video. You posted a picture to *Instagram*. Why not the whole video?"

"Objection! It's irrelevant."

"*Shut the heck up, you arrogant fool!*" Denny shouted in his mind.

"Sustained."

"Thank you, Mister McFarland. That's all I need."

Bernie took his seat next to Denny. The cop was in shock.

"What the heck, Bernie?" Denny whispered.

"I got what I needed. That phone doesn't exist," the lawyer replied. "I'm going to try and weave that into the defense now. They have nothing but a screen shot and two opposing testimonies."

"And?"

"We have to rely on character witnesses now."

"Which I don't have," Denny protested.

"It'll depend on who's questioning them," Bernie whispered back. "That little twig what calls himself a man over there starts leading them on, I'm going to raise objections like crazy."

The character witnesses started with Chief Rondell Jackson.

"Detective Lawton was my number one man," Jackson replied to the probe into Denny's character. "Look, I have several detectives in vice. They've worked it for several years. All of them lost their marriages due to actual affairs. Not Detective Lawton. He had eyes for one woman, and one woman only. See, I could send him into a burlesque club to interview an exotic dancer, dressed in nothing but the tiniest top and a thong, and he'd keep his gaze directed on her eyes. I've never seen him even so much as touch another woman or look at any woman that would suggest he wanted to harm her or do anything to her. He was with PPB for eleven years and never received so much as a complaint until this past August."

That was for the defense. The prosecution went at Chief Jackson hard, as if he were the one being tried for rape.

"Dennis Lawton was under investigation for rape, was he not?" Curtis Ford pressed Jackson.

"Well, yes he was."

"Don't you generally keep tabs on officers who are under investigation for a crime?"

"Generally, we do."

"Then, please tell the jury why you would not only transfer the accused to a different police agency, but transfer him out of the country."

"Like I said before, we were certain he was innocent. He gave no reason for us to doubt it. We get so many frivolous complaints that one against an officer who's never had any issue in eleven years was a non-issue. It was only after Detective Lawton had been overseas for a couple months that the seriousness of the accusation was escalated. I mean, shoot, the man came back here willingly when we ordered his extradition. What does that say about him?"

"I would think you'd be more responsible than that," Ford shot back, "seeing that any accusation should be taken seriously. Might I remind the jury that we must believe all survivors and take crimes against women seriously. I submit to you," he turned to the jury, "that the rape and subsequent delay in arrest of Dennis Lawton is a top-down failure of the Portland Police Bureau."

"Objection!" Bernie shouted.

"Sustained," Judge Jessop begrudgingly said.

"It was my belief that only DC Lawton was on trial," Bernie explained, "not the whole of the Portland Police Bureau."

"That may be well and good, Mister Bernie," Ford hissed, "but the fact remains that we are observing where these failures happened, so that we can get to the root of what happened and prove unequivocally what we already know about that man," he pointed at Denny, "that he is an opportunist who will take advantage of a woman at any chance."

"Hey, screw you, Ford!" Denny suddenly shouted.

"Order! Order!" Judge Jessop shrieked as she banged her gavel. "That is one outburst and one only, Mister Lawton. One more, and I swear I will hold you in contempt of court."

"My apologies, your honor," Denny said, almost in a subdued whimper. "I just can only take so many lies told about me in one day."

The day was growing long. The lion's share of the testimony lay squarely in the prosecution's favor. Even Chief Jackson had to admit that letting Denny go for almost six months was a huge mistake.

The last witness for the day was Talia. She took the stand boldly, bolstered by Rick's encouragement.

"How long were you married to the accused?" the prosecution asked.

"Eleven years." Her voice was small and shrill like a mouse, as if the whole world were watching, and some deep, dark secret of hers was on display for them all to see.

"In that time, were you ever worried about Denny seeing other women?" Ford asked.

Great, he's using my nickname to make her think he's her friend, Denny groaned within himself.

"I never did," she replied.

"Missus Johnson," Ford addressed her. Denny shuddered at the name change. "Did the accused ever beat you?"

"No."

"Did he ever hit you?"

"No."

"Ever verbally abuse you?"

"Never."

"So, he never gave any indication of what he was until the day he came home from attempting rape on Michaela Roberts?"

"He…" she trailed off before continuing. "There was one thing," she almost whispered.

"What was that one thing, Missus Johnson?"

"He could never look me in the eyes," she said slowly, as if the realization was just dawning on her after nearly twelve years. "I thought it was just a nervous tick, but he never looked me in the eyes. I never said anything, but I didn't think anything of it. It was just a thing with him."

"So, you're saying he could never look at you?"

"I don't know," she continued in that meek, slow tone. "He looked at me plenty, just never directly in the eyes. It was always worse when…" she trailed off again.

"When what?"

Talia was now blushing. Denny knew exactly what she was thinking. All of the times he had made love to her, and he could never stare into her baby blues because they were the exact same eyes of his abuser – nothing she could control as she was at the mercy of her genetics. Every time he was with Talia in that way, it always took him back to the sexual abuse and coercion carried out on him by Talia's own mother, Jana Crockett.

"When we were making love," she replied, tears beginning to well up in her eyes. "He never looked at me."

"What the actual heck?" Bernie mouthed at Denny.

"That's all I have," Curtis Ford said coldly.

"Does the defense have any questions for Missus Johnson?" the judge asked.

"Not now, and I think it best Missus Johnson not be pressed for any more questions today," Bernie replied solemnly. "I think I've heard all I need to hear from her."

Both Denny and Bernie glared at Curtis Ford as the smug prosecutor took his place. Even as cold-hearted as he could be, Bernie was appalled at the cruelty the prosecution had just displayed on poor Talia. It was almost as if now the prosecution was attacking anyone who may have shown any bit of small kindness toward the accused, no matter how they currently felt about him.

"Then if that's all," Judge Jessop said, "this court will be adjourned until tomorrow morning." She smacked the gavel and stood up from her throne.

The county mounties cuffed Denny and led him out. As they led him out, for the first time, he made eye contact with Talia – actually looked her directly in the eyes. It hurt. The pain he felt from all those years of exploitation from her mother returned in an instant. Every threat from that woman, every feeling of pain and pleasure was palpable. But he forced himself to look at her. He could read Talia. She was confused, but all at once, she knew. It was as if she could see the pain in his eyes. Then, they led Denny out and into the waiting van.

Chapter 26
Eyes Wide Open

The prison cell seemed even colder than the courtroom. If there ever was a time for Denny to feel total desolation, it was now. Even though the first day of the trial had gone as bad as expected, it all still felt so unreal.

He pinched himself. Maybe this was all a dream. He'd wake up in bed next to Talia some early morning before that fateful Sunday, and the text from Michaela Roberts would never come. Better yet, he would wake up as an innocent twelve-year-old now well-equipped with the ability to say "no", thus retaining his innocence and sexual purity. It was no use. This was real life, and now he was left with a throbbing pain in his arm.

After he changed back into his Prison Blues, they brought him dinner. He let his dinner grow cold next to him. Heck, it was already cold when he received it. He decided he would go hungry for the night – perhaps, feed a rat that may or may not scurry into his cell.

"Look alive, Lawton," barked a voice.

Denny stood to attention. It was getting late. There was no reason for him to leave his cell for any activities.

"You have a visitor," the guard told him.

That was even stranger. Why would anyone want to talk to him in the middle of a trial? He waited to be led out to the meeting hall.

Denny's heart skipped a beat as he sat down. Across the glass sat Talia. Up close, he could see how much she had changed in the last seven months. Her cheeks were rosier, a little fuller, all framed by her short golden curls and corkscrews. Her new husband had turned her into some perverted version of his late wife, and she let him do it as if in some sick zombie resurrection fantasy. And look, there was the very zombie lover looming over her like some oversized mutt protecting his bowl of dollar store kibble. Denny picked up the phone.

"If you have anything to say to me, he needs to leave," were the first things Denny said.

Talia looked back at Rick, wordlessly asking his permission to be left alone.

"This isn't a negotiation, Talia," Denny continued. "Either he leaves, or we don't talk. Look at me. Do I look like I pose any threat to you? Seriously, there's a big piece of glass between us. I so much as look at your wrong, those guards will be on me quicker than you could say 'Bob's your uncle'."

Talia looked back at Rick again. Wordlessly, he left, but not before shooting a sneer Denny's way. Denny returned the sneer in kind to his former friend.

"Now, what do you want?" Denny asked as Rick slammed the door behind him. "Doesn't this somehow force me to violate the restraining order?"

"Look at me, Denny," Talia told him.

Denny looked up at her, his eyes focused on some ambiguous point on her face – the beauty mark she had always concealed from him, now worn proudly out in the open, another similarity she shared with Julia.

"Look me in the eyes, Dennis."

Denny tried, but he could not bring himself to set his eyes on that one single point.

"Why? Why can't you do just this one simple thing?" she moaned. "It's not rocket science. It's not music theory."

Denny was at a loss for words. His brain said one thing, but somewhere between the part of it carrying out instructions and the other part doing what was instructed, there was a wide gulf.

"Eleven years, and not once did you look me in the eyes. I made love to you for eleven years, and not one time did you look into my eyes. I gave you myself, and couldn't see it. Why? Just why? Was the thought of those other girls just too much? Was I that ugly to you that you just had to pretend to enjoy me?"

"Talia, I loved you more than life itself," Denny began.

"Is that so? I can't believe I actually fell for that once. Like, how are you unable to look me in the eyes and connect with me? I made love to you, and you couldn't even give me your heart."

"What do you mean I couldn't give you my heart? You were my everything."

"Yeah, I thought that for eleven years, but it's all become so clear to me. You can't change my mind. I just want to know why. Why would you go into that profession? Why vice, if not to see naked women? Why would you force yourself upon that poor woman?"

"I didn't do that," Denny protested.

"You keep saying that," Talia argued, "but the evidence says otherwise. Seriously, was a regular patrol not enough? Heck, was staying in Astoria not enough? Did you drag us out to Portland so you wouldn't have to be accountable to our families? Was it so that your infidelities would be easier to cover up? Was it so that you could hurt me without fear of being caught out?"

"I moved us because of your mother!" Denny burst out.

"Great, blame my mom, the grandmother of your children."

"My abuser!" Denny shot back.

"Oh, that's rich," Talia groaned. "So, now she's your abuser. You have some nerve making that accusation. All just to get the heat off of you, I suppose."

"It's not an empty accusation," Denny protested with a sigh. He then broke down, tears falling from his eyes.

"You're impossible," Talia grumbled. "Are you seriously giving me crocodile tears."

"You freaking want to know why I could never look you in the eyes when we made love, why I ran away from Astoria the second I got the chance? Your mother groomed me when I was a teenager, Talia. She took my innocence away from me and covered it up."

"You take that back."

"I'm done hiding it. I'm done pretending it didn't happen because it's not supposed to happen because it was woman on teenaged boy. Your mother, I can't believe I'm saying this, is a predator. She set us up to make sure I stayed close."

"You're lucky you're on the other side of that glass, or I'd scratch your eyes out," Talia hissed.

"I wouldn't blame you," Denny said with a sniffle, drying his tears, "but that's the honest truth. I wouldn't lie to you. I didn't lie to you back in August, and I'm not lying to you tonight. I never laid hands on Michaela Roberts except to stop her from falling into me, and your mother groomed me and had sex with me when I was fifteen. Nobody would listen to me back then, not my mom, not my dad, not our pastor. They all laughed me off."

"Again, with the lies," Talie moaned.

"Talia, you were different. You weren't your mom. I wasn't lying when I said she put us together because she wanted to get close to me. Instead, I fell in love with you because you were the only good thing about her. Not only are you beautiful, but you're smart and caring. You make everybody around you a better person. Shoot, I'd hate to imagine even how bad your mom would have been if you weren't around. But the thing is you're the spitting image of your mother, and..." Denny trailed off.

"Denny, I can't do this," Talia muttered.

"The reason I could never look you in the eye," Denny continued, "the reason I felt so distant when we tried to connect was..."

242

"Please, don't be dramatic."

"My gosh, Talia, have you ever been abused? Have you ever actually been manipulated into believing what you're doing that is so heinous and dishonorable is right because an authority figure said so? Every time I look into your eyes, I'm fifteen again. Your mother is touching me everywhere that feels good. I'm scared and at the same time aroused. I don't know what's going on as she forces herself on me. I feel pleasure but at the same time, I feel shame. Frick!"

"If my mom is the monster you say she is, then why did you never tell me? We were married for eleven years. We tell each other about things like this. That's what couples do."

"Why? And ruin our marriage? Find out that not only were you not the first, but also the fact that your own mother was my first?"

"You've already done a great job at ruining our marriage."

"Rick ruined our marriage, Talia. He lied to you. You believed me at first. Remember?"

"Shut up! I don't know who to believe."

"And how fast did you lose your trust in me? I loved you. I protected you. And the second things got tough, when my integrity was called into question, you let a sick man worm his way into your mind so that you kicked me out of your life."

"Don't talk about my husband that way!"

"Do you actually want me to be guilty?"

Talia paused at this.

"Seriously, Talia, did it ever occur to you that maybe what I'm saying is true?"

"Oh, like what you said about my mother?" Talia sneered.

"Truth."

"Bull."

"I wish it was," said Denny. "I really wish your mother just left me alone. Then again, I wouldn't have been able to do the good I have been able to do."

"What good? What good ever came of your life?"

"I met you, for one. I had three beautiful children with you. By the way, your mother's abuse led me to join vice. See, when kids are abused in the church, they tend to hate God, and their lives often end up even worse from the abuse. I saw that, and vice was a way I could make contact with a lot of these people who were abused when they were younger and convince them that their abuse didn't define them. I got so many kids off the streets and to safety because I was able to understand them."

"Gosh, Denny, you're so unbelievable. Like, I think you must have hit your head."

"I don't blame you for not believing me. Look, I didn't do anything to Michaela. She and Sticky lured me to her hideout where they ambushed me."

"Why would they want to do that? Seriously, what good would come of that?"

"No good came of it. Sticky wanted to discredit me because I was getting his girls off of the street. Michaela was an informant of mine. He found out she was snitching on him and set us both up."

"Why were you there in the first place?"

"She sent me a text saying she was in trouble, remember?"

"It's been almost eight months."

"Yeah, and that was enough time for you to dump me, have our daughter, get remarried, and get busy. How long was Rick whispering in your ear?"

"Shut up and just look me in the eyes, Denny."

"Why?"

"Because I want to know what you're truly thinking."

"I've already told you what I'm thinking."

"No, you haven't. Now, look me in the freaking eye, Dennis. Your eyes tell me what your words can't."

There seemed to be some physical resistance, as if Denny was about to look into the eyes of a Gorgon and be turned to stone. It was almost cartoonish the way he pulled his eyes toward Talia's.

The moment Denny locked eyes with Talia, she could see everything, as if she were looking straight into his soul. It was more than just some metaphor. The whole truth had been revealed to her. Her eyes had been hard on him the whole meeting, as if he would have noticed that; but now, they were softened.

"Oh, my," she whispered to herself.

Talia put her hand on the glass, as if reaching out to her ex-husband.

"I, I need to go," she said as she slammed the phone on its receiver. Without a word, she stood up and stormed out the door.

"I guess that's it, guys," Denny said to the guards.

He was returned to his cell with more questions than answers. Had he actually revealed and convinced Talia of the truth? He had never wanted to bring her world crashing down, and he had convinced himself that he could live the rest of his life with her never knowing what had been done to him.

He sat on the edge of his bed for a good hour, nibbling at the edges of his cold sandwich. (The rats and mice had chosen to stay away from it.) Now that Talia knew, what would she say? Would Jana be receiving a call from her? Would she be giving Rick a piece of her mind?

After another hour, the sandwich was gone, and Denny laid back down on his bed. As he hit the pillow, he noticed an envelope stuck under it. They must have left it there while he was visiting with Talia. He opened it. It was another letter from Verity.

It was good news. The whole force in Lancashire was pulling for him. At least he had some encouragement.

Michael Lorde had attempted suicide twice and was now on suicide watch. Patrol officers were taking bets on whether or not he would be "Epsteined" before his actual trial. Hassan was being tried. It was more than likely he would serve most of the rest of his natural life and, if he survived his prison sentence, be released an old man, and exiled back to Afghanistan.

Ian Love was still leading in the polls for MP, far and away from any other candidate. Michael Lorde's interim was basically neutered, powerless in his own constituency.

The slums were being cleaned up. Without fear of gangs, even though there were still gangs, residents had time to take pride in their homes and flats. The gangs were reduced to some young migrants who verbally harassed women occasionally from the front porch, a far cry from the sexual assaults of the last forty years.

Verity ended the letter as usual, telling Denny how much she loved and missed him. Denny could smell her perfume on the letter. He missed her too, but he had just had a taste of his old life. Who was he kidding? She was remarried and pregnant with her new husband's kid. That ship had sailed. They had both moved on. Any attempt to return to the status quo would only cause more grief and heartache to the multiple parties involved. This right here, this letter, was his new life.

Denny curled up for bed, cradling the letter close to him, smelling Verity's perfume as he drifted off to sleep.

Chapter 27
Talia's Choice

Talia sat at her vanity later that evening, rolling curlers into her hair. It wasn't natural. Her hair had always been a full head of golden strands, as if created by the touch of Midas, cascading down her back almost to her waist. As of recent, and after many months of begging from Rick, those golden locks had been shortened to about shoulder length and required curlers every night, all to keep her new husband happy.

This wasn't natural either. She looked down as she put her hand on her belly. It was all so soon. She had only given birth in September to Denny's youngest. All so soon. Had she been that eager to move on that she felt the need to create a fourth child in Rick's image, before she was even physically ready?

A single tear fell from her eye as she continued rolling her locks into the hot curlers. That was another thing – Denny. The last seven months, she had shut him out completely. She had sold the house as soon as she could, moving the kids with her into Rick's house right after the wedding. She had tried to rid herself of every last vestige of Denny, but the kids, oh, the kids. Rickey, despite his step-father's namesake was every bit Denny, even down to his looks. He carried himself with the same confidence and cool demeanor his father possessed, even at such a young age. Despite a fairer complexion, compare a picture of the two side-by-side at that age, and you'd think they were twins. So, she would have to see Denny every day that boy matured. And Hudson? There were even some of Denny's mannerisms. Even absent the man, the boy was becoming his father. There was nothing Rick or she could do to change that.

Another tear fell as she cleaned the makeup off from her face. What was Rick turning her into? She knew this wasn't her. And Rick, completely oblivious. Was he always like this? Did he treat Julia like this? Sure, he was protective, but even tonight, she could tell it was more like some mutt over a food bowl than actual love. The man gave tacet love to her and Denny's children, but there was none of the warmth that Denny showed to them.

And then there was their time alone. Was it always going to be like this? Five minutes and going about their day? No passion, no connection? With Denny, besides the lack of eye contact, it still always seemed meaningful, like he wanted her close, like there was something he was hiding but knew she could make right, like they were both a comfort to each other.

"*No, why are you thinking about this, Talia*," she said to herself. "*You're not married to that man anymore. Rick is your husband now.*"

As if summoned by her thoughts, Rick walked into the room. He was still pale and gaunt from the cancer treatments, but he had been cancer-free for well over a year. He walked up behind her and kissed her neck, sending shivers down her spine.

"Ah, there she is," he rumbled, watching Talia transform herself into Julia right before his eyes.

"Bella down to sleep?" she asked. Bella was her newborn from Denny. She had been begging for help from childless Rick, only recently convincing him he actually possessed the ability help put the kids to bed.

"Sleeping like a baby," he replied proudly.

"Which means she'll be up screaming in a couple hours," Talia ruefully joked.

"Well, let's hope she sleeps through the night," Rick said.

"Can you feed her tonight if she does wake up?" Talia asked, batting her eyes. "It's just been quite the day."

"Of course, of course," Rick unsuccessfully assured her. "I get it. Long day, having to relive that horrible marriage."

"Yeah, that was exhausting," Talia replied, not without a hint of hesitation.

"So, what did he want anyway?" Rick asked. She hadn't been upfront with Rick and had told him that she was summoned to the jail, not the other way around.

"He just wanted to talk," she said, "one more chance to vindicate himself."

"Idiot," Rick spat.

"Hey, you're talking about the man I was married to for eleven years and the father of my children."

"I know, I know. Just knowing how he had us all fooled for all that time, you know, it just does something to me."

Talia looked at herself again in the mirror, Rick now looming over her. There was that hungry mutt again. Not tonight. She didn't want him tonight.

"He told me some things," Talia went on.

"Oh, I bet," Rick muttered, anger simmering under his breath.

"Some things I didn't know."

"Makes sense. If he was hiding the fact that he's a sex-crazed opportunist, then what else wouldn't he hide?"

"Well, he says my mother... My gosh, I can't bring myself to repeat it." She burst into tears.

"He's not making it back to court if I have anything to say about it," Rick growled.

"No, he got very personal," she continued through sobs. "He said, he said that my mother..."

Rick sat on edge, waiting for the words that just would not come out of Talia's mouth. Whatever this was, it was horrible.

"My mother," Talia moaned. "Mommy… How could you?"

"What's wrong with your mom?"

"She…"

"Yes? Talia, you can tell me."

"Denny told me that when he was a teenager," she began, slightly composed but still shedding tears, "he said she groomed him and took his virginity."

"Bull!" Rick shouted.

The baby started crying in the other room.

"Of course, I did," he grumbled as he turned to leave.

"No, let me," Talia said, dabbing her tears.

She stood up from her vanity and headed to the baby's room. Rick followed.

"Shh," she hushed the girl as she picked her up from the bassinet. "I know, Papa Rick got a little loud."

"I'm so sorry, Talia," Rick apologized as he tripped into the room after her. "I just don't get it. Your mom? That's preposterous! She's the sweetest woman I've ever met!"

"Can you keep it down please so we can get Bella back to sleep?"

"Right," Rick whispered. "There's no way that happened."

"He says that's why he could never look me in the eye," Talia went on to explain. "Oh, Rick, it was terrible. I've never seen someone physically unable to drag his face to make eye contact. He says it's because I look exactly like my mom."

"Well, you are the spitting image of her."

"I know, and he said that he moved us to Portland to get away from her. You know, he never talked to her when we went home. He'd just wave, never any conversation. He was always so disengaged whenever she was around. Heck, he wouldn't even go to church when we went back to Astoria to visit family."

"Unbelievable," Rick muttered.

"I thought so too," said Talia, "but then he did look me in the eye. Like, he physically struggled, but he brought himself to do it. Rick, he's hurting."

"He'd better be hurting. He tried to rape a woman. God knows what's actually become of her."

"Did he though? Or did that McFarland man make this all up like Denny says he did."

"You're actually going to buy that?"

"Sure makes for a great headline, especially when the city government is so opposed to not only the police, but to people like us."

"And you're saying they're just using you?"

"I don't know, Rick. I really don't know. Part of me still wants to believe that Denny was the man I thought I married all those years ago."

"You don't have to," Rick tried to reassure her, as if he was starting to fear losing her back to Denny. "You've moved on. I'm here." He stroked her cheek.

"Rick, what am I doing?"

"You're helping me raise a family," Rick confidently explained.

"Don't you see how wrong that sounds? 'I'm helping you'. It's not 'us'. It's me helping you."

"We're raising a family."

"Are we, Rick? You barely spend any time with my children. I have to practically beg you for help with the baby. You come home from work, crack open whatever book you're reading or turn on some gay football game while I'm left doing everything else."

"You said you wanted to be a homemaker," Rick shot back.

The baby was asleep now, and Talia put her back down. Without a word, she turned and walked out of the room, shutting the light off and leaving Rick in total darkness before he decided to give chase.

"Are you serious right now? You're walking away from me? From your husband?"

"Do you actually think I'm your servant, Rick?" she turned back onto him. "Denny may or may not be who they're saying he is, but he at least took care of me and loved me."

"I do love you," Rick protested.

"Oh yeah, you 'make love' to me every other night," she said "make love" with air quotes. "Meanwhile, I'm left feeling empty, and unloved, and used as you roll back over and go to sleep. You don't

251

connect with me. You just do whatever you need to do and ignore me. Is this how it was with Julia? Maybe that's why you never had any kids!"

"You shut your dang mouth!" Rick hissed as he raised his hand.

"Oh, do it! Come on, hit me! If that's what it takes for you to feel like a man!"

Talia now burst into tears, first leaning up against the wall, and then falling down along it, curling up as much in a fetal position as much as possible for her.

"I thought you'd be different," she sobbed. "I didn't know. I didn't know."

Rick gazed stupidly at Talia from his increased height over her. He sneered at her, actually curled his lips into a sneer as she sobbed like a hysterical woman.

"Did you actually believe the accusations at first?" she asked Rick through the sobs. "Or were you planning this long in advance waiting for the moment for him to slip up and for me to be at my most vulnerable?"

"Talia, you're being ridiculous and melodramatic."

"Answer the question, Rick!" she came back forcefully.

"I don't know," said Rick timidly. "It seemed somewhat preposterous, but I put two and two together."

"You could believe that the man I loved attempted rape on a woman, and yet you don't believe my own mother groomed and raped my ex-husband?"

"One makes sense. The other doesn't," Rick explained. "That kind of thing, a woman like your mom on a kid like Denny, it just doesn't happen."

"You're right about that, but not in the way I think," said Talia as she dried her still-flowing tears.

"You're not actually going to believe him!"

"I don't know, Rick!"

"Look, this is almost over. They've got him. It'll be proven in a court of law, and we can put this all to rest tomorrow."

"Rick, I need you to sleep in the living room tonight," Talia said solemnly.

"Wait, what?"

"I need you to grab the knitted blanket and your pillows and sleep on the couch."

"Okay, now you're not making sense. Is this some pregnant lady thing I don't know about?"

"Rick, I'm asking for alone time. Gosh, you convinced me so well that Denny was a rapist, and now I can't even believe how dense you are."

"I still don't get it. Look, if this is about my raising my hand at you, I didn't mean it. I'm sorry," he blubbered. "I wasn't going to hurt you, I promise."

"Rick, I just need some time to think to myself."

"Not in my house," he grumbled, as if another Rick had entered the room.

"What?"

"This is my house. How dare you presume to tell me what to do in my house."

"Our house," Talia fought back.

"Really? Whose name is on the title?"

"Fine, screw you. I'll sleep on the couch. I guess we're not one flesh in this marriage if this is just 'your house'. Hope you sleep well knowing your pregnant wife has been relegated to the living room."

"You made the choice to sleep apart from me. I'll sleep just fine."

"Did you actually treat Julia like this?"

"Julia never talked to me like this."

"Yeah, probably because she was afraid of you! Well let me tell you something, mister. I'm not afraid of you!" she hissed as she slammed the bedroom door.

That had made Talia's decision for her. For all of the accusations against him, Denny would have never raised his voice to her, let alone his hand. She thought back to that afternoon when she told him to pack his bags. It had taken her less than a week to lose all faith in him. What was she looking for? Had Rick really played her that easily?

Talia walked out to the couch, her feet hurting from all of the walking around already. She curled up and cried. What had she done? This was all wrong. This was not natural. It was all broken, and there was nothing she could do about it.

253

Chapter 28
The British Are Coming

Denny's heart nearly stopped as the gavel pounded loudly. Any other day, it signaled the coming of justice for evildoers, but there's just something about that sound when it's your head on the chopping block. This time, it was only to begin the day's proceedings. Judge Jessop was sat upon her kingly or queenly throne – whatever she thought she was.

The spring rains had worsened overnight, turning the Willamette River into Willamette Lake. In many places, she had overflowed her banks up to three quarters of a mile. In Portland, the water had just about reached street level in places, nearly rising to the road surfaces of some of the lower bridges, sweeping bicyclists off of the road and carrying their unmanned bikes away in the torrent. On top of that, it was a cold rain, chilling anyone stuck out in it right down to the bone. Did that convince Multnomah County to turn on the heat in the courthouse? Not a chance in Hades.

Julian Bernie was sweating, actually sweating like he had just biked from Hood to the Coast – a very reassuring vote of confidence for Denny. Of course, there was Curtis Ford, relaxed all smug in his chair. Today would be the last of the testimony as well as closing arguments. Then, the jury would deliberate and consider all facts and falsehoods, expectedly returning in about a grand total of three whole minutes and finding Denny guilty because, well, look at him.

"How the heck are you sweating in here when it's colder than your heart?" Denny whispered to Bernie.

"I have a witness that's supposed to be here," Bernie trembled.

"And let me guess, said witness is not here?"

"One last witness that could very well get you off the hook," Bernie explained, "was supposed to be here a half an hour ago. No communication whatsoever."

"Let me tell you something," Denny hissed, "I don't want to merely be off the hook. I don't want to be the rapist cop that got off because of some stupid nonsense technicality. I want the real story to be known, okay. I want them to know that Sticky not only staged this whole rape story, but also probably killed Michaela Roberts to shut her up."

"I'm sure you do," Bernie tried to reassure his client.

"Dang tootin' I am," Denny spat.

"Counsel for the defense, please make your statements," Judge Jessop ordered, her icy glare glued onto Denny.

"Here goes nothing," Bernie chuckled nervously.

As soon as Bernie had his back turned to his client, said client mouthed an expletive at him. So much for all that money he spent on a good lawyer.

"La… I mean, people of the jury," Bernie began, "you've been presented with the facts of this case. It all seems pretty straightforward, and really all we have is two opposing stories. You have seen that Detective Constable Dennis Carlos Lawton has maintained the same story from August 10 until this present day without a change in any detail. His upstanding character has been attested up until that fateful

255

day of August 10 as well. We've heard from witnesses that he has been the same man they all knew and loved. He maintained an upright and moral character in an occupation where it is nigh impossible to do so, without one single complaint for over ten years. There has not been any viable sign that he is who the county claims he is. So, what changed on August 10? Nothing. And that is why my client is innocent. And now we have this man who calls himself Sticky. How does this story add up? Are we really to believe he was just walking around, minding his own business, and just happened to stumble upon DC Lawton assaulting Michaela Roberts? Why should we believe his story? Possible, I'll give you that, but highly unlikely. Make it make sense. People of the jury, your job is to prove beyond a shadow of a doubt that my client, Detective Constable Dennis Carlos Lawton, is guilty of the assault and attempted rape of Miss Michaela Roberts. And as Miss Roberts is not here, how are we to hear her side of the story?"

Denny surmised the man was stalling, actually stalling. Did he still bank on this surprise witness? Did he find Michaela alive?

"Furthermore," Bernie went on, now turning red from his oratory, "I concur that this trial is a sham and an attack on the very foundations of Christianity in America."

"Crap, he went there," Denny groaned in his head. *"He's going to get himself arrested for rhetoric like that."*

"Were my client, Detective Constable Dennis Carlos Lawton, a Muslim, would he have been held to this standard? We have countless examples the world around, if not right here at home in these United States, that that standard you have set here in Multnomah County, Oregon would have not been held if my client, Detective Constable Dennis Carlos Lawton, were a Muslim. What if he was a gay man? Would he have been held to the same standard? We have countless examples the world around, if not right here at home in these United States, that that standard you have set here in Multnomah County, Oregon would have not been held if my client, Detective Constable Dennis Carlos Lawton, were a gay man."

"Objection!" Curtis Ford shouted. "Irrelevant! He's clearly attacking the most vulnerable of our communities."

"Sustained," Judge Jessop monotonously drawled.

As the judge spoke, the back door to the courtroom opened.

256

"Forgive me," the visitor said in a familiar voice. "I've never been here, and traffic is horrible with all the flooding."

Denny turned around and nearly had a heart attack, for there, walking to him, was Verity. She seemed to be glowing, seemingly melting the ice the judge had brought to the room, despite her constant banging of the gavel and screams of "Order". She dropped a backpack next to the table.

"Forgive me, your honor," Bernie apologized, "with your permission, I'm afraid I have one more witness."

"You may proceed," the judge relented, visibly and audibly done with this trial.

Before she could make it to the stand, Verity turned and embraced Denny. She was different – she seemed a little softer around the midsection.

"Why? Why are you here?"

"Shh, we've got this now, lah," she comforted him before walking up to the stand.

The bailiff brought out the old Bible and held it out for her.

"Left hand on the Bible," he instructed the Englishwoman. "Raise your right hand. Do you swear to tell the truth, the whole truth, and nothing but the truth, so help you God?"

"Yes," she squeaked.

"You may be seated."

Bernie wiped whatever sweat was left from his forehead. It was time to blow this thing out of the water.

"Please state your full name for the court, ma'am," Bernie instructed.

"Verity Eloise Baker," Verity answered.

"And what is your current occupation, Miss Baker?"

"I am a detective constable for the Lancashire Constabulary in Preston, England."

"Good, and how long have you been there?"

"Nine years with the LC," she answered, "if that's what you mean. In Lancashire itself, all thirty-one years of my life."

"Very good, and how do you know my client, Detective Constable Dennis Carlos Lawton?"

"He was my partner?"

257

"Professionally, right?"

"Yes, professionally," she replied, trying to hide her blush. "He was assigned my partner with the Lancashire Police."

"About how long was your professional relationship with Detective Constable Dennis Carlos Lawton?"

"Roughly three months," she answered.

"And in those three months, did he mention he had raped an informant?"

"No."

"Did he mention being under investigation for said crime?"

"Yes."

"And you willingly worked side-by-side with him, knowing he could potentially do the same to you?"

"Yes."

"Can you tell the court why you spent three months with my client, knowing full well he could be the monster he's accused of being?"

"Because he's not that monster. He didn't do it."

"And can you tell us why you think he didn't do it?"

"He never laid a hand on me," said Verity.

Denny cringed at that. He had definitely laid hands on her, but she had let him. Gently, albeit, but the fact was the same that he had been intimate with her. That might come back to bite him.

"He also fought for truth harder than any person I've ever met."

"He fought for truth? Can you explain that to the court?"

Verity took a deep breath.

"Our first assignment was a high-profile murder. All of the signs pointed to one particular suspect, but we were encouraged to forget it and basically chase our tails until they just decided that it would always be a cold case. Denny was having none of it. We were told to lay off because, frankly, the man we were pursuing was a migrant from Afghanistan. It was an open secret what he was doing to girls around the area, particularly underaged girls. Ultimately, we exposed not only the murderer, but a grooming gang that went all the way up to our local MP. We exposed the MP for the murder, since he was the one whole pulled the trigger, and he and the gang leader are currently in prison all because of Denny's actions. He fought for those girls to make them safe. If that's the kind of man who would rape a random woman for no reason other than to satisfy some weird sex addiction, then I'm the bloody Queen of England. He had the opportunity to have a go at any of the girls there in Crenshaw-on-Ribble, and he never laid hands on them. In fact, he was so distraught at the sight of one of them all bruised and abused that he waited there and sang her a lullaby like he was her dad until the medics could show up. What kind of psychotic rapist does that?"

"And that's your testimony?" asked Bernie.

"Only mine," Verity replied as she gestured to the bag she set by the table.

Bernie walked over and picked up the bag. Denny wanted to stand up and applaud Verity's testimony. Truly, it was the best he had heard the whole trial.

"Can you tell me what this is, Miss Baker?"

"If you open it up," she turned to the jury, "you'll find it's all personal testimony from every member of our precinct, as well as friends from Crenshaw, where we lived. It all attests to Denny's honesty."

Bernie walked the bag over to the jury foreman to have a look. The foreman picked a letter out and opened it. It was one from Fat Terry – a glowing compliment to his clean living and friendship.

"I submit this as evidence to our jury," said Bernie. "That's all the questions I have for you Miss Baker."

Verity stood up and walked over to Denny. He stood up and hugged her. There was so much he wanted to say, but he was far from out of the woods.

"As you can see," Julian Bernie concluded, "my client, Detective Constable Dennis Carlos Lawton, has a strong character witness. It would be foolhardy to even believe the slightest notion that this crime was perpetrated by him. I rest my case."

Now it was time for Curtis Ford to make one last effort to put his nemesis away. While Verity's arrival brought clarity to the situation, he had observed a few things during the cross examination that brought him pause.

"I would like to call Miss Verity Baker to the stand, your honor," he told the judge.

Verity approached the stand again, her eyes longingly on Denny.

"So, you say you worked with Detective Lawton for three months, right?" he began his questioning.

"That's right."

"Not a very long time to get to know a man, I'd say. Were you ever more than work partners?"

She paused here. It was an open secret that they were dating. Now it would be on record.

"Tell the truth," Denny mouthed to her.

"We dated," she replied defiantly.

"And that baby is his?"

The jury let out a collective "oof". Everyone, doesn't matter if they're black or white, male or female, demon-self or dragon-self, knows you never ever, under any circumstances, even if the life of your own mother depended on it, assume a woman is pregnant. (She was, but the rule still stands.)

"Denny is the father," she croaked out.

"Hold up, so just a few minutes ago, so we're clear, you said Detective Lawton never laid hands on you."

"That's correct. He never did."

"But he had sex with you, am I right?"

"Yes, we made love one, and only once."

"So, he laid hands on you."

"I let him. It wasn't like that."

"So much for all of those Christian morals and upstanding character we were talking about."

"Objection!" Bernie shouted.

The jury shouted their objections too. The gallery joined the chorus.

"All I'm asking is…"

"Order!" Judge Jessop shouted as she banged her gavel until it snapped in two. "I'll sustain that objection. Mister Ford, what has gotten into you? That was highly inappropriate."

"My apologies, your honor. No further questions."

Verity was visibly distressed. She trudged back to Denny's table. The tension was palpable, like a water balloon about to burst. Denny stood up, and she collapsed into his arms, releasing a torrent of tears.

If this was just courtroom pageantry, it was very good pageantry. Not one person was not moved by Verity's emotion, save for DA Curtis Ford. Denny brushed back her hair and looked deep into her eyes.

"Please, don't be mad," she pleaded with Denny. "I meant to tell you."

"Mad? I'm going to be a dad again," he chuckled. "Chin up, girl. You did great. It was all going to come out eventually."

"But what if they decide you're guilty?"

"Then I'll write letters to that child every day until they let me out, and when I come home, I'll be the best dad I can to that child."

"Please have a seat, Detective Lawton," Judge Jessop barked coldly.

Denny and Verity sat down next to each other.

"Is the prosecution ready to deliver closing remarks?" the judge asked.

"Yes, um, we're ready," Ford stumbled over his words. "I put them around here somewhere."

Curtis Ford was redder than Julain Bernie could ever get.

"Ah, here," he attempted to compose himself before stepping up to the front. "People of the jury," his voice cracked, "you've heard all the evidence. You've sat and listened to every excuse one could make. However, you must consider the facts. That is your mandate as a jury of peers. Dennis Lawton is an opportunist. He took the job in vice to prey on the most vulnerable of our people and…"

"No, he didn't!" a voice rang out from the gallery.

"We will have order!" Judge Jessop bellowed as she emphasized every syllable.

"Please, he's innocent," that same voice cried out.

"One more outburst, whoever you are, and I will hold you in contempt of court!"

"Hold me in contempt then! He joined vice because he cared about those kids. He was abused like them too!"

"Who is that?" Judge Jessop angrily asked.

"It's his ex-wife, Talia Johnson, and I want to put it on record, if I can that he could never look me in the eyes because he saw my mother in them. My mother groomed him when he was a teenager."

"Sit down and shut up in my courtroom!"

"He loved me," she cried, "and I, I, I…" she burst into tears before collapsing back into her seat.

"If anyone else has anything to say, you'd better say it now," Judge Jessop growled, "otherwise, I'm calling this and sending the jury to deliberate. No? Good."

Judge Jessop banged what was left of the gavel and stood up to go to her chambers. Talia was in her seat bawling her eyes out, Rick standing over her trying in vain to comfort her. He knew he had messed up the night before. He was at least making an attempt to be the husband he should have been this time.

Denny watched as the jury pensively filed out for deliberation. This was it. His life was on the line. He once again embraced Verity. If there was any solace in this moment, it was the fact that she was here for him. Like he had explained all the months ago, partners have each other's backs, and she more than held up her end of the bargain.

Epilogue

The sobs had subsided. Now, it was just the sound of tapping feet and pattering rain. From time to time, someone would blow their nose or cough. Nobody said a word. It was as if breaking the silence would bring a curse upon the whole land.

Denny silently prayed for a miracle as he ran his fingers through Verity's hair as she rested her head on his shoulder. They savored the moment, knowing this could very well be the last time they saw each other. It would take a while for the jury to read the letters Verity, the Lancashire Police, and the villagers from Crenshaw had submitted, so they both hoped that it would just take a couple readings to convince them that Denny was innocent.

In the gallery, Talia had dried her tears, but she hurt even more. She could see how Denny and Verity looked at each other. She could see how Denny held Verity. She hated it all. She hated her mother for what she always somehow knew deep down. She hated Rick for deceiving her. She hated herself for throwing away the love and protection of a man who truly cherished her, personal demons aside. Now, here she was in a sham of a marriage, seeing in real time what she had thrown away. Rick could do all of the "nice husband" things, but it didn't change the fact that he had led her into living a lie. Where do we go from here? Who are we going to hurt? Was there any way to make this right?

Brian and Marisol Lawton attempted to get in on Talia's consolation. In response, she swatted them away with a few terse words that Denny couldn't hear, but what looked like "You could've prevented this whole thing". And that was true. Had they taken Denny seriously and taken care of the problem of Jana Crockett's abuse of their son, the whole trajectory of his life would have been different.

"Mom and Dad," Denny whispered to Verity as he pointed them out to her.

"Glad they finally know the truth," she commented to him.

"About twenty years too late," Denny sighed. "Anyway, better late than never."

Sticky had decided to drag his butt to court today, if only to see the final piece of his puzzle fall into place. Without the man who wouldn't shut up, business would be booming, the politicians would ignore him, and he, not the mayor, would run this town. That hope began to fall apart with Verity's tears. Then, it began to collapse like a Jenga tower with Talia's outburst. His eyes started shifting left to right as the courtroom sat in silence. All of a sudden, it seemed like every law officer in the courtroom was staring at him. He hadn't told anybody about what became of Michaela Roberts. Why would he? But now, would an exoneration of Denny Lawton bring the heat down on him? Quite possible, and that would open up the question back up on Michaela's whereabouts. It was time to leave.

What Sticky didn't know was that an sheriff's deputy was, in fact, keeping an eye on him. Call it profiling all you like, but something just never sat right about Sticky with this particular deputy. As Sticky hurriedly left the courtroom, the Multnomah County deputy discreetly followed him out. Not three seconds after the doors swung completely shut, shouts were heard out in the hallway.

"You ain't takin' me! I ain't do nothin'!"

"Stop resisting!"

"Man, I was just leavin'!"

"Hands behind your back!"

"Let me go!"

"Taser, taser, taser!"

That was followed by the pop of the taser and Sticky screaming like a spoiled child as he lost all control of his body, bowels, and bladder.

"I guess that proves your innocence on one front," Verity chuckled with a sniffle.

"If only the jury could've seen it," Denny ruefully mused aloud.

What seemed like all day was only a duration of about fifteen minutes. The jury returned to their seats. Judge Jessop, clearly fed up with this trial, returned to her almighty throne.

"We will have order," she barked as she banged the half of her gavel. "Will the foreman of the jury read the verdict?"

The jury foreman was a plump coffee-colored woman in her early fifties. She stood up and cleared her throat. She shot a quick glance at Denny, knowing his life was in her hands, in the hands of all twelve of the jurors. Hidden behind the foreman's glance was a soft smile, a smile that said "It'll be alright". Denny hadn't realized he had tensed up in the last fifteen minutes, but all of a sudden, his body just released that tension. Verity could feel it and gripped his hand tight, fearing something was wrong.

"I'm right here with you," she whispered.

"It's alright, Princess," Denny whispered back. "It's all going to be alright."

"We, the jury, have found," the foreman began, "that on the count of rape in the first degree, we find the defendant, Dennis Carlos Lawton," the court held their collective breath, "innocent. On the count of assault in the second degree, we find the defendant, Dennis Carlos Lawton, innocent."

If Denny hadn't felt reassurance from the foreman before, he did now as he embraced Verity. He was a free man. No more words were needed. In fact, Denny could not hear any more words that were spoken. He kissed Verity on the forehead. Verity burst into different tears now. He caressed Verity's cheeks with both hands as he leaned his forehead into hers. He was officially free and clear, and that's all that mattered.

Denny had prudently asked Julian Bernie to make sure that his belongings were ready to go, on the off chance he was exonerated. The lawyer handed him the duffel bag with a firm shake of his hand as they stood on the shallow steps of the courthouse.

"I'm going to be honest, Brother Bernie," Denny said, "you had me freaked out there for a hot second."

"You're a peculiar case, Brother Lawton," Bernie replied. "It seems you have a lot of support from the people that love you."

"Well, it took a little pressure for some," Denny chuckled as he put his arm around Verity's shoulder and held her to him.

"Well, thank you for letting me represent you," said Bernie.

"No, thank you," Denny returned. "I think the script here lies clearly in my favor. Not just innocent in law, but innocent in the eyes of man."

And with that, Bernie walked off toward wherever he had parked his car, dodging a homeless man who was alternating between begging for change and preaching an oratory to the wind that even rivaled one of Julian Bernie's legal sermons.

"So, this little one is actually mine?" Denny asked as he turned back to Verity.

"I'm so sorry," she apologized. "I wanted to tell you, but then with the whole arrest and all that."

"Don't apologize," said Denny. "That was completely understandable. I guess Whit knows about our little night together?"

"Cat's out of the bag."

"How did he respond?"

"Happy for us, sad you missed the announcement, even sadder he didn't find out sooner. I guess I'll be on light duty here pretty soon."

Denny began to lead her down the steps.

"And Elliott?"

"He's found some other man to throw all of his cares and sorrows on after I told him I was having none of it. Livin' down in Manchester with the new boyfriend, I believe, now."

"I guess this means I'm stuck with you for life now," Denny admitted.

"Not unless you have some secret boyfriend in San Francisco or Brighton I don't know about," Verity chuckled.

"Ah, I think he's moved on," Denny joked with a snap of his finger.

"Denny, a word!" cried a voice.

Denny turned around to see Talia beckoning him. She stood aloof from Rick and the Lawtons. It was clear that she wanted to talk to him and only him.

"Excuse me a minute," Denny said to Verity. "I promise, it'll only take a second."

"Better not run off with her," she chuckled.

Denny winked at Verity as he left to meet Talia halfway. They hadn't been this close in nearly eight months. The warmth he felt all those months ago, the last time they had met on good terms, was back, but it was diminished. There were tears in her eyes, mascara running down her cheeks.

"I hope this isn't some ruse to get me to violate that restraining order," Denny half joked.

"I'm ripping that thing up first thing when I get home," Talia confessed. "I just wanted to..." She completely broke down, throwing her arms around Denny and embracing him as hard as she could. Denny just stood there motionless. "I'm sorry," she bawled over and over. "I didn't know. I was scared."

Denny reached a hand up and cupped her chin. He slid his palm up and held her cheek in his hand, looking into her blue eyes. It was as if whatever weight had kept his eyes everywhere but there was dropped – the final hold Jana Crockett still had on him finally gone.

"You did nothing wrong," Denny tried to comfort her.

"I should have known," she sobbed. "You're such a wonderful husband, and I believed the lie. I pushed you out. I ruined our marriage. I ruined the lives of our kids."

"Hey, I'm not going to lie and say that there's irreparable damage done," Denny said, "but I'm not mad at you."

Somehow, Denny's absolution only made her cry harder, as if all the world's oceans were held captive in her eyes. She buried her face in Denny's chest.

"Hey, chin up," Denny whispered. "You did what you thought was best for our family. What if it was true? The last thing I'd want is for you and the kids living with a monster. If a man is willing to sexually assault a random woman, what kind of danger does that put his family in? Seriously, I understand."

"But my mom," she tried countering.

"That's true," said Denny. "I'm sorry I didn't tell you. I guess we weren't ever the best at giving each other our whole hearts."

"I'm never leaving the kids alone with her ever again," Talia declared, drying her tears with her wrist.

"That might be a good idea," said Denny.

"And speaking of our kids," Talia continued, dabbing at her eyes with the sleeve of her blouse, "there's someone who needs to meet you."

"I can't wait."

"They all ask about you, you know. Now I can tell them, Daddy's coming home."

"I'll make sure to drop in," said Denny.

Talia could read something in Denny's face, something that began to darken her mood again.

"But you're not staying, are you?" she muttered.

Denny looked back at Verity, herself carrying his new child, waiting patiently for him.

"Talia, we moved on," said Denny. "Our marriage ended. You remarried. You're carrying his child. Don't ruin another kid's life like that. Don't take its father away. Don't make another child grow up in a broken home."

"He's not you," Talia countered.

"Rick, he's…"

Talia waited on the precipice of Denny's declaration.

"Rick's a good man," Denny declared.

Talia scoffed.

"Now, hold on. I know what he did was rotten, but consider how broken he was, and consider how awesome you are. It's an unfortunate

268

thing. We are given forgiveness but forced to live out our choices. Come on, if a man after God's own heart can rape a woman and kill her husband, can't we have a little grace? King David lived with much worse consequences than we ever will, but he was still a man after God's own heart. We just have to make the best of what God's given us."

"God gave me you, and I threw you away," she sobbed.

"You did. You did. But you have a second chance with Rick."

"So, you're not staying?"

"Something tells me I need to leave Oregon. I have a new life in England." Denny looked back at Verity, noting the life growing inside her. "I don't know what the future holds. I promise I'll be back. Shoot, I'll even fly the kids out to see me and their new step mom and step sister. I promise. We'll work it out."

Talia hugged Denny harder. This time, Denny embraced her.

"Is that a promise?" Talia asked him.

"That's a promise."

Talia let go and started making her way back to Rick.

"And hey," Denny called back to her, "take good care of Rick. He may be a good man, but he can be dumber than a pallet of bricks sometimes."

Talia tried in vain to hide the giggle as she returned to Rick.

That seemed to go well," said Verity as Denny returned to her. "You okay?"

"I think so," Denny replied. "We really screwed things up, but I think this was the first step to fixing things."

"So, free man," said Verity, holding up the key fob with a running horse stamped on it, "where to from here?"

Denny's heart raced. He was so focused on the conversation that he hadn't noticed that Verity had led him to the curb, right to where a brand-new red Mustang Dark Horse was parked.

"Rental company didn't have gray, but I thought red would suffice," Verity chuckled as she tossed Denny the key fob.

"How long is the rental?" asked Denny.

"They want it back on Thursday when I fly out," she replied. "Thought I'd do some sightseeing if anything else."

Denny pondered the proposition as he opened the passenger door for Verity.

"You know," he began, looking up at the bright blue sky, the storm clouds gradually drifting east off toward the Cascades and unobscuring Mount Hood, "the sun sets in about six hours or so. I hear the view from the Astoria Column is a must-see."

"You're in command," Verity chuckled.

Denny smiled as he closed Verity's door and walked over to the driver's side. He slid in behind the wheel and started the engine. As Denny placed his hand on the gearshift, Verity placed her hand on his. He looked into her eyes. She was all his, and he was all hers. Oh, there would be struggles and complications, but for the first time ever, Denny could truly say he loved someone, and all of them, not holding anything back. Denny turned his attention back toward the road as he put the car in first. He dumped the clutch and peeled off into the coming sunset.

Acknowledgements

I never thought the last several months of writing would be such a rollercoaster. I'm also surprised with how consistent the narrative remained. But I'm also surprised at how much more relevant the story of *Blameless* became during the writing process.

On September 10, 2025, Charlie Kirk was assassinated in cold blood at Utah Valley University while having a civil and honest conversation with someone he wildly disagreed with. Charlie had a family – a wife and two kids. He had everything to lose, but he stood for the truth. Following his death, I thought about how this alluded to Denny's story in *Blameless*. Denny didn't care what happened when he told the truth, only because everything that meant something to him had been taken away.

I dedicated this book to Charlie Kirk, because the truth is too valuable to ignore. In truth is the only place where we find freedom and mercy. Charlie died defending truth. Why can't we all do the same.

First off, as always, I need to thank God for giving me the ability to write. Without Him, I'm nothing. My wife, Stephanie, has been a constant encouragement for me to continue writing.

My friends with the Guild of the Pen: Nicholas M. Krohn, C.H. Gordon, and Awdrey Laine are always an encouragement to me to keep writing, offering some advice along the way.

Finally, I'd like to thank my beta readers who took the time to look over my work: Chris Braswell, Jacob Johnson, and Steve Mabrey.

Speak truth, do justly, love mercy, and walk humbly.

In Christ,
Sam Sitler